MW00339461

The Working Folding Knife

by Steven Dick

Stoeger Publishing Company

TITLE:	*The Working Folding Knife*
EDITOR:	*Ruth Guillet Fields*
EDITORIAL CONSULTANT:	*Bill Jarrett*
BOOK DESIGN AND LAYOUT:	*Laura A. Marsala*
COVER ART DESIGN:	*Ray Wells*
PRODUCTION COORDINATOR:	*Dominick Sorrentino*
ELECTRONIC IMAGING:	*Robert C. Marsala*

Copyright 1998 by Steven Dick
All rights reserved. No part of this book may be reproduced or transmitted in any form
or by any means, electronic or mechanical, including photocopying, recording, or by any
information retrieval system,without permission in writing from the publisher.

Published by Stoeger Publishing Company
5 Mansard Court
Wayne, New Jersey 07470

IBSN: 088317-210-0
Library of Congress Catalog Card No: 97-062008
Manufactured in the United States of America

Distributed to the book trade and to the sporting goods trade by Stoeger Industries,
5 Mansard Court, Wayne, New Jersey 07470.

In Canada, distributed to the book trade and to the sporting goods trade by Stoeger Canada, Ltd.,
1801 Wentworth Street, Unit 16, Whitby, Ontario L1N8R6.

INTRODUCTION

The history of the knife actually started thousands of years before our own species, *Homo Sapiens*, ever arrived on the scene. The first cutting edge was probably a fragment that broke off a rock used for pounding. This sharp stone flake opened a wide range of new survival possibilities. Some modern anthropologists feel early humans quickly found they could use their new cutting tool to rapidly reduce a large kill into smaller pieces. This, in turn, allowed them to carry the kill into the trees before large carnivores could show up and take their meal away from them.

Pounding stones were typically picked up off the ground, used and then discarded. Stone knives, were different in that they were actually manufactured for specific tasks and often retained for later use. For well over a million years, humans have depended on a sharpened cutting edge as their most vital survival advantage. Even today, there is hardly a manufacturing process that doesn't require at least a few cutting edges to produce individual parts that are assembled into our most advanced machines.

Despite advances in technology, personal cutting tools in the form of steel-blade knives remain nearly as important as the chipped flint blade was to our cave-dwelling ancestors 50,000 years ago.

For many, the most convenient and portable form of cutting edge is the folding knife. While the styles and uses may vary from one region to the next, the knife that folds into its handle is always there when needed.

One of the earliest marks of adulthood I can recall while growing up on a farm was that grown men all carried good pocketknives. My grandfather and uncle both used their three-blade stockmen folders constantly around the shop, barn and in the fields.

I acquired my first knife — a tiny, inexpensive single-blade shell-bolster folder with the edge ground off — when I was about four years old. Several more low-end, shell-bolster knives were to follow, but I dreamed of the day when I could own a quality multi-blade folder made by someone such as Western, W.R. Case or Camillus. In other words, I wanted a real man's knife.

Indeed, most of my spare time during the teen years was spent trying to earn enough money to buy knives. By the time I graduated from high school, my modest knife collection amounted to 30 blades or so, most of them folders.

That summer, I enlisted in the Army and soon found myself bound for Vietnam. I remember passing through O'Hare Airport in Chicago and noticing a Swiss Army knife in a gift shop. The can opener and screw driver blades of that Swiss folder looked useful, so I added the little red-handled pocketknife to the Western three-blade stockman I was carrying.

Thus began my love affair with Swiss Army folders. I carried that same knife throughout a tour in Vietnam with the 82nd Airborne

Division, plus four years of college and several summer forestry jobs.

I sold my first knife article to the old "American Blade" magazine in 1979 and within a few years found myself evaluating new knives for several cutlery publications. Over the next several years I carried and worked with just about every basic pattern of folding knife on the market.

I'm no longer a full-time forester, but I still hike, backpack, camp, canoe, hunt, fish, cross-country ski and generally explore the great northwest.

My small ranch in Washington continues to graze several head of cattle and produce vegetables and fruits in abundance. Through all these years, I've used a folding knife as an everyday tool for a thousand and one uses.

It long since became obvious to me that authors of many cutlery guides such as this one have never used most of the knives about which they write. Thumb through the photos in the pages that follow and you will clearly that many of the knives illustrated have been used, some quite heavily. In most cases, you'll be looking at knives I've been carrying around on a daily basis long enough to understand and appreciate their strong points and weaknesses.

This book is meant to be used and enjoyed by all who own and appreciate folding knives in all their various forms.

Steven Dick

About the Author

Steven Dick was raised on farm in central Illinois. He enlisted in the army in 1967 and spent the next two years in Vietnam as a member of a long range patrol team in the

Airborne 75th Ranger Infantry. Returning stateside, he served for another 18 months as a paratrooper in the 82nd Airborne Division. He left the service in late 1970 and moved to the state of Washington, where he earned a degree in forestry and worked for a private timber company for several years.

In 1977, Dick has his first article on knives published in The American Blade magazine. From that point on, he branched out into writing about firearms, survival and cutlery for a wide range of publications. In 1994, Harris Publications asked him to be editor-in-chief of a new knife magazine, Tactical Knives, which has since become the world's leading cutlery publication.

Along with a continuing interest in forestry — he and his wife own a tree farm — Dick remains an energetic outdoorsman. His favorite pastimes include hunting, fishing, hiking, bird watching, kayaking, cross-country skiing and camping out throughout the Pacific Northwest, Canada and, whenever possible, Central America.

THE WORKING FOLDING KNIFE

Table of Contents

1

A BRIEF HISTORY OF FOLDING KNIVES

Like many utilitarian tools of daily life, the folding knife never received much attention from historians until recent times. Those who studied knife history knew about the "gladius" short sword and "pilum" spear used by the Romans, but few were aware that ordinary people in that period carried simple folding knives offering several advantages.

For example, folding the blade into the handle eliminated the need for a sheath or belt in which to carry the knife. The folding knife was also considered a basic tool — not a weapon — by those in power. While openly carrying a dagger or other large sheath knife might get a farmer or sailor in trouble with the law, a sturdy folding knife was not viewed as a threat. It was, in fact, used as an eating utensil for many hundreds of years. Dinner guests were expected to bring their own knives (and sometimes spoons) with them. Folding a knife blade into its handle was simply a more convenient way to carry one's eating utensil.

The typical early Roman knife consisted of a blade, pivot pin, and a one-piece handle of either metal, wood or horn. Without a backspring or lock, the only thing that held the

Two knives shown below are replicas of the springless "penny" knife from the 18th century. The non-locking knife (top) utilizes an exterior spring that runs along the back of the cattle horn handle. All three designs are probably French in origin.

blade open was friction against the handle or pressure against the edge during the cutting process.

Eventually, this type of basic folder became known as a "Penny Knife" (because of its low price). Even the lowest paid worker could afford this basic tool, and most were worn out and discarded many times over during the course of one's life. While better designs have evolved, the penny knife remains a standard pattern in less developed areas. The famous French Opinel (see chapter 8) of modern times is basically a penny knife with a simple blade lock added.

About three centuries ago, various back springs and locking mechanisms became common features on folding knives. By the time of the American Revolution, slip-joints, ring pulls, back mounted springs and lock knives were common and inexpensive. American Continental militia were required to provide

and carry a folding knife as part of their standard field gear, and more than a few have been found on Revolutionary War battlefields.

For those settlers who pushed the frontier westward, the folding knife was an everyday necessity. It made and patched horse harnesses, built furniture, carved spoons and kitchen bowls, fashioned foot wear, whittled the pegs that held buildings together, skinned trap line catches, and performed a thousand other homestead chores. Fur trading company records have revealed that thousands of folding knives were sold and traded to mountain men and various tribes of Native Americans.

The homesteading movement following the Civil War formed a largely rural population in the United States. This movement, combined with favorable tariff laws, created a huge demand for pocketknives produced domestically. As a result, large numbers of

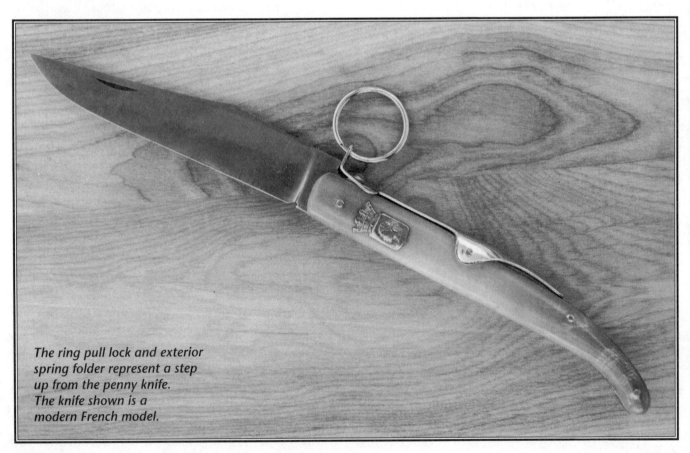

The ring pull lock and exterior spring folder represent a step up from the penny knife. The knife shown is a modern French model.

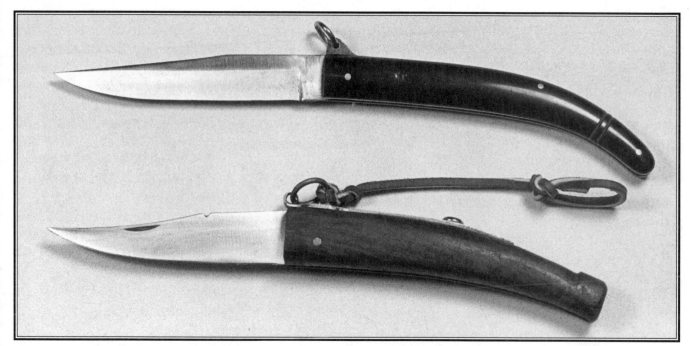

Two replicas of 18th century ring pull locks made for the modern muzzleloading trade.

unemployed European cutlery makers immigrated to the United States, causing one new factory after another to open.

Modern knife collectors now consider the years between 1890 and 1940 the "Golden Age of Pocketknives." The years after World War II, however, saw a steady decrease in the number of rural households, and with this development went much of the demand for folding knives. This downward trend was offset to a certain extent when folding knives gradually replaced the sheath knife as the favorite cutting tool of outdoorsmen.

The Vietnam period of the 1960s was to be the start of a renaissance in American cutlery. The was created a demand for custom combat knives that far exceeded the potential market for handmade sporting cutlery during that period. New custom knifemakers sprung up by the dozen and many still owe their fame to the battle blades they made during those years.

At about the same time, Buck's Model 110 folding hunter proved that a locking folder could be an excellent everyday working tool. Next, collectors gradually rediscovered

the handcrafted workmanship of pre-World War II folding knives. A "gold rush" of sorts soon followed as collectors searched high and low for previously unsold older pocketknives.

The end of the conflict in Vietnam saw many cutlery buffs switch to collecting custom combat and survival knives. The cutlery industry, encouraged by the success of the Buck 110, quickly introduced hundreds of new single-blade locking folders designed for every conceivable use a knife might be put to.

As the numbers of custom knife makers grew, individual makers sought greater challenges to set themselves apart from the crowd. For many, this proved to be the manufacture of handmade folders. By the 1980s, folding knives had once again become normal, everyday tools. Interest in collecting continued to grow until the market was able to support several cutlery magazines. More and more factories approached custom makers in their search for new and better designs.

Soon Spyderco had accomplished for one-hand opening knives and the serrated edge

Long bolster clasp knives such as these replicas (top and bottom) were common in Revolutionary America. Most Minutemen were required to carry one as standard gear. The top knife (stained by blackpowder while being carried in the author's muzzleloading hunting bag) has field dressed at least one deer. The center knife is a modern Italian folder of centuries old-design.

what Buck had done earlier for lockbacks. Thus was a new market born.

The 1990s have so far seen increased collaboration among custom- and factory-made projects, a renewed interest in auto-opening knives, and the rise of the folding self-defense knife movement. Basic knife-building materials and techniques continue to improve; and, while the fit and finish of an average factory folding knife may not equal those of the golden era, its modern counterpart is often a much better tool.

On the other hand, a small handful of custom knife makers are busy proving that the old masterpieces can be equaled — and even exceeded. This represents, without a doubt, the dawn of a new "Golden Age of the Folding Knife."

2
STEEL: THE HEART OF THE BLADE

Some knife users prefer plain carbon steel over stainless. Why? They believe stainless is too hard to sharpen, doesn't take as keen an edge, or is too brittle, soft or hard. Contradictory as they are, these opinions fail to consider an important fact: carbon steel and stainless come in different alloys, each with its own strengths and weaknesses.

Steel, in its most basic form, is iron with a small amount of added carbon, which allows the steel to be heat-treated to the desired level of performance. Steel with less than .5 percent carbon is considered low carbon and has little use in cutting edges; machetes are often made of this grade. Steels with .5 percent to 1.5 percent carbon are high carbon and are found in most common cutlery.

For many centuries, plain unalloyed carbon steel was made by iron ore smelters, who used charcoal as a heat source. Later, metal workers learned to add small quantities of:

- manganese, which increases strength and improves reaction to the heat-treating process;
- nickel, for toughness;
- vanadium, to retard grain growth at high temperatures and improve shock resistance;
- molybdenum, for greater toughness and responsiveness to heat-treating;
- silicon, for tensile strength and hardness;
- tungsten, to retain a small, dense grain structure and keen edge.

The most controversial of added elements,

however, is chromium. When used in larger quantities (more than 13 percent), it creates what is commonly known as a "stain-less" steel.

Cutlery makers often claim proprietary steel-making processes, assigning names such as surgical stainless, razor steel and Swedish tool steel. A tiny number of manufacturers are experimenting with traditional Japanese methods in smelting their own steel from iron ore. As exciting as this sounds, the end product is still basically a simple carbon alloy. While most custom knifemakers experiment more than commercial knifemakers, they are both generally restricted to those alloys supplied by the large steel companies.

Working folding knives are often used under more harsh conditions, and with less care, than fixed blade knives. Folding knives, usually

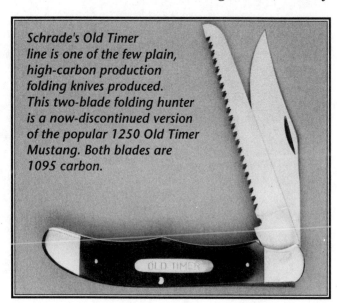

Schrade's Old Timer line is one of the few plain, high-carbon production folding knives produced. This two-blade folding hunter is a now-discontinued version of the popular 1250 Old Timer Mustang. Both blades are 1095 carbon.

Cutlery steel hardness is measured on the Rockwell C scale. A diamond point is pressed into the side of the metal under a set number of pounds. The depth of the dent produced is then measured and matched to the scale. Cutting tools run from approximately 45 for axes and machetes up to the mid-60s for hard custom knives. An average factory knife will register 52 to 56. Modern high-end factory blades and most custom blades run in the 58-60 range. While there are other factors to consider, generally the harder the knife the longer it will hold an edge. This also makes it harder to sharpen and may produce a brittle edge.

carried in a pocket, are exposed to body heat and corrosion-causing perspiration. Thus, the vast majority of folding knives today, both factory and custom made, are produced from a small group of stainless alloys. Carbon steel blades are still available, but in a smaller range of alloys.

1095 CARBON STEEL

The top carbon steel used in domestic commercial folder is 1095 or one of its foreign steel mill equivalents. the "95" indicates a .95 percent carbon content. This is a low alloy steel with just .30 percent to .50 percent manganese added to the carbon and iron. It is a popular steel and, with proper heat-treating, performs well. It seldom appears in custom knives, though.

0-1

This "tool steel alloy" contains .09 percent carbon, 1.0 percent manganese, 50 percent chrome, .30 percent nickel, .30 percent vanadium and .50 percent tungsten. Occasionally used in commercial folders, 0-1 is favored by custom makers when a plain carbon steel is considered desirable. It is generally considered to have better edge-holding qualities than 1095.

A-2

A-2 is considered a custom knifemaker's steel. This alloy, with 1.0 percent carbon, 5.0 percent chromium and 5.0 percent molybdenum, is tough and shock resistant. It's a good choice for fixed blade combat knives as edge-holding

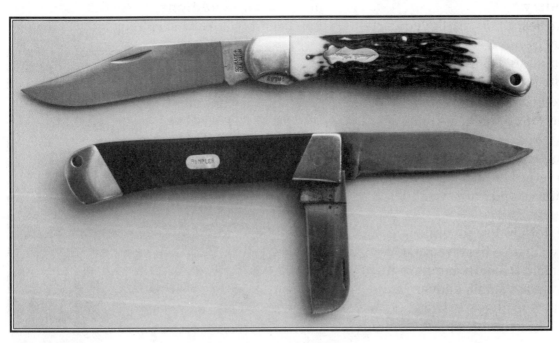

The knife at the bottom was custom made by Rimpler to the author's personal design, with A-2 blades for added strength. The knife at the top is a discontinued Schrade Uncle Henry folding hunter with a 440A blade.

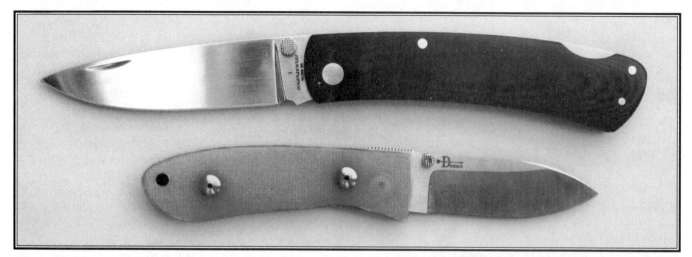

The top folder was custom made from 440C for the author by Phil Boguszewski. The bottom folder comes from the shop of Bob Dozier, one of just a few knifemakers who uses large amounts of D-2 in his folding knives.

is excellent. Like 1095 and 0-2, it rusts easily without special care.

D-2

D-2 is considered a semi-stainless alloy with its mixture of 11 to 13 percent chromium. Other ingredients are 0.45 percent manganese, .03 percent phosphorus, .02 sulfur, .60 percent silicon, .30 percent nickel, 1.10 percent vanadium and .7 percent molybdenum. Because of the difficulty of using D-2 steel on a production basis, its use in commercial cutlery production is limited, although many custom knifemakers consider it the best edge-holding steel available to the stock-removal maker.

The downside of D-2 is that it can be hard for unskilled users to sharpen; and its "almost stainless" quality can be tricky. If you grow lax in maintenance, speckled rust spots may appear.

5160

5160 spring steel is popular with hand forgers, who use it for larger bowies and hunters and, to a limited extent, for custom folders. It is one of several modern steel grades that contains lower carbon levels yet still makes an excel-

lent blade. The carbon runs .56 to .64 percent, manganese .75 to 1.0 percent, phosphorus 0.35 percent, sulfur 0.4 percent, chromium .7 to .9 percent, and silicon .15 to .30 percent.

VASCO WEAR

Vasco Wear is a steel used when knifemakers are looking for extreme edge retention, although it is hard to grind and polish. Users will tell you that when the blade does get dull, sharpening is difficult. During the 1970s, Gerber made limited runs of at least two Vasco Wear models, but these blades seldom appear on the market. The content: 1.12 percent carbon, 1.2 percent silicon, .30 percent manganese, 1.10 percent tungsten, 7.75 percent chromium, 1.60 percent molybdenum and 2.4 percent vanadium.

440 SERIES

In the stainless alloys we find the 440 series of steels: 440A, 440B and 440C. Carbon content is the difference — .6 to .75 percent in A, .75 to .95 percent in B and .95 to 1.2 percent in C. Chromium, the component that makes the steel "stainless," is a relatively high 16 to 18 percent in each.

Gerber uses 425 Modified stainless in many of its standard folders, such as these Gators.

All three are used in commercial cutlery to some extent, but 440A's easy working qualities make it the favorite of large scale knifemakers. Each of the grades offers corrosion-resistance that is desirable for use around salt water and for pure collector pieces.

440C once had a reputation for brittleness, more of a problem on large fixed blades used for chopping than light-duty folding blades. Recent advances in sub-zero quenching during heat-treating have mostly solved this problem.

425 MODIFIED

A more recent addition to the 400 series of stainless steels is 425 Modified. It contains .54 percent carbon, 13.5 percent chromium, .35 percent manganese, .35 percent silicon and 1.0 percent molybdenum. Despite the relatively low carbon content of this alloy, it seems to have a good reputation for holding an edge.

CAST DENDRITIC

Cast Dendritic steel is a subgroup of the 440 family. Its carbide crystal structure protrudes along the cutting edge, which in turn creates a microscopic serrated edge. Knifemakers have claimed that there is extraordinary edge-holding with this steel.

Logos and elaborate designs can be cast easily into the blade blank. The David Boye

While there are probably a few customs circulating, about the only production folder made from cast Dendritic steel is the model from David Boye. Casting allows blade decorations not possible with conventional steel.

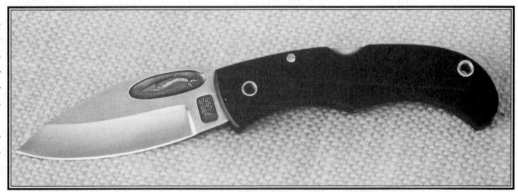

The Swedish company EKA uses San Vik 12C27 stainless on all of its stainless folders, such as this Super Swede.

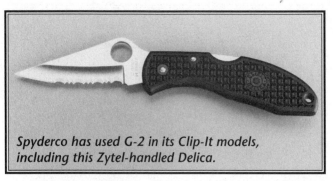

Spyderco has used G-2 in its Clip-It models, including this Zytel-handled Delica.

Lockback shown may be the only available dendritic steel folder.

SAN VIK 12C27

San Vik's 12C27 from Sweden is popular in European-made knives and, again, serves in the U.S. as a substitute for 440A — when the price is right. Carbon content runs .58 percent, chromium 14.0 percent, manganese .35 percent, and silicon 3.5 percent. There is good edge-holding ability with this alloy and corrosion resistance is reasonable, although not as good as the 400 series.

AUS-6 AND AUS-8

AUS-6 and AUS-8 are Japanese steel grade equivalents to 440A and 440B, respectively, but with slightly lower chromium levels

(13.0 to 14.5 percent) and vanadium (.10 to .25 percent). Both are commonly found in high-quality Japanese export lines such as SOG Specialty, Spyderco and Al Mar. Use among U.S. custom knifemakers is limited.

G-2

G-2 is a high alloy stainless popularized by Spyderco in its Clip-It folders. Benchmark also uses this grade in many of its knives, as do some custom folder makers. With a content of .90 percent carbon, .60 percent manganese, .02 percent phosphorus, .03 percent sulfur, 15.5 percent chromium, .37 percent silicon and .30 percent molybdenum, G-2 is nearly as good as the best stainless: ATS-34. The G-2, however, is easier to work with and has excellent corrosion resistance while maintaining a good edge that's easily sharpened.

Al Mar's Passport (top) is made from Japanese AUS-8. The Spyderco stainless steel-handled Delica is AUS-6.

One of the first production knives to use premium ATS-34 was the Al Mar Lightweight Sportsman.

154CM AND ATS-34

A couple of decades ago, an American steel created for jet engine parts, called 154CM, was considered the ultimate in a stainless alloy for knife blades, but steel mills stopped making it in dimensions suitable for custom knifemaking. The Japanese countered by introducing ATS-34, a clean alloy very close to the composition of the original 154CM.

ATS-34 quickly became the preferred stainless for most custom folders and many high quality commercial knives. Its composition — 1.05 percent carbon, .40 percent manganese, 0.3 percent phosphorus, 0.2 percent sulfur, 14.0 percent chromium, .35 percent silicon and

4.0 percent molybdenum — produces a stainless steel that provides fine edge-holding and corrosion-resistance properties, along with ease of resharpening. It's ideal for knives that come in contact with salt water.

CPM 440V

An alloy that is fast gaining favor among knifemakers and users is CPM 440V. It contains an amazing 2.15 percent carbon and 17 percent chromium, with 5.5 percent vanadium, .04 percent molybdenum and .04 percent silicon. Among the knives using CPM 440V are the Spyderco Military model. This alloy is known far and wide for holding an edge and for being exceedingly hard to resharpen. CPM is now producing a 420V that experts predict will exceed the 440V in quality.

300 SERIES STAINLESS

The 300 Series of stainless steel is sometimes used in knife production. The low carbon, high chromium steels were created for maximum corrosion resistance. They make poor cutlery steels but are popular among salt water divers who feel the resistance to corrosion is worth the poor edge-holding found on knives used

Spyderco's Military model was probably the first production knife to be made from CPM 440V.

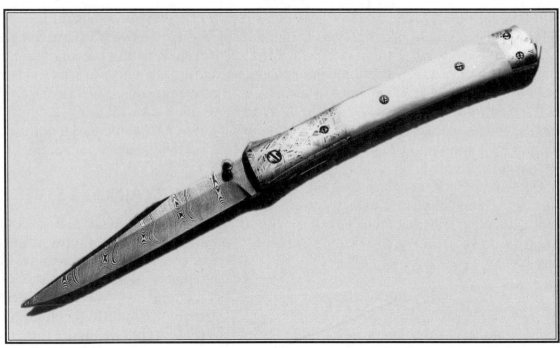

Damascus steel offers the knife-maker a wide variety of visually appealing options. It also provides an extremely strong, flexible blade with a high degree of edge bite. Knife by Jason Williams.

(PHOTO BY WEYER TOLEDO)

primarily for scraping, sawing and prying. The 300 Series knives are also used by cutlery makers in fittings, bolsters, handguards and similar knife components.

DAMASCUS

Damascus is not as easy to describe as the previous alloys. Modern Damascus, which is not necessarily the same as the original Damascus steel, consists of two or more steel types that have been heated, twisted and forge welded together. Usually this means one high and one low carbon steel, but there are no set rules. The end result is a blade with visible layers and patterns in the steel.

Performance-wise, Damascus steel provides greater strength and flexibility to the blade,

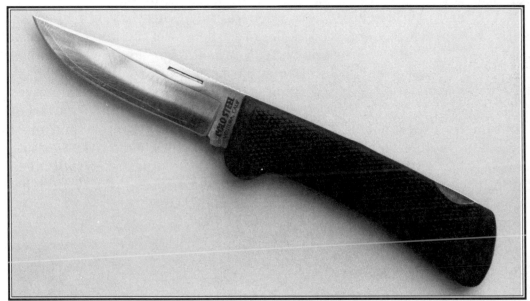

Cold Steel once produced this folder with a laminated blade. The lamination line is visible along the edge.

with the soft-hard layering giving the edge a microscopic serrated effect. These laminated blades are also easy to resharpen. Most Damascus blades are plain carbon steel mixes, but a few are made from laminated stainless. It is the custom knifemaker who is most likely to create blades using Damascus steel, although commercial shops do produce limited edition Damascus folders.

One commercial company, Bear MGC, forges its own Damascus steel as a standard part of its line. Bear sells bar stock to other cutlery makers in the United States, Germany and India.

LAMINATED STEEL

Laminated blades are made by layering hard, high alloy steel between two layers of softer, more flexible steel. Scandinavians and Japanese have used this method for many years to produce high-performance, low-cost blades.

The theory behind laminated steel is that the hard layer would be too brittle to stand up to normal use by itself, but by sandwiching it between the two soft layers it is allowed to flex. Cold Steel once made these two groups of laminated blade folders under the names of Shimubo and Clip-Mate. They have been discontinued. Currently, no known folder makers use this process.

CERAMIC

Commercial makers continue to experiment with non-traditional ceramic blades as an alternative to steel. Ceramic is harder than the hardest steel and holds an edge over an extremely long period of use.

But ceramics remain fairly brittle, inflexible and expensive. Resharpening usually requires a return to the manufacturer, as standard diamond sharpeners are too coarse for the ceramic edge. Still, a ceramic folder can, with care, be a useful investment. Boker offers an interchangeable folder with one ceramic blade and two made of conventional steel.

STAINLESS STEEL REIGNS

Modern stainless steel alloys have, for the most part, replaced plain carbon steel on both commercial and custom knives. Stainless edges stand up to such acidic foods as tomatoes, are easy to clean and resist corrosion. While in absolute terms carbon steel might, or might not, take a "sharper" edge than stainless, the average user will notice little difference in actual cutting performance between the two steel types.

The geometry of a knife's edge bevels and the skill of the user who resharpens the blade have more to do with its sharpness than whether it's stainless or carbon steel. Softness, hardness, flexibility, brittleness and ease of sharpening are all determined by factors other than whether the steel alloy has a high chromium content.

As a general rule, when buying a commercial knife of carbon steel the odds are that it will be 1095 or its foreign equivalent. A carbon steel custom knife will usually be 01 or 02. Working grade stainless commercial knives will be either 440A, 440C, 425, 12C27, AUS-6 or AUS-8. Premium grades of factory and most custom cutlery will utilize either ATS-34, 440C, G-2 or possibly 440V stainless steels. Between these basic blade materials there is a folding knife that will handle any job.

3

BASIC FOLDING KNIFE BLADE DESIGNS AND MATERIALS

One blade style, generally a spear or leaf shape, was once considered adequate for all cutting functions. As the cutlery industry evolved, specialized blade patterns appeared. During the Golden Age of pocketknives, there were several dozen different blade styles, each with its own name and supposed special use. This has now been condensed to a small handful. The designation for any pattern may vary among cutlery companies, but the actual style seldom does.

SPEAR POINT

The spear blade is probably the most frequently used design worldwide. The spine forms a curve that meets the edge at the center line or slightly below. At one time, the majority of American work folders utilized the spear blade as the master blade (the "master blade" on a folder is normally considered to be the largest). At the start of the 20th century, the clip point replaced the spear as the predominate master blade on most North American folders, but the spear remains extremely popular in Europe and in many other parts of the world. The Swiss Army pocketknife, probably the world's best selling folder, has long featured a spear as its master blade, as do the traditional Boy Scout and electrician patterns of folder.

The spear offers the advantage of a fairly strong point style for knives that may see hard use. A disadvantage is that the common wide spear blade is a poor tool for situations where a piercing point is needed, such as punching holes in leather or fabric, boring holes in wood, and when field dressing game. Some knives, especially those designed as weapons, overcome this weakness by elongating the point. While this improves piercing power, it also removes much of the edge belly (the curve formed by the edge bending up to meet the spine of the knife) that is essential to many utility uses of a folding knife.

For some, bluntness is considered a plus for the spear point. The spear point on a Boy Scout knife, for instance, is generally thought of being more utilitarian, and less dangerous and aggressive in appearance, than some other blade patterns.

Most modern spear points are flat ground from the spine to the edge. Earlier makers

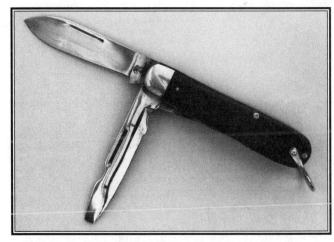

The standard master blade for electrician knives has long been the spear point.

also offered "saber ground" spear points. A saber ground blade is left full thickness to somewhere near the center of the blade, and then abruptly beveled to an edge. This gives the blade a more aggressive appearance, and the increased thickness strengthens the knife. However, saber ground blades don't always cut as well as a flat ground version, and are now mostly reserved for clip point blades and knives designated as survival or combat models.

Pen blades are small spear blades backing up the master blade when an edge is needed for fine work. They were once used to sharpen feather quill pens, hence the name, but this function has long been obsolete. Very small

dress knives often use pen blades as their master.

Daggers are spear point blades with top and bottom sides fully sharpened. Because the top side of most folding knife blades is exposed when the knife is folded, true dagger blades are not practical for most conventional designs. A few folding knives, such as the Applegate/Fairbairn folding combat, get around this inherent design weakness by having the entire blade enclosed in the handle when in the closed position.

DROP POINT

The drop point has the best claim to being a modern invention. It is a spear blade on which the edge meets the spine somewhere above the center line. The spine in turn forms a gentle, convex curve down to meet the edge. Bob Loveless popularized the drop point on his fixed blade hunting knives during the late 1960s. This blade style was soon considered

As these two pages from a 1930s Remington cutlery catalog show, there are many variations and names for the same basic blade patterns. With a few exceptions, such as the Remington can-opener, all of these blade patterns are still in use.

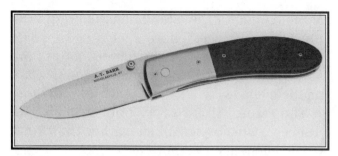

The drop point has become the accepted blade pattern for knives intended for field dressing game. This Liner-Lock is from A.T. Barr.

(PHOTO BY WEYER OF TOLEDO)

mandatory on custom sheath knives intended for hunting.

There is now a vast selection of both custom and commercial folders in this blade style. The primary advantage of the drop point is that it gives the blade a little more belly for skinning and slicing than the traditional spear, but it also provides a blunt point for opening game. The curve of the spine helps prevent the point from snagging the internal organs of large game animals when the blade is used edge up during field dressing. In the early days of the modern drop point, this blade style was described as "like putting zippers on deer."

CLIP POINT

The most common blade style found on American folders is the clip point. Here, the spine runs straight for part of its length and then either forms a straight downward slant or is ground into a concave curve to the spot it meets the point. By varying where the slope to the point starts, makers create long and short clips in a wide variety of patterns.

A few years ago, I was shown the prototype of a new folding hunter model by a large knife manufacturer. The point on the knife was a very useful looking drop style that I thought would have wide appeal with hunters. When the knife actually entered the market, I found

it now had the traditional clip style of point. I asked the factory design engineer what happened? His response was that their market research had shown that the drop point was thought of as a hunter's blade, while the clip was considered an everyday work knife. Since there were far more potential customers among working people than hunters, they went with the clip. The folder in question went on to become one of the best sellers on the market, the Gerber Gator.

The clip point has two primary advantages over the spear. It is much sharper and pierces materials much easier. This is important on knives that might be used as weapons, but it is also useful on an everyday utility blade. Any time a hole needs to be punched or reamed, the clip comes into its own. The second advantage of the clip point is more esoteric: It simply looks more appealing than the average spear style, and looks sell more knives than any other feature.

Buck's family of titanium handled folders are perfect examples of the classic American clip point folder.

Clip point blades come in a wide variety of patterns and the names sometimes blur. Most trapper and muskrat pattern folding knives have a long, narrow style of clip blade, sometimes referred to as a Turkish clip, a California clip, a lance blade, or as a skinning blade. They all serve the same functions.

SHEEPSFOOT

After the spear/drop point and the clip, the most common folding knife blade is the sheepsfoot. This is a blade with a perfectly straight edge and a spine that curves all the way down to meet it at the "point" (there really isn't a point on this blade in the conventional sense).

In the past, a blade known as the Wharncliffe was also popular on folders. Basically, this is a sheepsfoot with a longer, more drawn out curve to the spine that forms sometimes closer to a real point.

Sheepsfoots are a standard backup blade on stockknives and other utility pattern folders. This blade style is excellent for woodworking tasks, opening packages and cutting patterns out of flat materials like leather, canvas, cardboard, rubber, etc.

Large, single blade sheepsfoot knives were the traditional cutting tool of the sailor. Legend has it that this blade style was required because it didn't provide a point for stabbing during the altercations that arose on long sea voyages. There seems to be some truth to this story as sheepsfoot knives are still common among both civilian and military nautical knives.

The issue British Army pocket knife also utilizes a sheepsfoot blade rather than what would seem like the more useful spear or clip. Some researchers of sheepsfoot nautical knives have stated it's better not to have a point on a knife that might be dropped from the ship's rigging to the deck below. Makes sense.

In addition to the safety factor, a large sheepsfoot is an ideal blade style for cutting rope on a sailing ship. The straight edge is simply placed on the line and struck with a belaying pin.

For those who have access to something that will serve as a cutting board surface, this is still the best way to make a clean cut in rope with a knife. Any light wooden club will work for the belaying pin.

Horticultural knives also feature large and small sheepsfoot blades. Most grafting blades are sheepsfoot, as are some types of pruning and flower cutting knives.

SPEY

The third standard blade in most multi-bladed knives is the spey. The standard spey is a

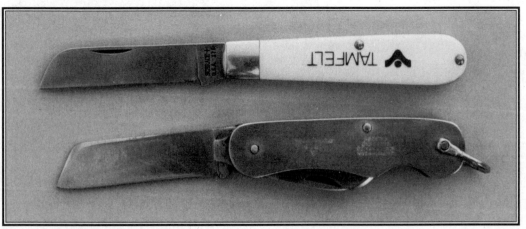

Both the top knife, a Schrade single blade, and the bottom, a British Army issue model, feature a sheepsfoot blade for their master. The British Army knife was carried by an American Green Beret for several years of duty.

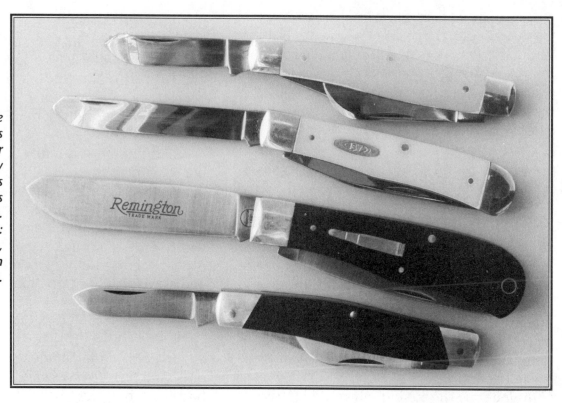

The spey blade on knives was designed for surgical use by livestock raisers and as a trapper's skinning tool. From the top: Queen, Case, Remington and Buck.

small blade with what might be called a stubbed-off clip point and a well-rounded edge belly.

Originally, the spey was used for castrating male animals and performing minor livestock surgery. Because of this, its edge was kept extra sharp and reserved for special duties. Some cutlery companies ground the spey blades extra thin and etched them "For Flesh Only." Having grown up on a farm and still working as a small time cattle rancher, I have regularly used the spey blade for its intended purpose. The blunt tip is also useful in the prevention of accidental stabbing of struggling animals, and the curved edge slices well if it's kept extremely sharp.

Some hunters and trappers have also found the spey blade is useful for the fine skinning work around the head and ears of game. Still, the majority of spey blades are not used for their original purpose. Modern non-livestock raising knife users are more likely to reserve the spey blade for rough work and abusive cutting than for delicate tasks.

Along with the standard spey, there is the long spey blade, which is discussed in more detail in the section on trapper pattern folding knives.

HAWK'S BILL

As their name indicates, hawk's bill blades are shaped like the beak of a predatory bird. The majority of hawk's bill folders have been marketed in horticultural circles for pruning fruit trees and shrubs. In fixed blade versions,

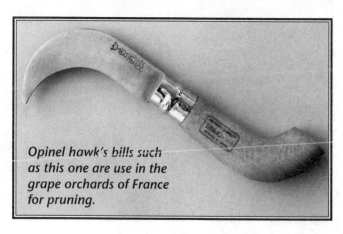

Opinel hawk's bills such as this one are use in the grape orchards of France for pruning.

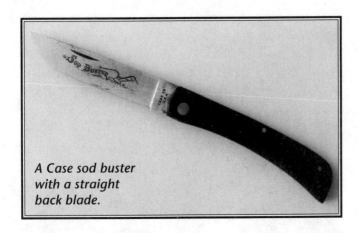

A Case sod buster with a straight back blade.

the hawk's bill is also popular for cutting carpeting, linoleum, and roofing. It is useful for weeding in tight areas around flower and rose beds, and also has a reputation as a street fighter's weapon. I have met at least one ex-U.S. Navy SEAL currently working in international security who prefers this blade style for self-defense.

In general, the inside curved edge of the hawk's bill makes it a specialist type of tool that you either have a need for or you don't. If not kept very sharp, the hawk's bill tends to hang up in a cut rather than slicing on through.

STRAIGHT BACK

While not all that common on anything but sod-buster folders and a few customs knives, the straight back blade actually is a fairly useful pattern. The second blade on the classic two-blade folding hunter is usually very close to a straight back, and several of Gerber's early lockback models were basically straight backs.

As the name indicates, the spine of this blade pattern runs straight all the way to the point. The edge parallels the spine for most of its length and then abruptly curves up to meet it at the end. What you end up with is a blade with plenty of straight edge for whittling and utility, a good belly for skinning and slicing and a reasonably sharp point for piercing.

RAZOR POINT

Razor point folder blades (sometimes called one-hand man's knives) are one of those blade patterns that have remained on the market for a long period of time without any good explanation. Basically, the blade has the general appearance of a straight razor blade, but without the thin hollow grind. This blade appeals to those who think that simply looking like a razor blade means the folding knife blade is literally as sharp as a razor. Actually, a straight razor is much too thin at the edge to make a good utility tool.

The Boker knife, bottom, has the classic razor point, while the Bear MGC, top, is a more modern version of the design.

As its alternate name indicates, the razor point was once thought of as a blade shape that could be opened one-handed. The hooked point was somehow snagged on clothing, table top or other object, and the blade pried open. It may have worked, but there are now many easier one-hand opening folders.

CHISEL POINT

Among the modern blade patterns trying to find a niche in the market is the chisel point. Cold Steel may probably be given credit for starting this fad with its folding version of the popular Tanto fixed blade.

On the chisel point, both the spine and the edge run parallel to each other to a short distance from the point. At this spot, the edge forms an abrupt straight angle up to meet the spine. Normally, the blade grind lines reinforce this slanted point for extra strength.

In recent years, a second variation of the chisel point has become popular: the one-sided edge grind. In Japan this has long been used on specialized woodworking and horticultural knives. Ernest Emerson was probably the first custom maker to offer this Japanese edge on his folders. Benchmade quickly picked up on it for its Emerson designed CQC7 defensive folder. Since then, nearly all makers of tactical type folders have added a one-sided grind to their lines.

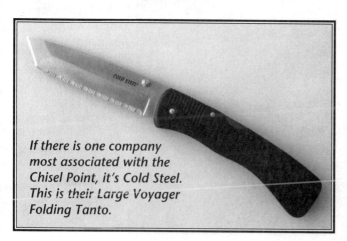

If there is one company most associated with the Chisel Point, it's Cold Steel. This is their Large Voyager Folding Tanto.

The advantages of the chisel point are primarily related to defensive use of a folder. First, the chisel point is relatively strong compared to other common folding knife blades. The slanted edge aids in penetration and cuts full width as it thrusts. One-sided grinds are more controversial and many makers have added them to their lines simply because they sell. Those who endorse the one-sided grind say they are easier to sharpen, take a supersharp edge and cut flesh extremely well.

Other knife users are willing to argue each of these points. Detractors say the edge is left unsupported on the flat side and is thus more fragile. Generally, one-sided grind knives are considered more delicate in Japan than two-sided edges.

HANDLE AND FRAME MATERIAL

Bone

Folding knife handle materials may be divided into three general categories: traditional, high tech, and exotic. For most folding knife users, the most traditional of handle materials was once bone, or as the cutlery companies call it, bone stag. The bone in question is sawed from the shin bone of a cow. Once rough shaped, it may be dyed to practically any color desired. A red/brown color, simply called red bone, was the standard but many other shades were tried.

In most cases, cutlery companies declared the bone a cheaper substitute for stag horn. To make this bone resemble stag horn, the surface was given a series of small gouges forming a pattern called jigging. With the exception of barlow pattern knives, practically all bone handles were jigged. A few types, such as Queen Cutlery's Winterbottom and the now-gone Robeson Cutlery's Strawberry bone, are easily recognizable as coming from one particular source.

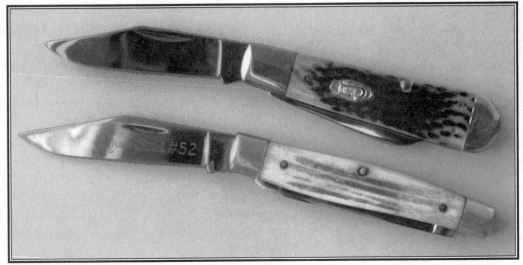

Bone may be dyed to about any color the maker feels looks attractive. The bottom knife is an old Queen Winterbottom bone. The top is a Case Red Bone handle. Case has long been known for using more bone than any other cutlery company.

With use, bone fades and wears in a manner many owners find appealing. On the down side, it's limited in supply, fairly difficult and expensive for the factory to work, and can be broken or cracked easily if dropped on a hard surface. As plastics have improved, more and more companies have switched from bone to a synthetic grip. Today, only Case Cutlery uses any real quantity of bone on standard line folders. Others, including Queen, Blue Grass, Camillus and a number of Solingen companies, produce special runs of bone handled folders with an eye primarily on the collector market.

Stag

Stag, the handle material bone long tried to imitate, was fairly common on even inexpensive folders during the 19th century. The depletion of natural sources for stag caused it to be limited to premium quality folding knives. One reason for stag's scarcity is that only certain types are considered suitable for

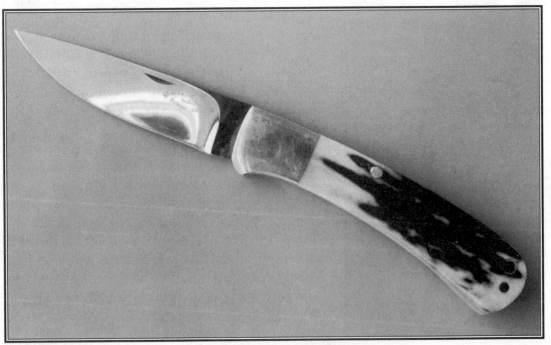

This Wayne Clay custom hunter has genuine stag handle slabs. Many feel this is the most attractive knife handle available.

knife handles. The first choice in stag horn is the Asian Sambar. These large deer drop their antlers each year and licensed collectors scour the forests for it. While the animals are fully protected in most countries, declining habitat is shrinking the size of the herd and the harvest.

Some European companies utilize native red deer horn (closely related to the American elk) and this seems to work fairly well. American elk and whitetail deer are considered too pithy for commercial purposes. Custom makers occasionally use elk and deer antler, and while it doesn't have the striking appearance of Sambar, it seems to be acceptable.

Generally, stag antler is more durable than bone but it is also more prone to shrinking and expanding, depending on the climate. Like bone, stag picks up its own individual wear and stain patterns over long periods of use that many knife carriers find appealing.

Wood

After bone and stag, the most common natural handle material is wood. Native walnut and tropical hardwoods such as rosewood were very common folding knife handles

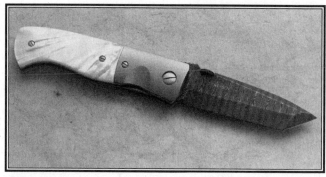

One seldom sees large pieces of pearl such as those used on this Emerson CQC7. While very attractive pearl, it is not particularly durable.

throughout the 19th century, but modern plastics quickly replaced them in this century. It may not be as durable as stag or bone, but wood has a great feel and appearance.

In recent decades, knifemakers have begun using large quantities of plastic laminated wood under various trade names on knife handles. These are normally inexpensive softwoods, dyed to a desirable color, and injected with plastic under great pressure. Pakkawood is one of the most common varieties, but there are many other proprietary names for similar products.

This material has the advantage of retaining some of the original natural appearance of

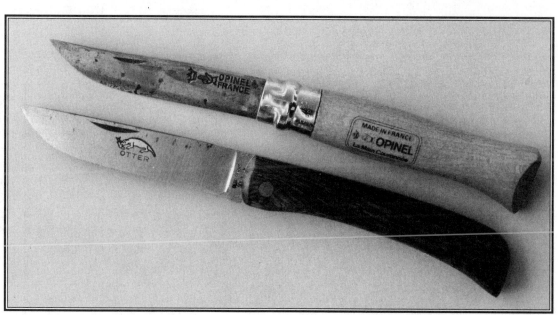

Probably the most common modern folders to use for a handle are the Opinel (top) ring locks, and various German made Sodbuster pattern folders (bottom).

wood, but with greatly increased durability and weather resistance. The down side is that it is normally much more slippery than untreated wood.

Horn, Tortoise Shell, Ivory and Pearl

Cattle horn, tortoise shell and ivory were once common folding knife handle materials. While the use of cattle horn has declined, it may still be found on a fair number of knives imported from third world countries. It is, however, less durable than bone or stag and subject to insect attacks.

Elephant ivory and tortoise shell are both considered products of endangered species and thus subject to government restrictions. Fossil ivory from mammoths and ancient walrus is legally available in large quantities and some knife users appreciate its mottled, stained appearance. Fossil ivory is generally more durable than modern elephant tusk.

Pearl was once popular on fancy pen knives and other folders that were considered for Sunday wear. It's not particularly strong, difficult to work and breaks easily. Natural sources have become limited, so not much is used today.

Celluloid

An early variety of plastic once popular on

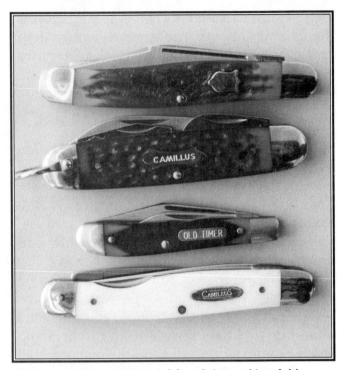

The most common material for plain working folder handles is Delrin plastic. From the top: Camillus Stockman, Camillus Camper, Schrade Jack, and Camillus Muskrat.

knife handles was celluloid. Available in a great variety of colors and patterns with names such as Christmas Tree and Candy Stripe, celluloid was a material you either liked or hated. Unfortunately, it was also highly flammable so it was quickly replaced as bet-

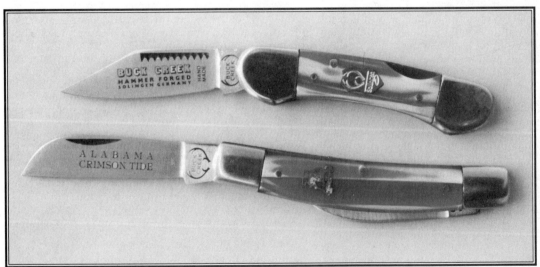

Real celluloid has been gone from knifemaking for several decades, but German makers such as Buckcreek sometimes turn out a Delrin copy. At the top, a Buckcreek lockback Canoe; at the bottom, a Buckcreek Congress.

ter plastics came along. From a collector's standpoint, celluloid handles are subject to a natural decomposition that eventually destroys them. This is hard on the pocketbook if you are buying old knives as an investment.

Delrin

The current standard plastic in the knife industry is Delrin. Delrin may be colored and molded to give a close resemblance to bone, stag, ivory, tortoise shell or just about any other natural material desired. Buyer beware: Knifemakers using Delrin substitutes for natural materials like to use confusing names, leading the buyer to think he is receiving real stag or bone. If it doesn't say "genuine" stag or bone, it probably isn't.

Delrin is much more durable than any of the above natural materials and much cheaper to work with. Still, very few serious knife buffs have much use for Delrin as it never quite captures the natural beauty of any of the materials it imitates.

Delrin may also be produced in about any

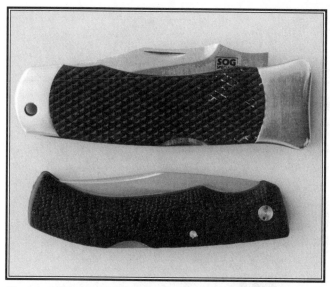

Kraton offers a semi-soft, durable substitute for rubber on knife handles. Top knife: SOG Tomcat; Bottom, Gerber Gator-Mate

color the maker desires, but the only shade that has ever been in demand from serious knife users is yellow. Trapper pattern folders, in particular, are traditionally offered in yellow Delrin handles, but most other styles may be found in this shade from time to time. This may be because the color is bright enough to be easily spotted if the knife is dropped.

Micarta

Micarta, a phenolic resin impregnated material developed by Westinghouse, has long been popular with custom knifemakers. Wood-based Micartas retain most of the natural grain and color, but become impervious to water and much more resistant to chipping and cracking. Linen-based Micartas are considered the strongest and are available in many desirable colors. Green, gray, black and camo colored linen Micartas are popular on combat and survival-style knives. Paper Micarta is considered an excellent substitute for elephant ivory and difficult to discern the difference. While paper Micarta is not as durable as some of the other Micarta types, it is much more stable than natural ivory.

Micarta has long been favored on custom knives for its durability. From the top: Atkinson, Boguszewski and Rimpler customs.

Zytel has quickly become the favorite thermoplastic for modern lightweight handle frames. Buck also uses Valox on some its older models. From the top: Katz Blackcat, Outdoor Edge Field-Lite and a Buck Bucklite.

Kraton

Except for a few very high quality commercial folders, such as those produced by Al Mar

G-10 is one of the latest high tech handle materials for heavy duty tactical folders. The material is a form of woven fiberglass. From the top: Spyderco Military, Benchmade AFCK and Benchmade/Emerson CQC7.

knives, Micarta is primarily a custom knife handling material. The large cutlery factories have developed a separate family of modern synthetic materials better suited to mass production.

Kraton, a semi-soft synthetic rubber, was once the odds-on favorite material for high tech folder handles. Many companies quickly found they had problems adhering Kraton to the metal frame of their knives. A few, such as Gerber and its highly popular Gator line, have created special knife frame designs that hold the soft material in place.

Kraton does offer a soft, comfortable, secure, non-slip gripping surface. On the down side, under hard use it may scratch and wear more than some of the other synthetics.

Zytel

Probably the most popular among today's synthetics is Zytel, a fiberglass-based thermoplastic. It is easily cast into any shape and handle texture, and is extremely durable under hard use. Because of its great strength, Zytel ideally lends itself to one-piece ultra-light weight linerless folders. Practically every major cutlery company has added at least one Zytel folder to its line in the last five years.

Valox

A similar but less common thermoplastic is Valox. Buck Knives has used this material on its lightweight models for some time with good results. Kraton, Zytel and Valox are all trademarked proprietary materials; a number of similar materials are starting to enter the market under various other brand names. The ones used by the better known cutlery companies are usually about as good as the materials they are copying, but beware the low-end knock-offs.

G-10

The "in" handle material for both custom and high-tech factory knives at present is another fiberglass-based synthetic called G-10. So far, the only colors available are shades of black, gray and olive. In addition to being extremely durable and lightweight, G-10 offers a textured, woven surface for an excellent grip.

Benchmade and Spyderco have used G-10 on most of their recent folding defensive knives. Custom makers such as Kit Carson, Allen Elishewitz and Bob Terzuola are also using large quantities of the material.

Bronze, Steel and Aluminum

A wide variety of metals have been used for folding knife handles over the years. Bronze was once fairly popular for sailors' knives because it held up well around salt water. The down side, of course, is that bronze is extremely heavy for anything but very small knives. In modern times, stainless steel has replaced bronze on a few all-metal sailing knives. Although not as heavy as bronze, stainless steel handles on folders of any size are still cumbersome. Spyderco has had good luck with stainless steel on a number of the original Clip-it models. One advantage of stainless steel is that it can be engraved much easier. For this reason, it is fairly popular on small dress knives.

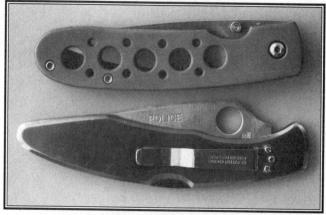

The top knife is an aluminum handled Benchmade Leopard; the bottom is a stainless steel handled Spyderco Police. Aluminum offers a trade off between light weight and reasonable strength, and heavy weight and high strength.

Aluminum weighs considerably less than stainless and I've been told by at least one knife company that there is no real loss in overall strength. Other than its unsuitability for engraving, the one disadvantage of aluminum for folding knife handles is that it is soft enough to easily pick up many small dings and scratches in use.

In general, these disadvantages are simply cosmetic, but not everyone appreciates the appearance of an aluminum knife handle after a year or two of use. There are various

Factory carbon fiber handled knives, such as this Spyderco/ Walker, are still fairly uncommon.

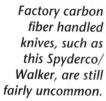

coatings to protect the surface of aluminum handles available on the market and most work to one degree or another.

Carbon Fiber

Another modern handle material that sells mostly on its "high tech" appeal is carbon fiber. Carbon fiber handles are extremely light in weight and are said to be ultra strong. The carbon fiber has a natural shiny finish some knife users may think looks cheap, and the surface tends to be overly slick.

At least one custom maker, Warren Thomas, is experimenting with composite knife blades made of steel and carbon fiber. The theory here is to provide a blade both thin and light weight while retaining its strength.

Titanium

The hottest trend in metal handled folding

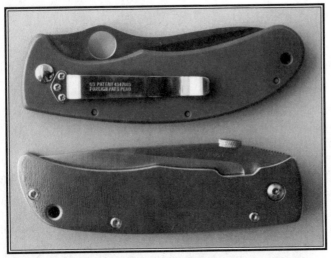

Titanium is valued for both its high strength and light weight. From the top: Blade-Tech Hunter and Wayne Clark Utility.

knives is the titanium frame. Although the difference is barely noticeable next to an aluminum knife handle, titanium is light weight. It is also extremely strong, non-corrosive and non-conductive (mainly an advantage for military personnel working around explosives).

On the down side, it is both expensive and difficult to work. Given its non-traditional appearance, titanium will probably never catch on for everyday work and outdoor folders. Nevertheless, it does have some good applications on survival, military and defensive folders.

Semi-Precious Stones

Other handle materials include a wide range of precious metals and semi-precious stones. Turquoise inlaid handles have a wide following, with David Yellowhorse setting most of the trends. Most of this group are primarily for dress as "show off" knives rather than being used as real working tools.

If I had to pick my favorite handle material, it would be natural antler stag. Zytel and G-10 work equally well on any of the ultra-lightweight high-tech folders, as does Delrin on everyday working tools.

Aluminum or titanium would be my choice for a folder requiring both light weight and high strength. Beyond that, it is a matter of personal taste and esthetics what handle material folding knife users carry. Practically all of the common modern handle materials will stand up to many years of use if they are not abused.

4
TRADITIONAL SLIP-JOINT POCKET KNIVES

Early folding knives generally lacked a back-spring because this made them cheaper and simpler to produce. Also, reliable spring steel was difficult to produce. In the mid-18th century, metal working technically advanced to the point that spring-back pocket knives became practical on a large scale. Soon the most common form of pocketknife mechanism became what is now known as the slip-joint.

A spring set into the back of the handle frame holds the knife in the opened or closed position without locking. By pulling (or pushing) on the back of the blade, the tang 'slips' by the end of the spring into position. From a legal standpoint, the slip-joint is considered less likely to be use as a stabbing instrument than knives with a lockback system. Concealed weapon laws frequently exempt ordinary pocket knives, which are usually accepted as slip-joint folders.

Long bolster "barlow" clasp knives such as the one on top were very popular in the New World around the time of the American Revolution. They eventually evolved into the standard 3⅜-inch closed pattern such as the Boker on the bottom.

The top knife is a modern Boker barlow and the bottom a Colonial. Both follow the traditional Russell pattern.

How safe and reliable the slip-joint system is depends both on the strength of the backspring and the care taken by the user. A very strong back spring can make the knife safer to use, but at the same time much more difficult to open. A weak backspring may cause the knife to fold on the fingers of a careless user.

By the time of the American Revolution, large, single blade, slip-joint clasp knives were in universal use in the colonies. Those called up for militia duty were required to carry a folding knife as well as a musket. As English clasp knives of the period had long bolsters, these knives are now referred to as early barlows. The original Barlows were said to be a family of knifemakers in Sheffield, England, from 1600-1800. What their knives actually looked like is not clear and the term seems to have become generic in the trade fairly early for long bolstered folding utility knives.

RUSSELL BARLOWS

In 1875, the American company of John Russell (of Russell Green River butcher knife fame) entered the pocketknife market with a line of single and double bladed barlows that quickly became the modern concept of what this knife should look like.

Basically, Russell split barlows into two groups: the standard 3⅜-inch closed size and a large 5-inch closed "Daddy" barlow. Blade patterns were either the spear or clip point, but sheepsfoot and razor point were occasionally used. The popularity of the Russell barlow grew because the company put a high grade steel blade into a very plain bone handle and sold the product for well under a dollar for several decades. The long metal bolster also added an extra margin of strength to a relatively small work knife. During a period when much of the United States was still rural, the barlow pocketknife became an everyday necessity.

As with every folding knife pattern, once the Russell barlow became a success the entire cutlery industry followed the lead and added similar versions to their lines.

The majority of these knives were pretty much exact copies of the Russell, but a few experimented with size, blade shape and handle material variations. The standard barlow has slowly lost popularity among knife users since World War II. Still, Queen, Camillus and Boker all continue to offer the barlow. The standard 3⅜-inch barlow remains one of the strongest working folders for its size. Many generations of farmers have proven that in the right hands the barlow will get the job done.

EQUAL END JACKS

Much of the remaining American folding knife pre-1890s market was dominated by simple equal end and swell butt two-blade jack knives. An equal end folder is just that; both ends of the handle are basically identical and usually capped with metal bolsters. On swell butt folders the rear end of the handle is larger than the front, with a straight taper in between. Swell butts are about equally divided between knives with two bolsters and those lacking a rear bolster.

Most of these folders were plain, stoutly constructed working knives with wood or bone handles and one or two blades folding from the same end of the frame. Although the now-popular clip point was offered, and the

The ultimate Equal End Jack would have to be the three blade Cattle Knife, such as this modern one from Bull Dog Knives. Most equal ends were simple one or two blade patterns.

Both these Queen Jack knives follow the swell butt pattern popular in the United States before the turn of the 20th century. While the style lingers on, it is nowhere near as popular as it once was.

square point or sheepsfoot had its following among sailors, the basic spear point seems to have dominated blade styles. While about every size imaginable was offered, the average jackknife of this period was between 3½ and 4¼ inches long closed.

The pre-1890s may be called the Model T period of the American cutlery industry. One could have any type of work knife one wanted as long as it was an equal end or swell butt (barlows are also swell butt folders), or a one or two blade spear-point jack.

While more elaborate pocket knives were available, with the exception of a few three-blade cattle knives, most were expensive letter openers for the white collar trade. This all changed almost overnight in the 1890s when Congress enacted a series of tariff laws against imported cutlery. Sheffield, England,

long the source of the finest folding knives, was suddenly priced out of the market place. Rather than starve in England, many of the best cutlery craftsmen immigrated to the United States and started new businesses.

The period between 1890 and 1930 is now considered by pocketknife collectors to be the golden age of folding knives. Companies such as New York Knife, Miller Brothers, Case Brothers, Napanoch, Holley and Schatt & Morgan began hand-crafting pocketknives that only in recent years have the best custom knifemakers been able to equal.

Not only were new companies springing up everywhere, their knife lines were expanding to incredible size. Many catalogs listed several hundred different patterns and each variation was frequently offered in multiple handle materials.

Strong working knives with one, two, three, four, five and occasionally six blades were available at reasonable prices in every hardware store. The majority of slip-joint knife patterns popular today originated during this period of rapid industrial expansion.

Most of these new folding knife variations did not perform any particular function better than a long list of more common models. Simply pleasing the visual preferences of a handful of customers was enough to keep a knife listed in the catalog. Unfortunately, the hard times of the Depression caused many cutlery companies to reexamine this policy. A good number of the finest companies closed their doors and those that remained started reducing slip-joint folding knife lines down to a core group of easily produced models.

All of which brings us to the subject of the slip-joint folders commonly available today and their uses.

CATTLE KNIVES

The cattle knife was an equal end pattern that normally came with a large spear point blade, a small spey and a sheepsfoot blade.

As the name indicates, it was once popular with cattle ranchers and farmers, but the Stockman pattern has come close to completely replacing it. Parker Brothers imports a few cattle knives in both 3¾-inch and 4¼-inch closed sizes under its Bulldog brand, and a few German Hen and Rooster brand knives in similar styles are occasionally available.

The primary advantage of the cattle knife or any other equal end style knife is that the rounded bolsters are comfortable to carry in a pocket.

Other than the barlow, the only taper side jacks that remain are a scattering of small- to medium-sized pocket folders such as the Queen Model 10 and the Boker Razor Jack and the standard electrician's knife.

Electrician's knives normally come on a 3¾-inch frame with a 2¾-inch spear point blade and a combination screwdriver/wire stripper blade that locks open by means of a brass tang block.

The military has long issued this pattern of knives as the Model TL-29 for use by radio operators and electricians. Camillus, Boker, Case, Kutmaster and Queen all still offer electrician knives.

WHITTLERS

Two other patterns that date from the pre-1890s are the whittler and the congress. The whittler, in particular, flowered into a wide variety of knife styles during the golden era of knives. To be a true whittler, a knife has to have one large blade at one end of the handle and two smaller blades at the other. Usually, the two smaller blades are a clip point and a coping/sheepsfoot, but pen and clip combinations are also common as are double pen or clip. The two springs functioning with the small blades merge at the opposite end to form a single spring on the large blade. Usually, this large blade has a relatively thick spine for heavy cutting while the smaller blades are very thin for fine work.

Along with being heavier than normal, the main blade of the whittler is centered in the handle frame rather than off-set like the large blade of a Stockman folder or two blade jack. The centered blade makes the whittler main blade a little easier to use when carving wood, but this tricky spring arrangement also makes the whittler an expensive knife to manufacture.

As a result, most whittlers models were dropped from knife lines after 1960. In a few cases, the standard three spring arrangement of a Stockman pattern folder is used on a model designated as a whittler. Case, Hen and Rooster Parker's KCS, Blue Grass and

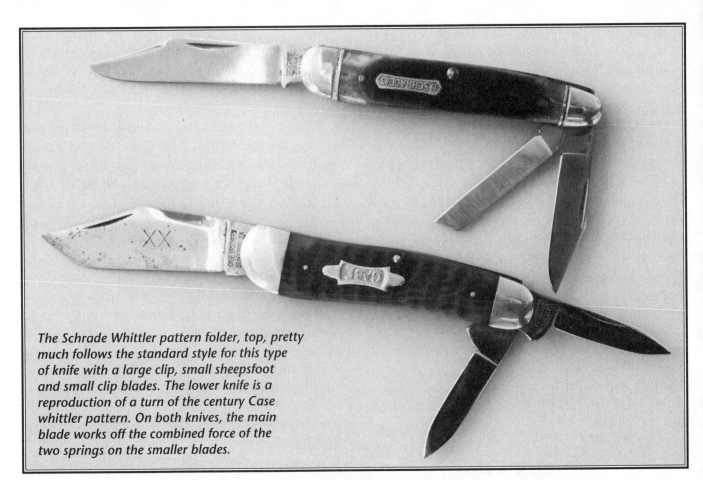

The Schrade Whittler pattern folder, top, pretty much follows the standard style for this type of knife with a large clip, small sheepsfoot and small clip blades. The lower knife is a reproduction of a turn of the century Case whittler pattern. On both knives, the main blade works off the combined force of the two springs on the smaller blades.

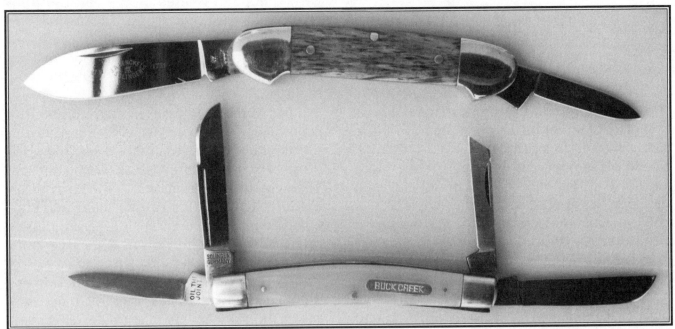

The top knife is a Henckel canoe pattern jack and the bottom one a Buckcreek congress. The congress was for many years a style of folder seldom seen outside the southern U.S. The canoe is more or less a fancy version of the equal end jack.

Queen have all produced limited numbers of whittlers in recent years, as the pattern is considered highly desirable by collectors.

CONGRESS FOLDERS

The congress is unusual among American pocketknife patterns in that it is a regional pattern seldom seen outside the southern states until recent times. The normal blade arraignment is two sheepsfoot and two pen blades paired at either end of a concave curved handle frame. Another common name for the congress is tobacco knife and it is said to have been use primarily for cutting a chew off plugs of tobacco. As a utility tool, the

larger congress models made fairly good woodworking knives.

CANOE KNIVES

Like many folding knife patterns originating in the golden era, the canoe's primary virtue is an appealing appearance. Rather than having anything to do with canoeing, the name comes from the fact that both front and rear bolsters curve up to give the frame the outline of a canoe.

The standard version is 3½ inches closed with a large spear point blade at one end and a small pen blade at the other. In years past, larger canoes with three and four blades were

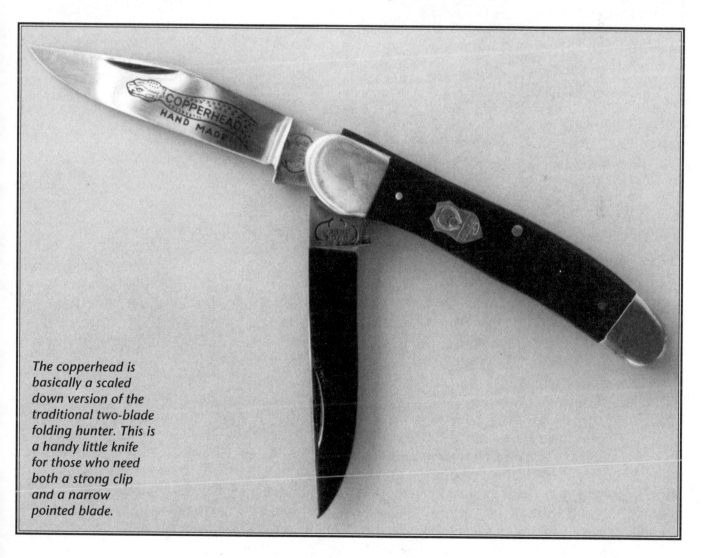

The copperhead is basically a scaled down version of the traditional two-blade folding hunter. This is a handy little knife for those who need both a strong clip and a narrow pointed blade.

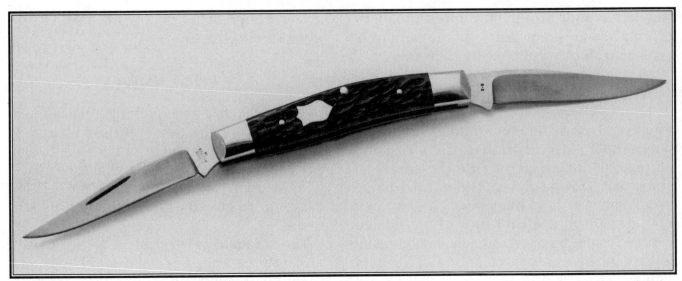

A muskrat pattern folder from the shop of folding knifemaster Tony Bose.   (PHOTO BY GARY LONG)

also commonly offered as an alternative to the plain equal end folder and cattle knife.

Other than looks, the only advantage to the modern canoe is that the opposing blade arrangement makes for a very flat pocket carry knife. The two blades will accomplish just about anything that can be expected from any other similar size folder. Boker, Buckcreek and Henckels all currently market examples of the canoe. Some of the older, large pattern Canoe knives have also been recreated in limited editions by Parker's KCS.

COPPERHEADS

The copperhead is one of the few slip-joint pocketknife patterns that can be called modern. Basically, the copperhead is a greatly scaled down (3¾ inches closed) version of the classic two-blade folding hunter with one clip point blade and one straight back skinner blade on a curved, horn-shaped frame.

Most copperheads are imported from the various Solingen, Germany, factories, but both Queen (Model 9165) and Camillus (Model 707Y) produce American versions. Function-wise, the copperhead is large and stout enough to survive fairly heavy use, but at the

same time remain comfortable to carry in a pocket. The blade combination is well suited to small game, birds and everyday utility use.

MUSKRATS

Among the more specialized forms of pocket cutlery is the muskrat, a jack pattern with two identical, long, narrow clip blades folding from both ends of what is usually a 3⅞- or 4-inch frame. Muskrat trappers tend to skin large numbers of small animals each day. The needle point muskrat blades are ideal for the delicate work of pelting small fur-bearing animals and the double blade feature gives the trapper twice as much use between sharpenings.

At one time, a style of knife on a frame under four inches (more than four inches and it is referred to as a trapper's or moose folder) with a long clip and a long spey was also called a muskrat. With the exception of a few special editions such as the Remington Bullet commemorative, these have pretty much disappeared.

Another muskrat variation is the Hawbaker with one long clip blade and one long sheeps-foot blade. This was a specialty item sold by a mail order trapping supply company up until recent times.

Given the current state of the trapping industry and the pressures on it from urban society, one wonders if the muskrat knife will be around much longer. The knife does serve equally well as a small game and bird dresser or in any other situation in which a narrow, fine point blade is useful. Likewise, it still provides double the edge life in situations where only one blade pattern is required.

THE STOCKMAN

This brings us to the one slip-joint pocketknife that outsells all other traditional patterns by a wide margin: the stockman.

The stockman is a descendent of the equal-end cattle knife. Most are built on what is called a curved serpentine frame with a combination of large clip blade, small spey and a small sheepsfoot blade. Bolsters come in both rounded and square versions with the round considered by some users to cause less pocket wear.

Occasionally, one of the small blades is replaced with either a leather punch or a pen blade. Even more rare are the four and five blade versions of the stockman. While four inches long closed might be called the standard size for a stockman, nearly any increment between 2¾ inches and 4¼ inches is available from a variety of sources.

The serpentine stockman handle frame is so

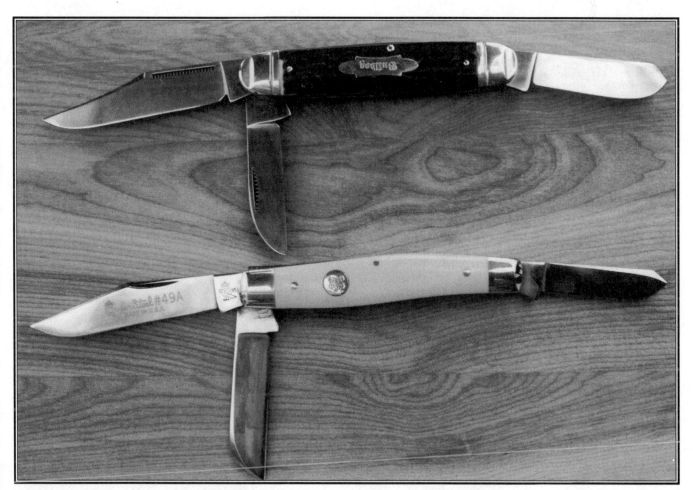

The stockman evolved from the equal end cattle knife sometime in the late 19th century. The top knife is a German Bull Dog brand; the bottom is an American Queen.

popular with the cutlery industry that it is also used as the basis for the majority of the smaller two blade jacks still cataloged.

As a kid growing up on a Midwestern farm during the 1960s, I held a strong belief there was only one knife really suitable for an adult to carry — the stockman. My grandfather, whom I admired greatly, used his Camillus stockman for everything from scraping spark plugs to castrating bull calves and peeling apples. Farm knives of this type were forced to work hard for their living and many had a very short life span. The goal was always to get the job done any way possible and worry about the tool later. Some years later I began carrying a Solingen, Germany-made 4¼-inch closed Buckcreek stockman while working as a

professional forester. The primary reason I prefer the largest of the common stockman patterns is that the handle is slightly longer than the width of my palm. This in turn means there is plenty to grip onto when using the knife for the type of heavy cutting expected of a serious working tool.

On the job, my Buckcreek sharpened stakes for research plot centers, cut forestry fire hose, sharpened pencils, cut the straps off tree seedling bags and made shavings for warm-up fires. Like most field foresters I know, my knife also field dressed a fair number of snowshoe hare, grouse and trout, plus a couple of deer taken during work hours. In short, it served daily to perform a hundred and one essential tasks.

The bottom knife is the heavily worn Buckcreek 4¼-inch stockman the author carried on the job as a forester for many years. Eventually it was put it into semi-retirement and replaced by the Buckcreek shown at the top. Knife carriers may find the large stockman to be the best utility pocketknife available.

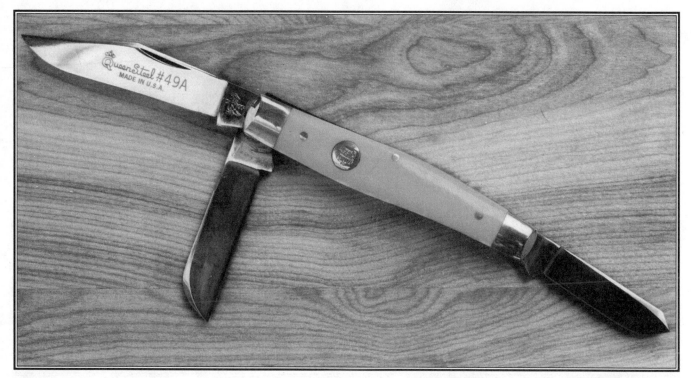

A 4¼-inch closed Stockman such as this Queen will do just about anything that can reasonably be required of a folding knife.

Back on our small ranch, I reserved a stainless bladed Buck Wrangler model stockman for cutting bull calves while using the Buckcreek for chores such as cleaning vines out of the tines of our Troybuilt rototiller.

Frequently, one reads that a good quality pocketknife should last several generations of users. All I can say is, those who believe it have never been around anyone who really works with a folder daily. I probably shouldn't use members of my family as examples because they tended to expect a pocketknife to do a lot more than simply cut, which often resulted in prematurely broken blades and discarded handles. Nevertheless, anyone who uses a knife frequently will need to resharpen the blades on a regular basis.

My own experience tells me that you can expect about 10 year's use from a folder, depending on when you personally consider it worn out. Most knife collectors have run across folding knives that have been sharp-

ened literally down to toothpicks. In my own case, I sharpened approximately 30 percent of the main blade on the Buckcreek away in eight years before putting it into semi-retirement.

If I were to be limited to one style of slip-joint pocketknife (not counting Swiss Armies, which are really pocket tool kits) for the rest of my life, I would chose the stockman without the least hesitation.

The 3¼-inch main blade of my large stockman is adequate for most outdoor chores and the sheepsfoot shapes wood, leather, cardboard, cloth and other materials requiring straight line cuts. The spey really doesn't see a lot of use, but when I need a surgical tool for vet work, it's there.

Over the years I've tried a variety of stockmen from many different companies. Most were the 4¼-inch closed pattern, but there have also been 3½-, 3⅞-, 4- and a couple (one stainless, one carbon steel) of now discontinued 4¾-inch Carl Schlieper Eye Brands.

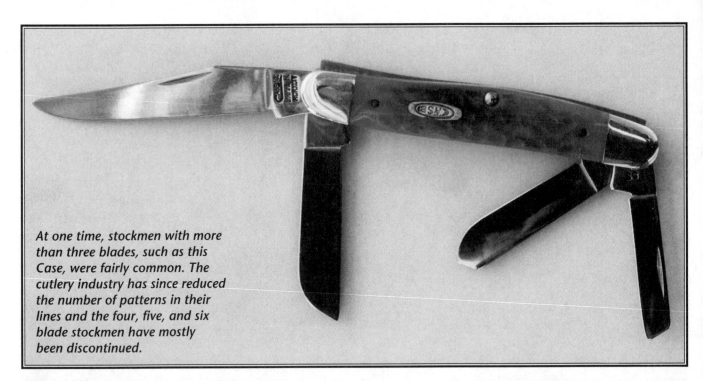

At one time, stockmen with more than three blades, such as this Case, were fairly common. The cutlery industry has since reduced the number of patterns in their lines and the four, five, and six blade stockmen have mostly been discontinued.

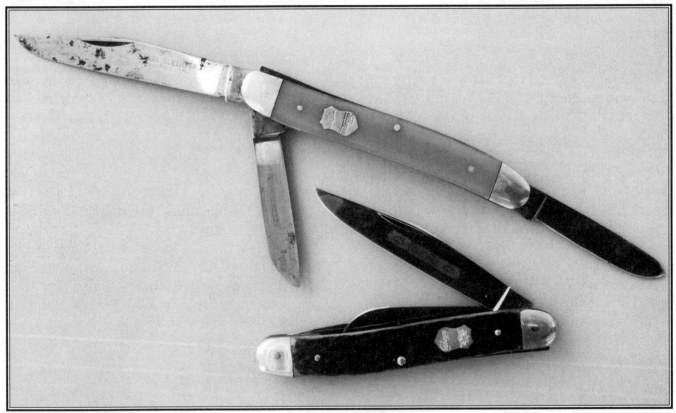

These two discontinued pattern Eye Brand stockmen are 4¾ inches long closed. This is about as large as this pattern ever went, but the author has found them to be outstanding tools that are still easy to carry in the pocket. The top knife is carbon steel and shows the effects of real field use. The bottom one is a less common stainless model. It is hoped that the company will put this model back into production some day.

I feel the 3½-inch frame is about as small as I would want to go on a serious work knife, but I do wish the Schlieper (a Solingen brand) had not dropped its extremely comfortable round bolster, extra large stockman. Had I still been working full time as a forester when I obtained my first Eye Brand, I feel fairly confident in saying it would have replaced the Buckcreek as my everyday companion.

Among American stockmen, I highly recommend the knives from Buck, Case, Queen, Schrade, Camillus and Remington. Excellent German brands include Schleiper, Buckcreek, Boker, and Hen and Rooster.

Despite its past popularity with professional outdoorsmen, the stockman has generally been replaced by the single-blade lockback folder among farmers, ranchers, foresters and game wardens. While the lockback has advantages we will go into in a later chapter, I still feel a stout stockman has much to offer for everyday field utility. Unlike the single blade, it still provides three different blade styles for varied uses. It can provide a second and third sharp edge when the user doesn't have time or equipment to re-hone the first in the field. Most stockmen are large enough to get the average job done but small enough that they don't require the belt pouch common to large lockbacks.

While the stockman may have lost its place as the sales leader in the American cutlery industry, I don't think we will be seeing it go the way of the equal end jack any time soon.

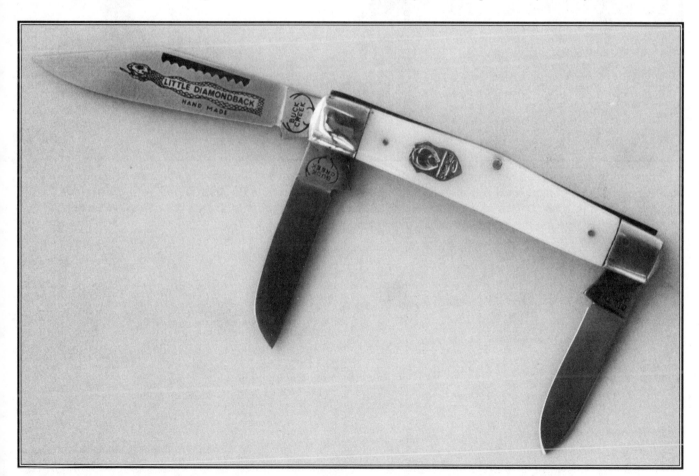

Stockmen come in a wide variety of sizes from under 3 inches closed up to 4¾ inches on some Eye Brands. For a serious working folder, I feel 3½ inches closed, such as this Buckcreek Little Diamondback, is about as small as a knife user should go.

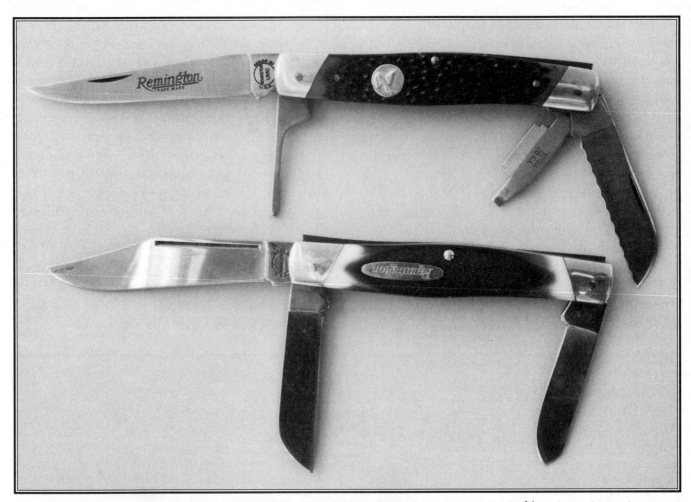

The top knife is a specialized waterfowler's folder offered by Remington on the standard 4¼-inch stockman frame. Among other blade options there is a shotgun choke wrench. At the bottom: Remington has the distinction of producing the only green Delrin-handled stockman I know of. The blades on this model are also plain carbon steel, which seem to be bucking the modern trend in folding knives to stainless.

5

TRADITIONAL SLIP-JOINT KNIVES: THE OUTDOOR PATTERNS

The knives in Chapter 4 were loosely defined as non-locking folders of pocket size suitable for everyday utility. The knives in this chapter were all primarily created for sporting and outdoor use. Many models, the trapper pattern in particular, have proven just as useful as everyday work knives. Up until the late 1970s, the three most popular knives among the foresters I worked with were, in order of use, the classic two-blade folding hunter, the two-blade trapper and the three-blade stockman. In the years that followed, many of the trappers and stockmen were replaced with sin-gle-blade lockbacks, but most of those large folding hunters continued to soldier on until they were lost or wore out.

THE TRAPPER

Next to the stockman (again, excluding Swiss Armies and Boy Scouts), the most popular pattern slip-joint folder is the trapper. This is a two blade jackknife built on what is commonly called a curved "dog leg" frame. The blade arrangement is always a long clip and a long spey blade.

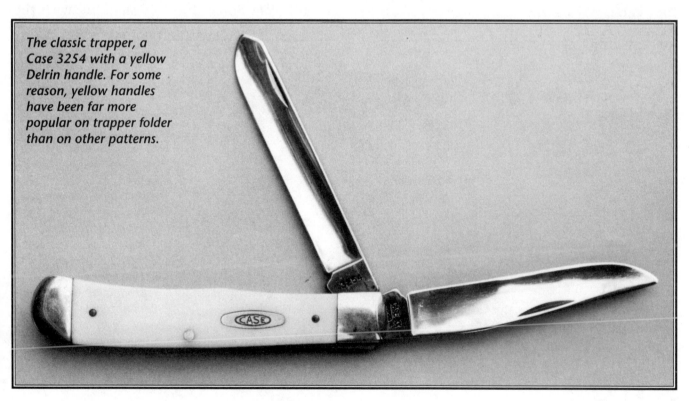

The classic trapper, a Case 3254 with a yellow Delrin handle. For some reason, yellow handles have been far more popular on trapper folder than on other patterns.

While the standard size is usually considered to be 4⅛ inches closed, a wide variety of other sizes have been tried over the years. The 3½-inch mini trappers are common, as are 3⅞-inch closed medium frame knives. In the 4⅛-inch models, both standard and slim line frames are often offered as variations. Handle materials may run the full range of options, but over the years yellow Delrin plastic has become a traditional favorite for trappers. During the 1920s and '30s Remington also popularized an extra heavy-duty, 4½-inch closed trapper pattern, usually referred to as "the bullet" because of the bullet emblem set into the handle. The heavy trapper has seen a revival in recent times and is once again a fairly common outdoor knife.

A well worn trapper remains the mark of a savvy outdoorsman, big enough in skilled hands to tackle any field problem without being too large for a pocket carry. The late Jack O'Conner, a hunting expert, recommended the trapper as the ideal hunter's knife, as have a number of other big game writers over the years.

Fur trappers in general, though, prefer a stockman knife rather than a trapper model folder. The trapper seems to be more popular with outdoorsmen and hunters than the profession for which it was named.

One of my favorite outdoor writers during my high school years was the late John Jobson. Based on the influence of his knife articles, I carried both a Case slim-line trapper and a standard size Ka-Bar trapper. Both knives saw extensive trap line use dressing small game and birds, cleaning fish and doing the usual farm chores. Next to the stockman, the trapper remains my personal favorite non-tool, pocket-size slip joint pattern.

One point about this knife remains a puzzlement: What purpose did the long spey originally serve? Most knife books and catalogs refer it for skinning. The curved edge at the tip of the spey blade does work well for delicate skinning but the long, straight edge section is of little use for hide removal. Trappers who do use this pattern are evenly split on how the two blades of this knife are to be utilized. Some do their skinning with the

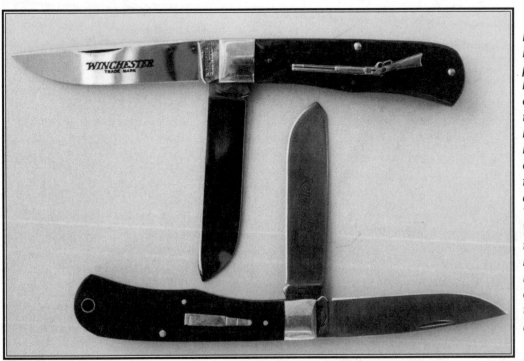

In the 1920s and '30s Remington made this pattern of heavy trapper highly popular with outdoorsmen. While these blades are a little large for skinning fur bearers, they are outstanding for general field work and field dressing large game. The top knife is a modern Winchester by Blue Grass; the bottom is a recent reproduction from Remington. Winchester actually never produced this knife so it can't really be called a reproduction.

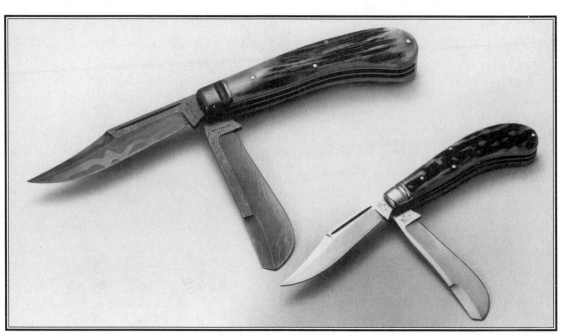

Tony Bose made his name in the custom folder business producing these Saddle Horn pattern trapper knives. The Saddle Horn was an early 20th century style of trapper that disappeared by World War II.

long spey and save the clip for rough work, while the others skin with the clip and save the long spey for rough jobs.

The heavy trapper is a better hunter's utility knife than the small fur bearer skinner. The spey blade on these knives is considerably wider than a standard trapper, giving the edge more belly and sweep for serious hide removal. Camillus once offered a double lockblade heavy trapper, while Parker's

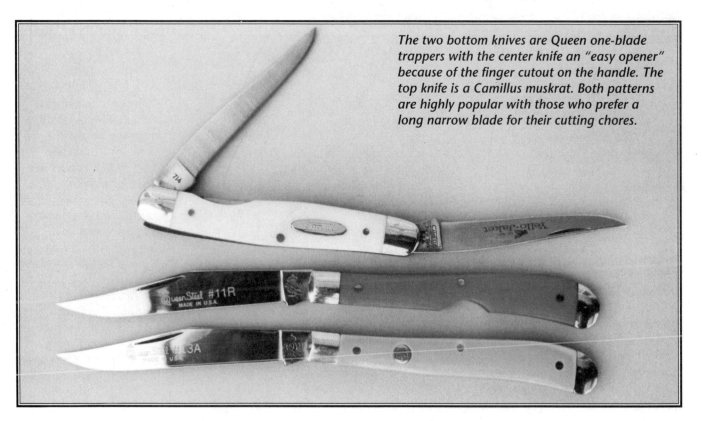

The two bottom knives are Queen one-blade trappers with the center knife an "easy opener" because of the finger cutout on the handle. The top knife is a Camillus muskrat. Both patterns are highly popular with those who prefer a long narrow blade for their cutting chores.

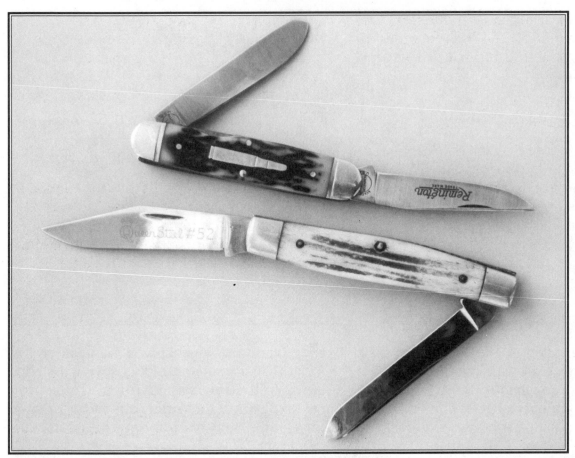

Knives with a large clip on one end and a long spey on the other are usually called moose patterns. The Queen on the bottom is another of my personal knives that has seen extensive use field dressing small game and birds. The top knife is recent limited edition Remington Bullet.

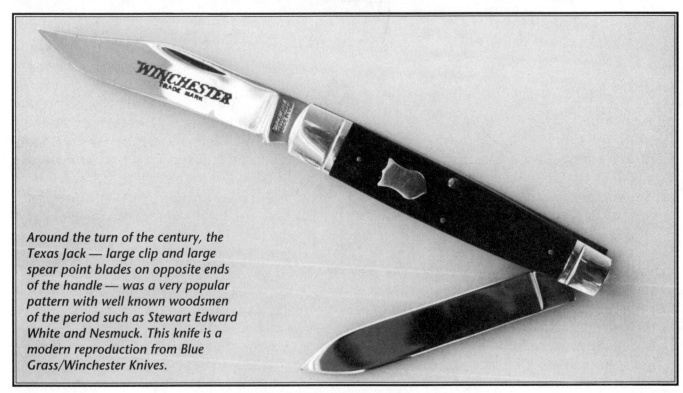

Around the turn of the century, the Texas Jack — large clip and large spear point blades on opposite ends of the handle — was a very popular pattern with well known woodsmen of the period such as Stewart Edward White and Nesmuck. This knife is a modern reproduction from Blue Grass/Winchester Knives.

KCS, Blue Grass Knives (Winchester) and Remington have marketed limited versions. This pattern is also a favorite of several custom knifemakers.

ONE-BLADE TRAPPERS

Take the spey blade off a slim-line trapper and you have yet another medium-sized outdoor knife that has seen a lot of use over the years. Going under many names — utility, sportsmen's, farmer's, one-blade trapper, etc. — these single blade folders provide a reasonably large cutting tool in a slim, light, easy-to-carry package.

The first premium brand pocket knife I ever bought was a Case XX Model 61048 farmer's knife, for the simple reason it cost around half what the two blade version of the same knife did at the time. This was in 1963 and that 61048 set me back the total of $3.50, money earned shooting groundhogs for the 50-cent bounty. I used the Case for much the same tasks as I did the two blade trappers mentioned earlier. If the truth were known, I could have probably gotten by just fine without the long spey option.

THE MOOSE AND TEXAS JACK

Another knife pattern closely related to the trapper is the moose, a double-end jack featuring a large clip and a long spey blade that is built on the large stockman frame. For those who wonder why a moose might be preferable to the trapper pattern, it's because the moose usually has the slightly wider and heavier blade of a large stockman rather than the long clip of a standard trapper. Some people simply prefer the stockman frame to the dog leg style of the trapper. At one time, practically all cutlery companies offered models of this same knife with a spear blade rather than a spey; they designated them as Texas Jack patterns.

Many classic woodcraft writers, including the legendary "Nessmuk" (George W. Sears), spoke very highly of the Texas Jack for outdoor use. For some reason, the knife fell out of favor around the 1950s and one seldom runs across it now.

THE SOD BUSTER

Moving up the size scale a bit we come to what is commonly called a sod buster folder. The origins of this pattern seem to be a stripped down German farmer's knife and the majority of these knives still come out of Solingen.

Basically, the sod buster is a single blade clasp knife with a straight back blade and a curved, unbolstered handle. Most German sod busters have plain wood handles while American companies favor Delrin plastic. The standard size is 4½ inches closed, but both larger and smaller sizes are common. While most sod busters are slip-joints, a few versions have been made with liner and rockerbar locks. Eye Brand manufactured a two blade version with a saw blade option.

The primary advantage of the sod buster is in providing a stout but plain work or outdoor knife at a very reasonable price. On game, the up-swept edge of the straight back blade makes the knife a better-than-average skinning tool. Most sod busters feature a very strong backspring that makes a blade lock relatively unnecessary. At the same time, the sod buster may be a little hard to open for those with weak fingers.

THE FISH KNIFE

Like the single blade trapper, the fish knife is a folder pattern with a dual personality. It is either a single or double blade folder five inches long closed with a long, narrow clip blade and a powder horn-shaped handle. As with most other patterns of folder, both larger

Sod busters seemed to have evolved from plain German farmers' knives. Usually inexpensive, they make excellent general purpose field knives.

and small versions of the fish have been produced but none have had the popularity of the five-inch. On two blade models, the second blade is normally a combination scaler, hook disgorger and bottle opener.

Because fishing knives in general tend to be abused more than other forms of cutlery, fish knives have long been a popular item in cutlery companies' economy lines.

My own first experience with the fish knife

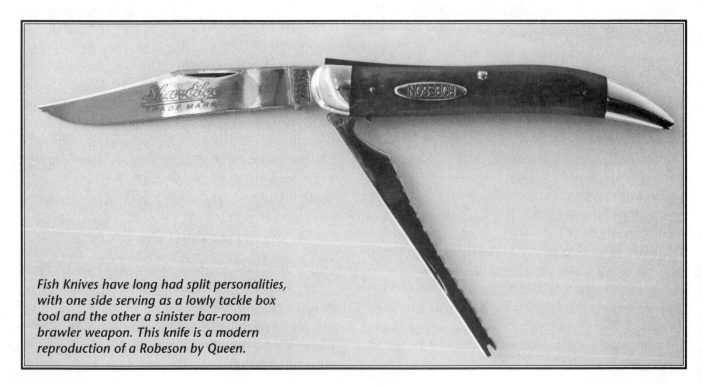

Fish Knives have long had split personalities, with one side serving as a lowly tackle box tool and the other a sinister bar-room brawler weapon. This knife is a modern reproduction of a Robeson by Queen.

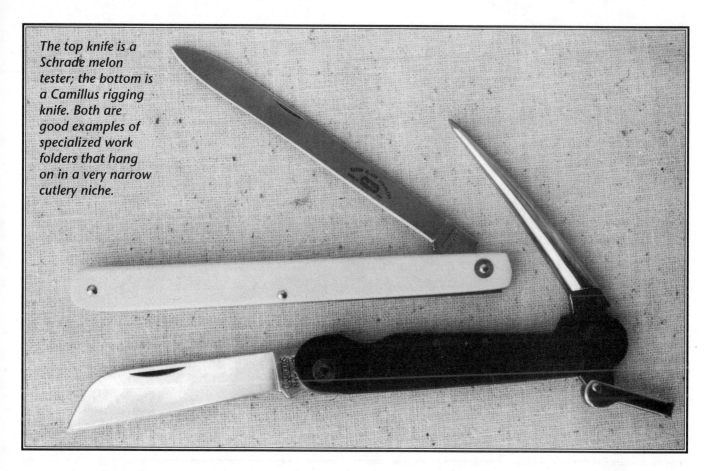

The top knife is a Schrade melon tester; the bottom is a Camillus rigging knife. Both are good examples of specialized work folders that hang on in a very narrow cutlery niche.

was with a 99-cent, two-blade Imperial I bought at Sears when I was around 13. Not being overly sure my dad would approve of such a large folder, I kept the knife out of sight and only used it on my lone-wolf fishing safaris to a local creek. About the third trek across our corn field to the stream bank, I lost the knife out of my back pocket and failed to recover it by retracing my steps. So much for my little secret.

The large size and low price led to the growth of the fish knife's reputation. Under the name Texas Tickler, Tango Knife, Saturday Night Special, Dixie Switch and a few additional designations, the fish knife was once considered a tool of the street thug. Many hardware distributors actually made a point of selling the knife under two different names, depending on whether their market was sporting or urban.

The folding fish knife seems to have started loosing popularity with outdoorsmen during the mid-'60s, about the time Finnish filet knives were introduced. While the traditional folding fish knife is both too stiff and too short for efficient filleting, it makes an excellent utility tool for the angler.

On larger fish — such as salmon and steelhead — that are normally opened and iced down in the field for later steaking, the fish knife works as well as any pattern. Queen and Frost Cutlery, along with an occasional special run from Case and Blue Grass, are the primary sources for the fish knife folder.

THE MELON TESTER OR SAUSAGE SAMPLER

The melon tester, or sausage sampler, is a rather specialized form of large slip-joint folder that normally features a narrow spear point blade between 3½ and 5 inches long. The

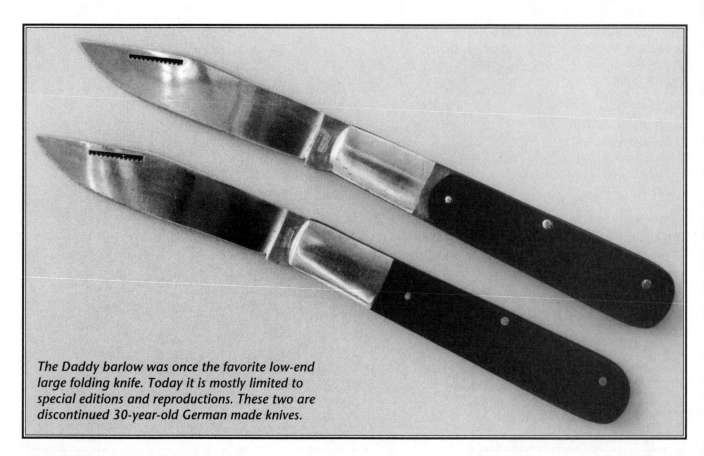

The Daddy barlow was once the favorite low-end large folding knife. Today it is mostly limited to special editions and reproductions. These two are discontinued 30-year-old German made knives.

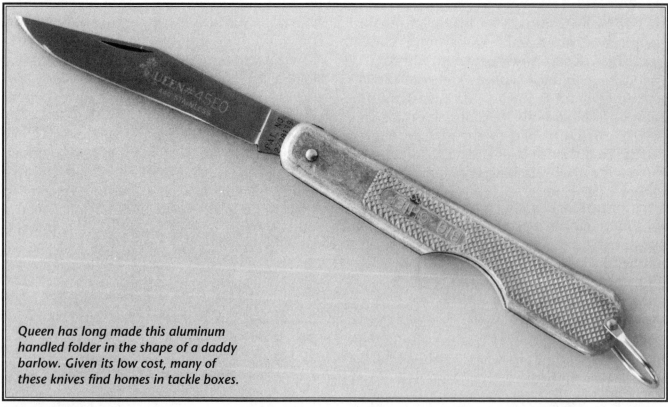

Queen has long made this aluminum handled folder in the shape of a daddy barlow. Given its low cost, many of these knives find homes in tackle boxes.

long, narrow blade allows a fruit tester to cut a core sample from the center of a melon. As the alternate name indicates, the knife was also once used to sample sausage in stores. Occasionally, these knives have a second fork blade folding from the butt end of the knife.

Melon testers are not as common as they once were. At one time, they were favored by farm and produce supply companies for advertising purposes, possibly because the handle provides considerable space for inscriptions. Along with its intended uses, the pattern make an excellent gardening tool and serves equally well as a folding kitchen knife for the hiker or picnicker.

DADDY BARLOW

Like the fish knife, the daddy barlow has been displaced by the modern lockback. Originally, the five-inch-long closed daddy barlow was one of the folders that made the Russell name famous in the United States. Just as with the standard barlow, the daddy was a very plain, low-cost tool with a long, heavy front bolster for added strength. Russell once offered rockerbar lockback versions as well as knives with fish scaler spines and easy opener notches in the handle. For a brief time, Remington marketed two-bladed daddy barlows with a second pen blade next to the large clip. Spear-point blades were also once as common as clip point models.

My own experience with the daddy barlow dates to a short time after I bought my Case one-blade trapper. A Case XX daddy in an Amish hardware store caught my eye and for another $3.50 I owned my second knife of this stamping. I should probably add that Case XX knives were about the highest quality items as could be found at the cutlery counter in the period. I just about wore that daddy out around the farm, trap line and hunting field. As plain as the daddy barlow may look, the handle is actually quite comfortable for

heavy use. I wouldn't mind seeing someone reintroduce a good lockback version of the old Russell. Currently, most of the daddy barlows available are limited editions, although Queen introduced one in its Robeson line.

THE TWO-BLADE FOLDING HUNTER

This brings us to the classic two-blade folding hunter. The standard size here is 5¼ inches long closed, with one wide clip point blade and one straight back skinner blade. Both saber ground and flat ground clip-point blades are common, but the skinner blade is always flat ground.

During the early part of my forestry career, the two-blade folding hunter was the hands-down favorite pocketknife of the professional outdoorsman. Belt pouches were not yet widely used, so most of these knives were carried in a coat or cruising vest pocket. Another common carry method was to run a cord through the lanyard hole found on the butt of most folding hunters at the time and stick the knife straight down in a front pocket. The lanyard was left hanging over the front of the pocket. A quick pull on the cord and the knife was in the user's hand. For some reason, the lanyard hole has been dropped from most of the folding hunters still on the market.

The potential uses of the clip blade are fairly obvious, but less obvious is why the second blade is called a skinner. Usually, skinning blades have rounded points and/or sharply curved, up-swept edges. The folding hunter's narrow skinning blade is more like a boning or filleting knife, and this is how most outdoorsmen use it. This folder pattern requires a little special care in use as the long blades can stick in a cut and fold across the fingers of the user.

Despite the non-locking blades, the two-blade folding hunter continues to be a favorite among conservative professional outdoorsmen. First, this pattern is the equivalent of

The classic two-blade folding hunter has long been highly popular with professional woodsmen. The top knife is a German Eye Brand; the bottom is a Case 5265.

If only knives could talk! these two Case 6265 folding hunters are approximately the same age (late 1960s). The top knife has been used very little, but the blades on the bottom knife are worn down to a fraction of their original size.

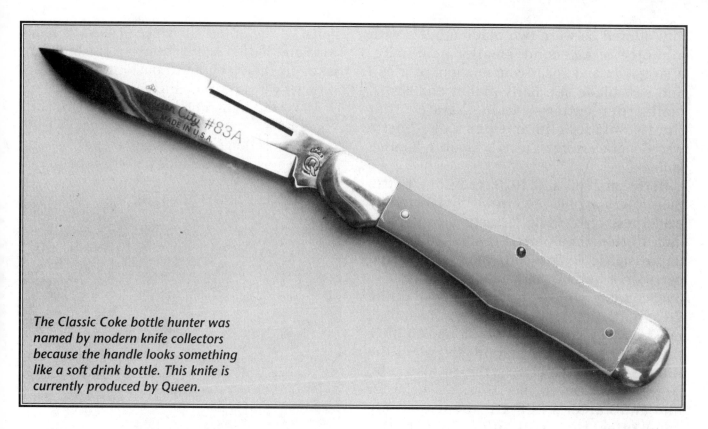

The Classic Coke bottle hunter was named by modern knife collectors because the handle looks something like a soft drink bottle. This knife is currently produced by Queen.

carrying two knives and thus doubles the work time possible between sharpenings. Secondly, in rare cases, it can provide a second knife if the first blade is broken. The two-blade folding hunter is large enough that it may be thought of as a serious wilderness survival tool and has the advantage of classic outdoor look. On the negative side, along with the non-locking blades (Boker actually marketed a locking blade version for a couple of years, but it didn't sell all that well and was discontinued.), the two-blade folding hunter is a relatively heavy knife; the Eye Brand tips the scales at 7½ ounces.

Most major cutlery companies — Case, Ka-Bar, Camillus, Schrade, Boker, Queen etc. — continue to catalog the two-blade folding hunter. Single blade versions on the same frame with only the clip blade were once very common. Schrade's Old Timer 125-OT Mustang, Queen's 9145, and Camillus's Cam-6 are about the only remaining models on the market.

The Schrade 125-OT differs from the others in that it is both a slip-joint and a liner lock combined. It is one of the better knives around for general outdoor use.

THE COKE BOTTLE HUNTER

A few years after the Civil War ended, cartridge-firing handguns made the full-size fighting bowie knife obsolete. Freed from the need to carry a short sword-size blade for personal defense, outdoor knives shrank to more practical sizes.

One of the knives to evolve out of this period was the so-called Coke bottle, or swell center, single blade folding hunter. Either designation is actually a modern collector's term, based on the general shape of the handle frame. Coke bottles are all large, heavy folders averaging between 5¼ and 5½ inches long closed. The most common version features a wide saber ground clip blade, but spear point knives were occasionally offered as were two blade models with a choice of a second, smaller pen blade, a large clip and spear combination, or a clip and saw blade set. Early Maher and Grosh mail order cutlery catalogs stated that the two-blade, clip and pen Coke bottle was General George Custer's favorite hunting knife.

Between 1880 and 1920, the Coke bottle hunter was a knife pattern highly favored by wilderness pros, while recreational outdoorsmen of the same period tended to choose impressive-looking sheath knives they could carry on a belt. As authentic wilderness and backcountry professionals disappeared, the Coke bottle hunter's popularity waned. Still, most cutlery companies continued to offer the pattern up until the mid-60s, when the Buck 110 lockback took the industry by storm. Today, Queen, Blue Grass's Winchester line and Parker's KCS are about the only companies that still offer Coke bottle folding hunters, with a choice of a slip-joint or rocker-bar lock models.

RIGGING KNIVES

There are a number of specialized large folding knives designed for working on sailing ships, the most common being the rigging knife, a 4½-inch closed folder with a large sheepsfoot blade on one end and a marlin spike on the other. The spike is used to splice rope and loosen knots. They are still standard issue in the Navy and Coast Guard and are popular with sport sailers.

All of the slip-joint knives in the previous chapters are time-proven designs that will still get the job done. Fad designs may come and go, but most of these knife patterns endure.

Technically, these Myerchin rigging knives are lockbacks rather than slip-joints. Myerchin currently makes a number of folders for the U.S. military. Many consider them to be the state-of-the-art in this type of tool.

6

ROCKER-BAR LOCKBACK FOLDING KNIVES

Preventing a knife blade from folding unexpectedly during use is a highly desirable design feature. An endless variety of blade locking mechanisms have been developed over time. Many proved to be solutions to what the knife-buying public saw as non-existent problems. A few have hung on to become industry standards.

For at least the last century and a half, the leading form of folding knife blade lock has been the rocker-bar lock. This lock consists of a notch in the blade tang into which a projection on the back spring snaps down under spring tension. The lock bar pivots on a pin set at point near or slightly forward of the handle center and is held in the open position by a spring that pushes up on the end opposite the blade tang.

This spring tension is enough to prevent the projection on the backspring from coming out of the notch on the blade tang, thus locking the blade in the open position. To close, the end of the backspring is pushed down, which raises the end sitting in the tang notch. It's actually a very simple mechanism and many knife companies have found it to be easier to manufacture than the traditional slip joint.

Although leaf springs are probably the most common, the type of spring used for the tension end of the rocker-bar lock varies with the maker. Occasionally, a maker changes the spring type or its placement and announces he has invented a new locking mechanism. While it depends on how one

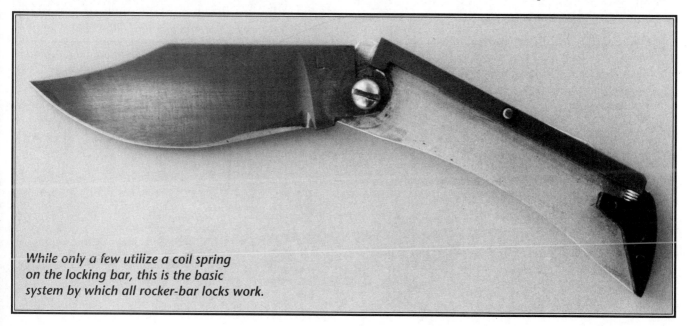

While only a few utilize a coil spring on the locking bar, this is the basic system by which all rocker-bar locks work.

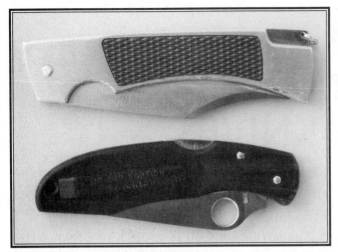

The top knife, a Spanish Aitor, features a rear release on its rocker-bar. The Spyderco Endura on the bottom uses the mid-handle release system.

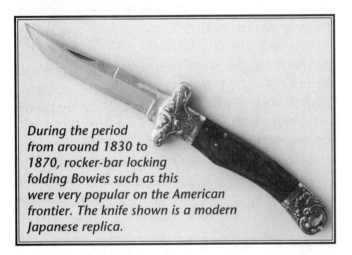

During the period from around 1830 to 1870, rocker-bar locking folding Bowies such as this were very popular on the American frontier. The knife shown is a modern Japanese replica.

defines "new," all of these locks work on the same basic principle.

Mid-handle rocker-bar locks have become popular in the last couple of decades. This is a shorter rocker-bar with the pivot pin moved forward and the blade release and tension spring mounted in the center of the knife frame rather than at the rear. A mid-frame lock release does have advantages for one-hand blade closing but this is not a new invention. Mid-handle blade releases have been around just as long, if not longer, than the full length rocker-bars.

It is not recorded in history who actually invented the rocker-bar blade lock. By the early part of the 19th century, rocker-bar locking folders were being imported from Sheffield, England to the United States on a wide basis. Many were in the form of the folding Bowie knives and dirks popular on the frontier from around 1830 to the 1870 period. Others were plain, single-blade, utility folders better suited to work on sailing ships, farms, ranches, trap lines and hunting camps.

The rocker-bar lock is best used as a safety device during normal utility cutting. For 99 percent of the use the average folder sees, this is more than adequate. Any unusually hard force pushing down on the back of the blade

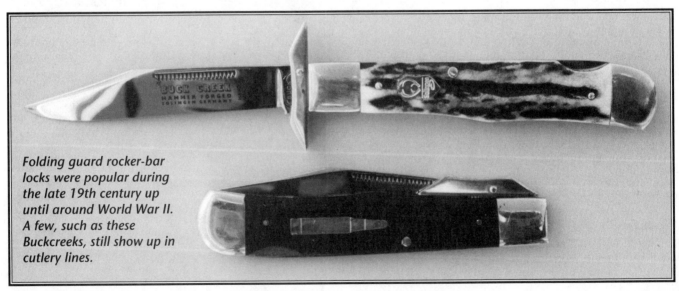

Folding guard rocker-bar locks were popular during the late 19th century up until around World War II. A few, such as these Buckcreeks, still show up in cutlery lines.

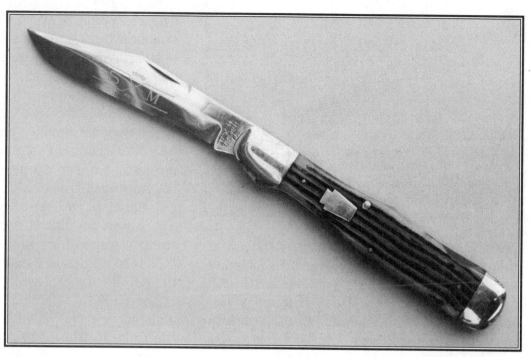

At one time, the Coke bottle folding hunter in both locking and non-locking versions was probably the most popular outdoor knife with expert woodsmen. This knife is a replica Schatt and Morgan from Queen Cutlery.

can override the lock on many models. Some of the less expensive and more poorly fitted imported models may hardly be considered lockbacks at all. All rocker-bars are also sensitive to bits of dirt, sawdust, sand, lint, etc. in the tang notch. Debris in this area can block the bar projection from fully seating in the tang notch and this can make the lock fail unexpectedly.

As a result of this inherent design weakness, care must be taken when selecting a rocker-bar locking folder for emergency uses. Those offered by Spyderco, Cold Steel, SOG Specialty, Katz and some of the other premium brands are designed to stand up to more downward pressure than others. A rocker-bar lock is unlikely to fail on a thrust, but the possibility still exists.

FOLDING GUARD

By the end of the 19th century, two rocker-bar folding knife patterns had become highly popular in the United States: the folding guard and the Coke bottle. Folding guard lockbacks feature a two-piece double handguard that

pivots on a pin on the tang of the blade. In the closed position, the guard lies flat against the handle frame. When the knife is opened, the guard swings with the blade into the open position. As with most knife patterns, folding guards were offered in several sizes, but the 4½-inch closed version seems to have been the most popular. Coke bottle hunters with folding guards were also fairly common.

The folding guard lockback remained a part of Case, Ka-Bar and a few European cutlery lines up until around the 1970s when it was replaced in popularity by the Buck 110-type folding hunter. Case still turns out an occasional limited edition with a folding guard and the German brand, Buckcreek, offers the model in several handle options.

LOCKING COKE BOTTLE

The rocker-bar Coke bottle lockback is a locking version of the once highly popular slip-joint folding hunter of the same name. As was explained in the chapter on slip-joint outdoor knives, the Coke bottle pattern of a clasp knife was the mark of the experienced hunter

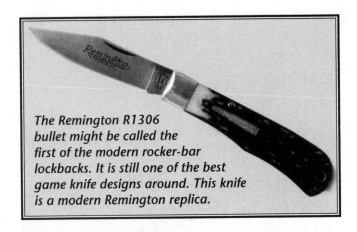

The Remington R1306 bullet might be called the first of the modern rocker-bar lockbacks. It is still one of the best game knife designs around. This knife is a modern Remington replica.

from around the 1880s up until the end of World War I. Currently, Queen is the only company turning out lockback Coke bottles on a regular basis, but Blue Grass, Parker Brothers and Case frequently offer the pattern as a limited edition.

The Coke bottle lockback has much to offer the modern hunter. It is large enough to handle almost any chore that can be expected of a folding knife, and the basic

In the 1960s the Buck 110 and its smaller brother, the Ranger, revolutionized folding outdoor and work knives.

frame is much lighter to carry than the more common Buck 110 style of hunter. Also, Coke bottles are simply attractive looking folders.

REMINGTON R1303 BULLET

While they were never completely abandoned by cutlery companies, the rocker-bar lockback models were forced into limited production in the years following World War I by the popularity of the Marbles-style sheath knives. There was one noted exception to this trend, the now-legendary Remington model R1303 bullet, so named because of the metal inset on the handle of a .30 Remington rifle cartridge.

The R1303 was a 4½-inch closed folder with a slightly curved frame and a swell butt. Like the Coke Bottle folding hunter before it, the Remington R1303 quickly became the mark of the experienced outdoorsman. This pattern is about the ideal size and shape for field dressing deer and other game. Unfortunately, Remington chose to sell its cutlery operation at the start of World War II and the new owner, Pal Cutlery, was only in business for a few short years. In recent years, Remington has contracted with Camillus to produce a series of limited editions of many of its original bullet models.

Queen Cutlery made an excellent reproduction of the R1303 during the mid-1970s but for some reason it never caught on. Since then, several companies have marketed the pattern as a special edition. All of the old Remington bullet patterns are also popular inspirations for custom knifemakers.

BUCK 110

With the flood of inexpensive surplus sheath knives, the years following World War II were lean times for lockback folders. Here and there, a company cataloged a folding guard or sod buster pattern lockback, but no one pushed them very aggressively. In April 1963,

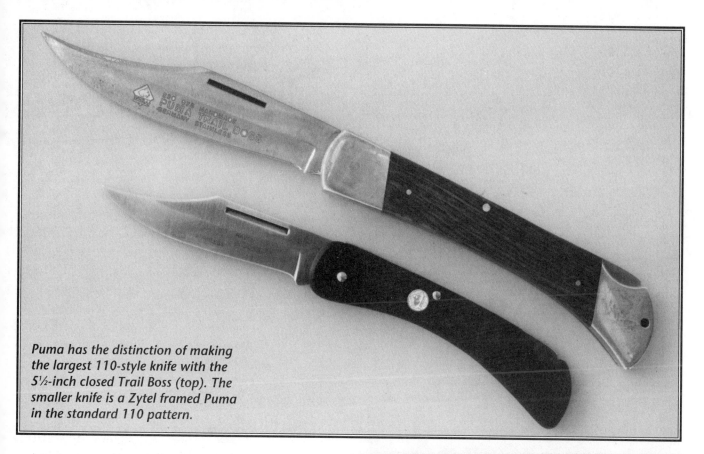

Puma has the distinction of making the largest 110-style knife with the 5½-inch closed Trail Boss (top). The smaller knife is a Zytel framed Puma in the standard 110 pattern.

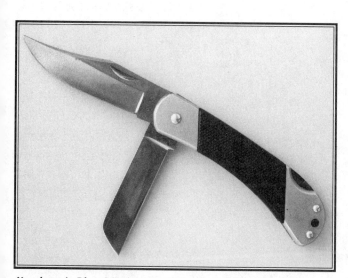

Kershaw's Blue Mt. is one of the few 110- style knives that have been made with a second blade. This large clip, small sheepsfoot combination makes an ideal everyday utility knife.

Cabela's imports this interesting three-blade Buck 110 style folder form Japan. Along with the standard clip point blade there is a bone saw and a European-style blunt point gutting blade.

Even more 110-style knives. From the top down: Schrade Old Timer, Schrade Uncle Henry and a Remington.

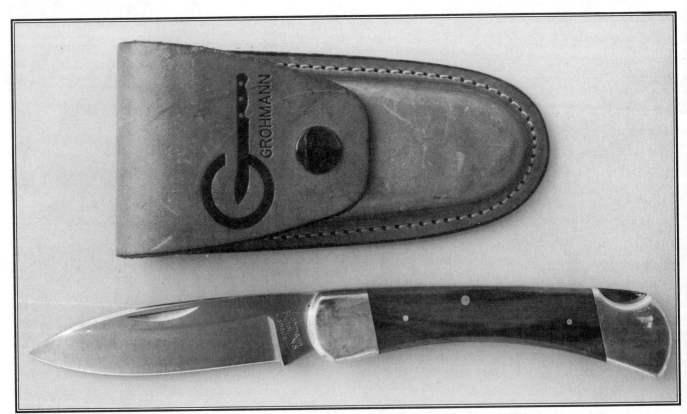

The drop point on this Canadian Grohmann 110-style folder makes it one of the better field knives in this pattern.

Buck Knives introduced what has become probably the most significant outdoor knife of the 20th century, the Model 110 folding hunter. At that time, the 110 — with its massive brass frame, tropical hardwood handle and stainless steel blade — was a totally new approach to the rocker-bar lock clasp knife.

Buck knew it could sell a reasonable number of its new model but it didn't expect the instant, overwhelming acceptance the 110 found. This popularity may be attributed to a combination of a strong, modern design; a well recognized and highly regarded brand name; and that the standard knife was offered with a belt pouch. Belt pouches for folding hunters had been around for years but they were usually only offered as an added cost option. The belt pouch made the new knife compact, low key and extremely handy to carry on a daily basis for both work and play.

Within a year Puma, a competing German company, introduced a Buck 110 look-alike. (Buck's joke is that Puma used a real 110 in its early promotional literature because it didn't have its own knife ready.) In the years that followed, practically every major maker of folding knives in the world added a version of the 110. There are Buck 110-style knives from the United States, Canada, England, Ireland, Spain, France, Germany, Italy, Taiwan, Hong Kong, China, Japan, Pakistan and Korea.

The original 110 was five inches long, closed with a 4-inch blade (this was later shortened to 3⅞ inches for legal reasons on many knives), but both Buck and its competitors soon began offering the basic style in a wide variety of sizes. While the standard 5-inch closed probably remains the most popular, you can find any size you desire between 2- and 5½-inches closed. Given the added safety of a locking blade, many of the smaller models have become highly popular as true pocket carry knives.

My own background with the Buck 110 began in 1967 when I purchased an early

Buck's Duke, a more refined 110-style knife, was one of the first drop point folding hunters to enter the marketplace.

model shortly before entering the Army. The knife went with me to Vietnam, where I carried the pouch under my jungle fatigue coattails as both a utility tool and a possible last-ditch weapon. I have been told many times that the Buck 110 was extremely popular with troops in Vietnam, but mine was the only one I ran across during the period I was in the country. Almost everyone who saw mine wanted to know where they could obtain one for themselves.

I had much the same experience in the fall of 1970 while working for the Washington State Department of Game removing the leg glands from deer as part of a research project. Very few of the hunters involved had seen a 110 before, but all of them liked its style.

By the mid-70s the Buck 110 and its look-alikes had become a standard part of thousands of working men's everyday gear. In fact, it started to replace the tried-and-true three-blade stockman and two-blade folding hunter among professional outdoorsman such as ranchers, farmers, foresters and game wardens. Buck has reported that by 1991 it had produced 11 million 110s and it continues to sell approximately 400,000 each year.

The Buck 110 caused several major changes in the knife buying public's taste. First, it convinced many that a lockback knife was a better idea than a non-locking folder. Second, it made the belt pouch an acceptable part of everyday working attire in many professions. Third, it generally raised the size of acceptable working folding knives across the board. Last of all, it converted vast numbers of outdoorsmen from fixed blade sheath knives to folders for their field chores.

Buck remains a first choice in a standard size 110-style folder, but Schrade offers good value in both its Uncle Henry Papa Paw and Old Timer Cave Bear models. For those looking for a larger-than-standard model, the 5½-inch closed Puma Trail Boss may be highly recommended. Queen, Case, Ka-Bar and Bear MGC all offer good "made in the U.S.A." versions of the 110.

DROP POINT LOCKERS

At one time, practically all American hunting knives had a bowie clip point blade. Bob Loveless's custom drop point sheath knives changed this in the 1970s and soon many felt all "real" hunting knives had to have some form of drop point blade. Among the best 110-style knife for field dressing game is the Canadian Grohmann. This knife features a wide DP blade with excellent belly for skinning and slicing.

The widespread introduction of drop point bladed folding hunters was probably the next

Gerber's LST folders were probably the first commercial Zytel-handled knives on the market. Their instant success led to industry-wide use of Zytel on light-weight knives.

Gerber's Magnum LST is a classic example of the modern drop point folding hunter.

major advance in rocker-bar lockers. Most of the early models, such as the Buck Duke, Gerber Folding Sportsman II D and the Boker 2000, were slightly modified versions of the 110 style that retained the double bolster metal frame, but in a slimmed-down form. These primarily appealed to hunters and were not overly popular with other knife users.

Once the Buck 110 had made the single-blade lockback folding knife an acceptable alternative to the traditional multi-blade slip-joint pocket knife, the flood gates were opened for a wave of new and innovative designs. Early on, a few custom makers start-

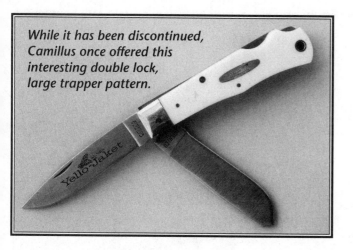

While it has been discontinued, Camillus once offered this interesting double lock, large trapper pattern.

ed experimenting with knives that replaced the metal frame and bolsters of traditional folders with a solid Micarta handle. This makes for a very light tool but care must be

taken to reinforce or line the pivot pin area, as Micarta tends to wear faster than some other materials. Most of the more recent Micarta-handled custom folders are now produced with thin titanium liners to avoid this problem.

ZYTEL ENTERS THE PICTURE

Cutlery factories needed something better suited to mass production than Micarta, and molded thermoplastics proved to be the answer. The first really good substitute was probably Gerber's Blackie Collins-designed Zytel-handled 3½-inch closed LST lockback. Zytel is a fiberglass reinforced plastic of extreme strength and durability that can be easily produced in any shape or color

The top knife is a 5-inch blade folding filet from Al Mar; the second and third folders are from Browning. All feature Zytel frames.

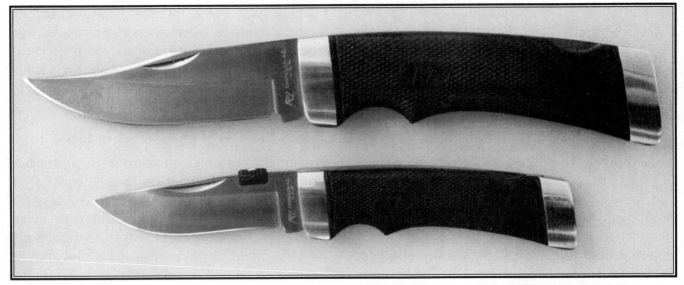

These Kraton and stainless steel framed folders from Katz are made for the person who feels a knife should have a distinct feeling of weight in his hand.

desired. The LST offered a high quality, flat, safe lockback of pocket size that weighed only 1.3 ounces and retailed for around $25.

The LST caught on like wildfire and Gerber soon followed up with a number of Zytel-handled folders, ranging from tiny key chain models to the massive Parabellum survival knife. Like the Buck 110, once thermoplastic-handled folders proved successful, everyone began producing them. Today the Zytel thermoplastic frame dominates a large part of the folding knife market.

Kershaw's model 1046 features a soft, highly comfortable handle of Kraton that gives a good non-slip gripping surface.

Thermoplastic handle frames allowed makers to offer any particular blade style for approximately half the price the same blade would cost in a traditional metal frame. When a knife buyer purchased a thermoplastic-handled folder from a quality knife company such as Buck, Cold Steel, Gerber, Al Mar, Case, Katz or Schrade, they received a first-class blade at a much reduced price.

Still, some doubted the ultimate strength of this construction when compared to brass and steel frames. The better quality Zytel knives are not noticeably weaker than those of traditional construction. No folding knife will stand up to much side pressure or prying without eventually loosening up in the joint area.

Cold Steel has gone to great lengths to prove its Zytel-handled line of folders can hold up to impressive amounts of weight hung on the butt of a knife clamped in a vice. The 6-inch blade Vaquero, for instance, had more than 100 pounds added to its handle without the lock failing. When used as the relatively light-duty cutting tool that all folding knives are, it will last the user many years.

The second objection to thermoplastic-handled knives — light weight — is strictly a matter of personal preference. Some knife users find the massive feel of a metal-framed handle reassuring, while others are only too glad to carry a folder they can simply forget until it's needed. This is why the original Buck 110 and the Valox handled BuckLites are still cataloged side by side.

KRATON

Along with the Zytel and Valox framed rocker-bar lockback knives, thermoplastics also enabled the creation of a family of folders that feature a combination of modern and traditional construction. Kraton is a plastic substitute for natural rubber that is easier to mold and more durable than the material it replaces.

On a knife handle, it creates a semi-pliable surface with a slightly sticky feel. Kraton is used as a handle scale material on a basic metal frame in place of the more traditional bone, stag and wood. Gerber, SOG Specialty, Katz and Cold Steel have had good luck with Kraton scaled knives.

In the last 10 years, the rocker-bar lock and Zytel revolution have taken still another major jump forward with the creation of the spring carry clip, one-hand opening, serrated edge folder. These knives have had a major impact on the market.

There are many quality spring carry-clip thermoplastic folders available. The original Gerber LST and LST Microlights are excellent true pocket carry knives. The Gerber Lightweight Bolt-Action and the Magnum LST models are equally proven knives for the hunter and outdoorsman. Browning's impressive new Signature series is an excellent working design. Buck's Mini Buck will serve a role similar to the LST, and the BuckLites are light-weight versions of the famous 110.

Buck's recent light-weight line includes the massive 5⅛-inch closed Goliath folding hunter. Al Mar's 6003 Airweight has long been a favorite folder to pack in a belt survival kit for extended wilderness canoe trips. Camillus's Kraton-handled Pro-Master series is unique with its double and triple lock blade system.

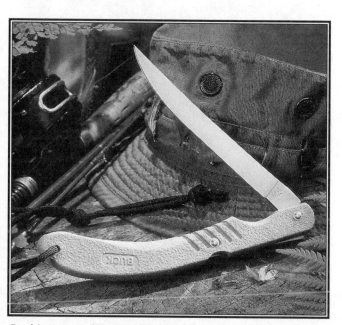

Buck's Kraton-handled folding filet knife is especially suited to wet, slippery conditions.

Buck's Proteges are examples of this company's efforts in the Kraton handle field.

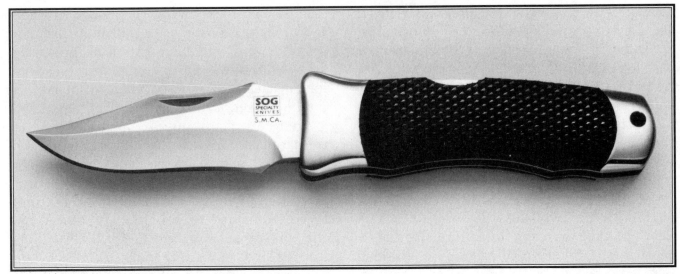

SOG Specialty's Tomcat features Kraton inserts on its handle.

(PHOTO BY WEYER OF TOLEDO)

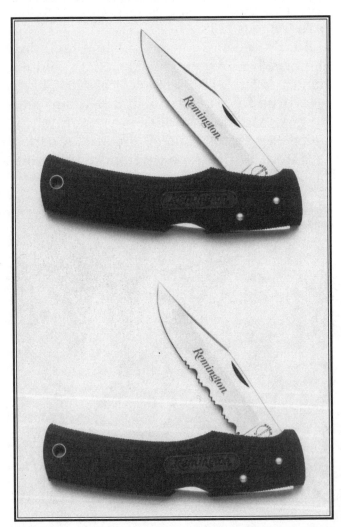

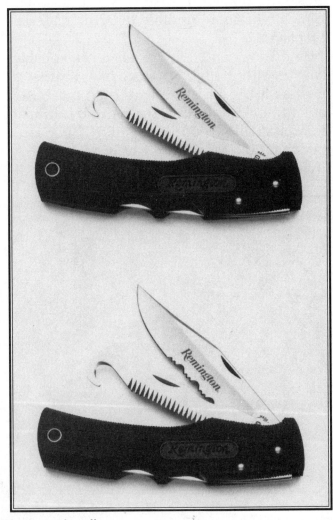

Remington produces this Grizzly series of folding hunters with Kraton handles.

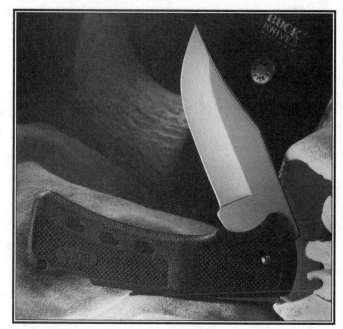

Buck's Zytel-handled Goliath provides a very large but light working folder.

Ontario's Parachutist folder is another big, heavy duty knife with a light-weight Zytel handle.

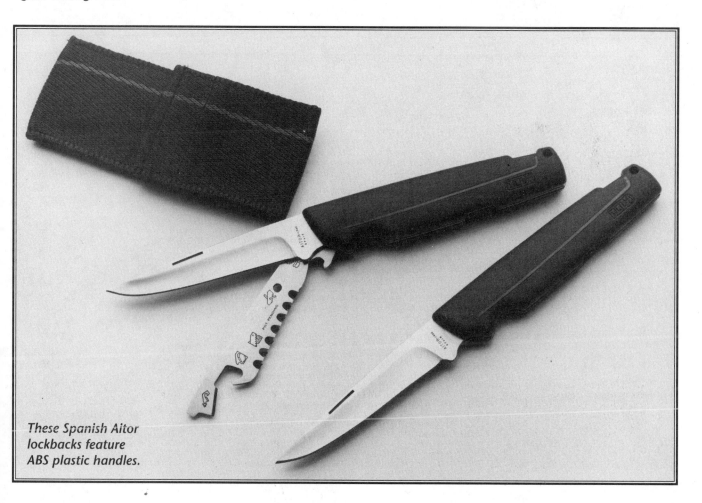

These Spanish Aitor lockbacks feature ABS plastic handles.

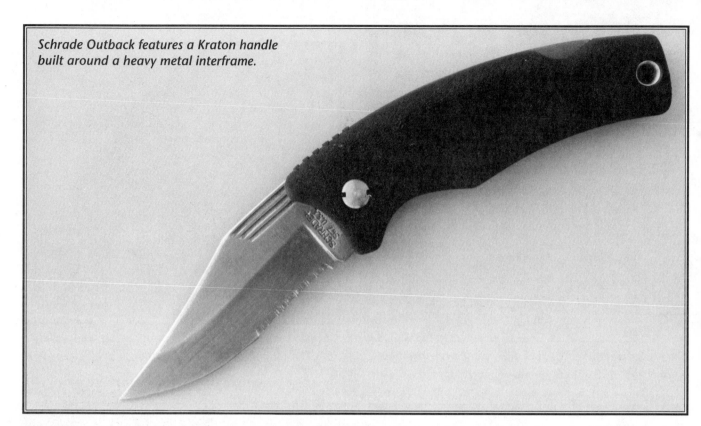

Schrade Outback features a Kraton handle built around a heavy metal interframe.

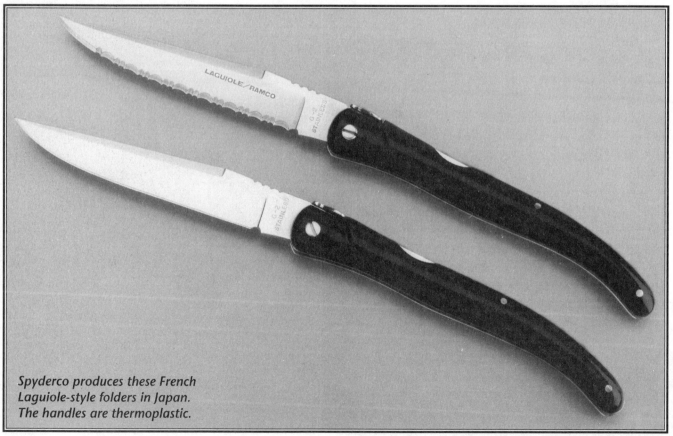

Spyderco produces these French Laguiole-style folders in Japan. The handles are thermoplastic.

Schrade offers the 2⅝-inch closed Nighthawk and the 3-inch Raider. For those looking for a heavier-duty field knife, Schrade turns out the TRP-handled Outback in both serrated and straight edge, clip and drop point blades. Puma has the 4¼-inch closed Featherweight series.

One of the best buys in a light-weight working blade is Colonial's Zytel-handled 4-inch closed Model LK95 Lite-Knife. Bear MGC produces a blaze orange Kraton-handled 5-inch closed lockback called simply the Deer Hunter. Case recently added a line of both slip joint and rocker-bar lockback folders under the name of Caliber pocket knives.

TRADITIONAL GERMAN FOLDING HUNTERS

There are many other rocker-bar folders on the market that don't necessarily fall into either the Buck 110 style or the modern thermoplastic frame system. German sportsmen have long utilized a modest-sized multiblade lockback that normally comes with at least one 3¼-inch spear point blade, a bone saw and a special blunt point gutting blade. Shell extractors, bird drawers, smaller blades and many other tools are also occasionally added to these knives.

Due to its fairly high cost, this type of outdoor knife is imported into the United States in relatively small numbers, but it is an excellent field tool for those who can afford it. Puma is the most common brand found here but there are others in Europe, and each year a few filter in as souvenirs.

EKA LOCKBACKS

Like most Swedish knives, EKA's lockbacks are designed for ease of production with almost no hand-finishing involved. While they lack some of the refinement found in most of the

SOG Specialty's Micro-Dot folder is one of a number of popular Zytel-handled key-chain folders.

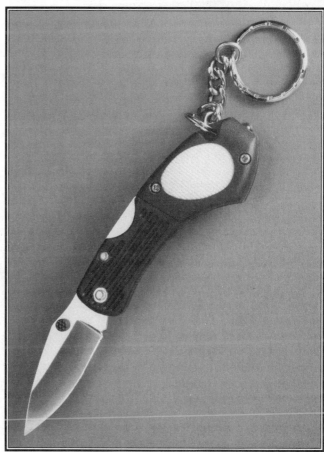

Spyderco's Firefly key chain knife features a red LED light in the handle.

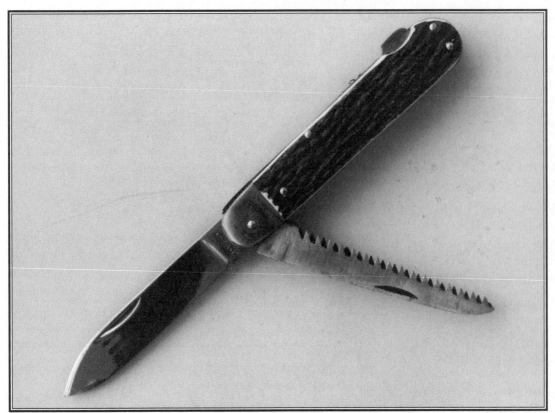

German hunters have long favored small folding hunters such as this model with a spear, saw, and often blunt point gutting blade. This particular knife is actually a Czech-made folder.

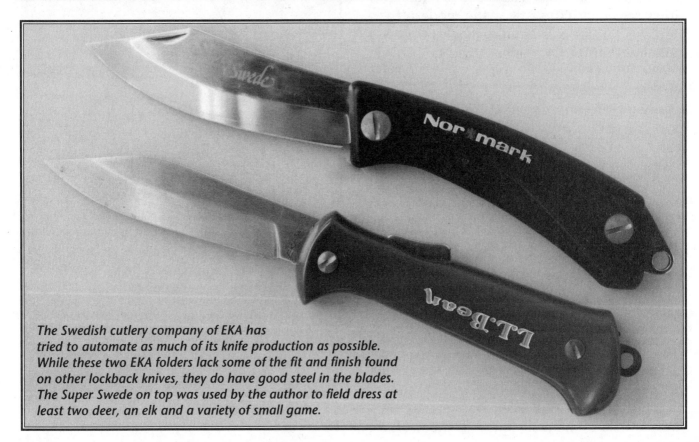

The Swedish cutlery company of EKA has tried to automate as much of its knife production as possible. While these two EKA folders lack some of the fit and finish found on other lockback knives, they do have good steel in the blades. The Super Swede on top was used by the author to field dress at least two deer, an elk and a variety of small game.

better quality American, German and Japanese knives, they are made of excellent Swedish steel and certainly get the job done. I carried a Super Swede model for a few months on the job as a forester, and field dressed both a blacktail buck and a fairly large elk during that time. I either lost the knife in the field or it was permanently "borrowed" by one of my tree planters. I never knew which, but I was sorry to see it go since several years passed before I found a replacement.

PRIVATE BRAND COMPANIES

Ten or 15 years ago, there were large numbers of medium-priced Japanese lockbacks being imported into the United States by several private brand companies. Many actually gave excellent value for the money. While the high-end lines, such as Al Mar, Spyderco, Katz, SOG Specialty and Outdoor Edge are still available, the poor exchange rate seems to have wiped out most of the mid-priced Japanese knife lines. In their place have come a variety of new Taiwanese brands.

One Taiwanese company that seems to be putting an effort into turning out a quality product at a reasonable price is Columbia Knife and Tool. Most of its designs are of the Zytel handle variety and several are of custom origin. The other Taiwan folders are acceptable tools — especially in situations in which the knife is expendable, provided the price is right.

PAKISTANI AND CHINESE IMPORTS

The lowest end of the lockback market is held by the Pakistani and mainland Chinese imports. A Pakistani copy of the Buck Ranger retails for under $10 in Europe. This knife sometimes ends up with other countries of origin stamped on the blade. One look at this lockback will convince you that the Pakistanis can produce a quality knife when desired. Yet, most of the knives from this country that land in the United States are simply made to sell for the lowest possible price.

Competition in the world market being what it is, mainland China seems to be pushing the Pakistanis out of the very bottom of the cutlery market. Again, none of this is to say that these countries can't produce high quality knives — if they desire.

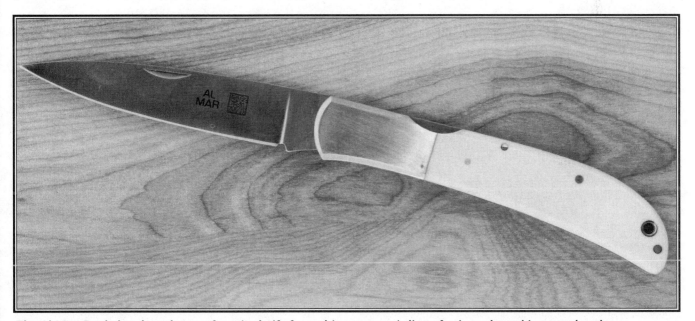

The Al Mar Eagle has long been a favorite knife from this company's line of private-brand imported cutlery.

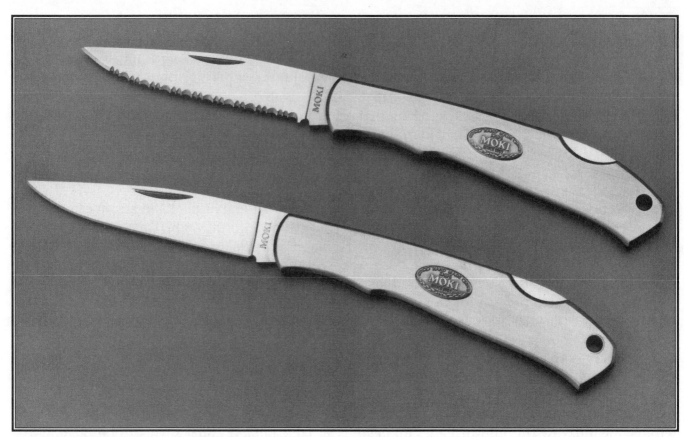

Along with the standard Clipit line, Spyderco imports several other Japanese lines such as these Moki Silver Feathers.

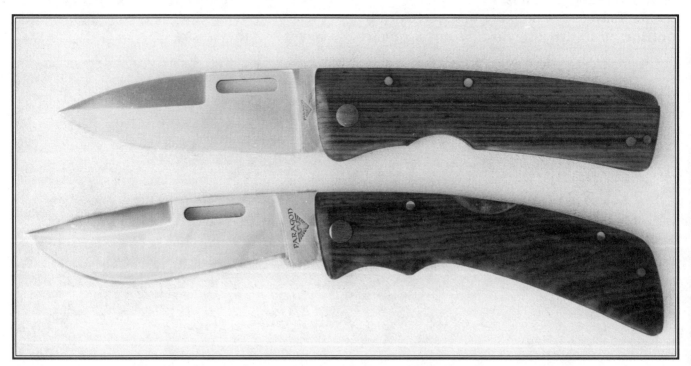

Paragon Cutlery had Blackie Collins design this pair of lockbacks, which are manufactured in Japan.

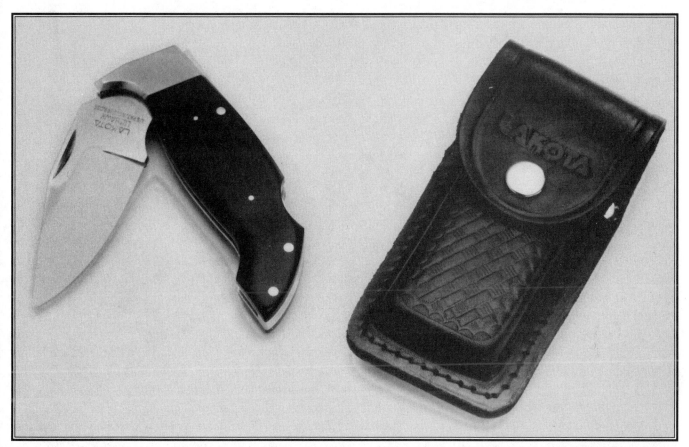

The Lakota ProHawk is imported by Brunton/Lakota from Japan. This Micarta-handled folder is especially popular with law enforcement personnel.

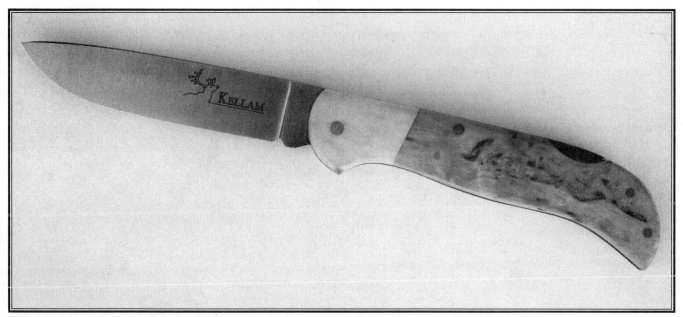

Kellam Knives wanted a Finnish Puukko-style folder, but none was available in Finland. The result was this Finnish-style knife made in Italy.

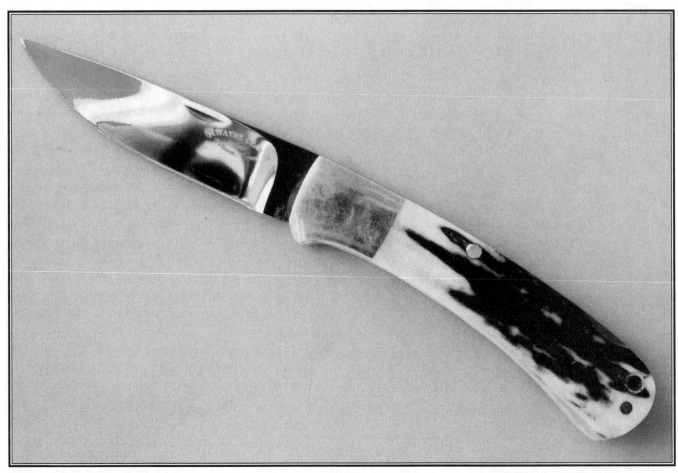

This custom Wayne Clay folding hunter is much lighter and stronger than it would appear at first, due to its state-of-the-art titanium frame.

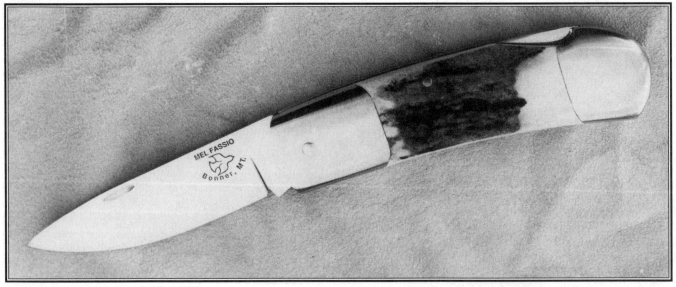

Custom rocker-bar locks have been overshadowed by new liner-lock models. A few makers, such as Mel Fassio, still turn out a good working model such as this hunter.

TITANIUM FRAMES

The trend in high-end quality custom rocker-bar lock folders is toward the use of titanium in the handle frame. This alleviates the handle-heavy feel found on traditional brass or stainless steel frame Buck 110-style knives, without any sacrifice in strength. A good example is the Wayne Clay folding bird hunter.

At first, the 4¼-inch closed stag-handled lockback looks to be a fairly heavy metal-framed folder that might be uncomfortable to carry in a pocket. Actually, its titanium liners allow it to weigh in at only three ounces.

Although a certain amount of absolute strength is lost, the better grades of aircraft aluminum can also serve this purpose at a greatly reduced cost.

As to the purpose of blade locks in general, some of the same people who serve as the movers and shakers of the anti-gun movement say that the only function of a blade lock on a folding knife is to convert an ordinary tool into a stabbing weapon. The actual purpose of a blade lock has long been a concern for the safety of the user. Non-locking blades can and do fold in the hands of careless users, sometimes resulting in a serious cut.

Boker offers a heavy-duty folder with exchangeable blades that includes one ceramic skinning blade.

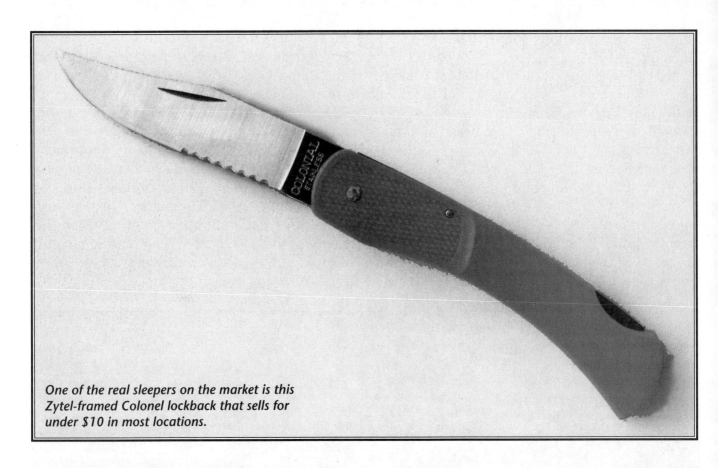

One of the real sleepers on the market is this Zytel-framed Colonel lockback that sells for under $10 in most locations.

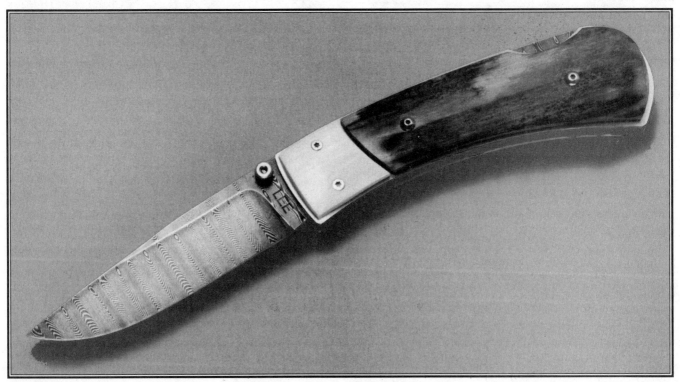

This Damascus blade rocker-bar is from the shop of custom knifemaker Tommy Lee. *(PHOTO BY WEYER OF TOLEDO)*

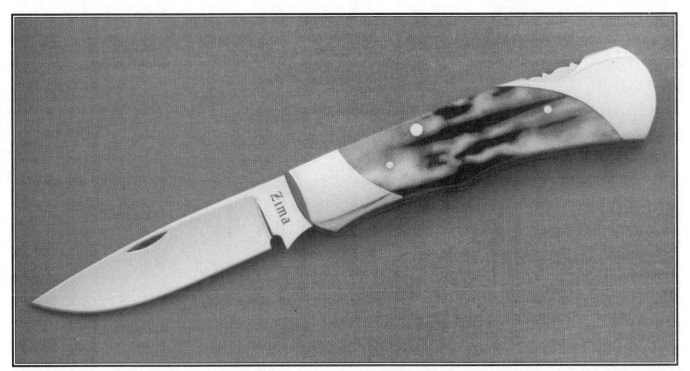

Mike Zima produces a number of very nice pocket-size rocker-bar folders such as this stag handled model.

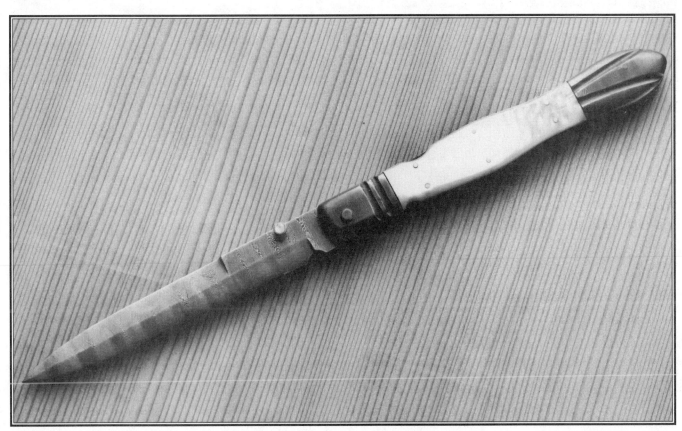

A.D. Rardon produced this decidedly 19th century-looking folding bowie   (PHOTO BY WEYER OF TOLEDO)

Lockbacks of any kind are safer with which to work for infrequent folding knife users, but they can never match a fixed blade for either strength or speed of deployment.

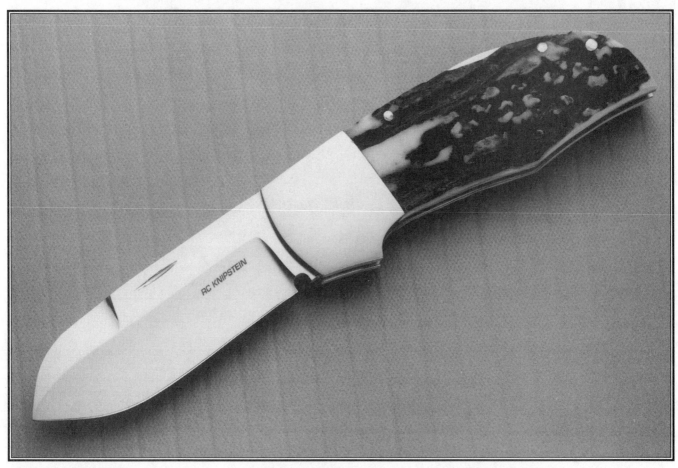

For those looking for a short and stout rocker-bar locking folder, there is the Sunfish- style knife from R.C. Knipstein.

7
LINER-LOCK KNIVES

The liner-lock system of securing a blade in the open position has been around since the turn of the century. The lock consists of one side of the knife frame forming a flat spring. When the knife is opened, the spring moves laterally in the handle frame to a position blocking the blade tang from folding. To release the lock, the spring must be pushed back along the side of the handle. Normally, a notch is provided on the handle frame to allow the thumb access to the spring, but occasionally buttons or flanges are installed to make the job easier.

Most early liner-lock knives utilized a brass liner and spring tang block on what was a conventional slip-joint folder. In practice, the liner-lock served as a back-up safety system to the normal force required to fold a heavy back-spring, non-locking knife. Simply adding a liner-lock to an already existing slip-joint folder was probably more cost-effective than designing a new model rocker-bar locking knife. Most likely, none of these early combination action liner-locks were intended for one-hand opening.

Both the Schrade Old Timer 125OT Mustang on top and the Imperial Sheepsfoot folder on the bottom utilize a brass liner-lock on a slip-joint folder. Woodcraft expert Cliff Jacobson feels this is one of the best factory knives around for the camper.

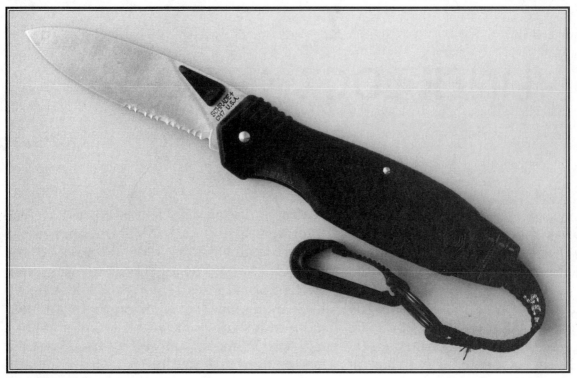

Schrade's new Cliphanger is basically the standard slip-joint with a liner-lock design, but the brass tang block has been replaced with stainless steel.

SCHRADE 125OT

One of my favorite wilderness work and sport knives was a 5¼-inch closed single blade Schrade 125OT Old Timer Mustang with a brass liner-lock. I worked that knife hard for a number of years, and would still recommend it highly for anyone looking for a reasonably priced backcountry folder. Schrade made this same knife in a stainless Uncle Henry version that offered certain advantages around water or in wet climates, but they chose to discontinue it.

Schrade continues to offer a smaller, 3⅞-inch closed single blade trapper pattern brass liner-lock and several models in its 'Made in Ireland' tradesman line. The company's new Cliphanger one-hand opener is another combination action folder, but with a steel rather than brass liner-lock. Bear MGC is another company that offers a group of Zytel-handled 4⅛-inch closed carry clip-style folders with a combination steel liner-lock and slip-joint action. For traditionalists, brass liner-locks are

still the standard system on most screwdriver blades used on electrician's knives and on many hawk's bill pruners.

While these combination slip-joint/liner-lock folders work well, most retain a certain amount of play between the point where the blade starts to fold under hand pressure and the spring liner blocks it. Under normal field utility use, this will seldom pose any real problem, but is probably one reason combination knives never really caught on as lockbacks.

In the mid-1980s, a new liner-lock system became popular with custom makers. In place of a brass spring, these knives used a high strength steel or titanium tang block. The design also eliminated the conventional slip-joint feature of earlier side-lock knives. When combined with some type of one-hand opening mechanism, the new liner-locks became the next best thing to an auto-opening knife for speedy deployment.

As the modernized tang blocking locks caught on, people started experimenting with lock strength. The old brass tang blocks had a reputation for bending and failing under heavy downward blade pressure. While not really a problem in normal use, it was a serious enough weakness to remove the tang block lock from consideration by those who think in terms of defensive or survival knife handling. Experiments quickly proved that the newer steel and titanium tang blocks offered major advantages in lock strength over the more common rocker-bar locks. Thus, the liner-lock became the accepted system for practically all custom survival and defensive folding knives.

PROBLEMS

Two problems with the liner-lock arose early on. Without the slip-joint back spring, only friction was holding many knives in the closed position. A slight snag or jar could partially open the blade in the pocket. Naturally, this posed a safety hazard to the user. The solution for most makers was to add a detent ball to the lock spring and a notch to the blade tang. When the knife is closed, the ball sits in the notch and provides just enough force to keep the blade from swinging open unexpectedly. A

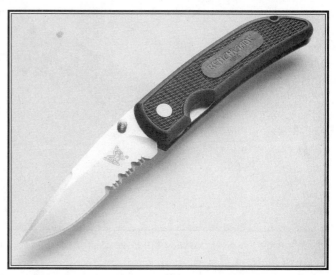

Benchmade was one of the first commercial knifemakers to use a detent ball on the tang block bar of models such as this Panther.

few of the really low-end imported liner-locks still lack the ball detent feature, so it pays to take a close look before buying.

To provide a backup system to the detent, many makers chose to put spring carry clips on the blade end of the handle. This ensures that the blade is pointed down in the pocket and, should it come partially open, the user won't shove his hand into the point on a draw.

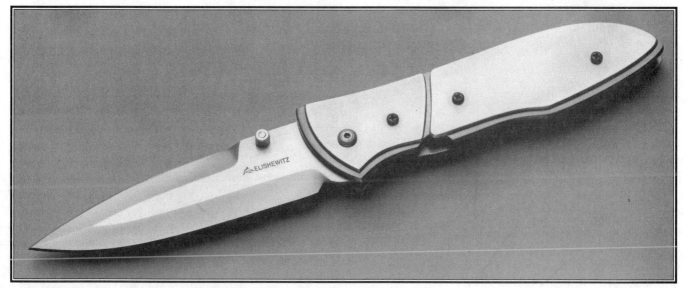

Experienced knifemakers such as Allen Elishewitz seldom have lock adjustment or flex problems. This is Elishewitz's Phantom model, which will soon be produced by Benchmade.

Benchmade's highly popular Emerson-designed CQC7 tactical folder.

On the down side, some knife experts feel rather strongly that the clip should be on the butt of the knife frame so that the user doesn't have to reverse the knife in his hand before opening. This is a matter of speed, which is primarily of interest to those carrying a folder for emergency needs.

The second technical problem with designing a modern liner-lock folder is the close tolerances required when fitting the lock to the blade tang in the open position. On the old combination slip-joint/tang block knives, this was not particularly critical since the back spring held the knife open. Without the back spring, it's up to the liner-lock bar alone to hold the blade securely in place.

A poorly fitted bar allows play between the blade tang and the lock. Using the wrong alloy on the spring bar often leads to the spring end wearing at its point of contact with the harder blade tang and, again, the blade develops

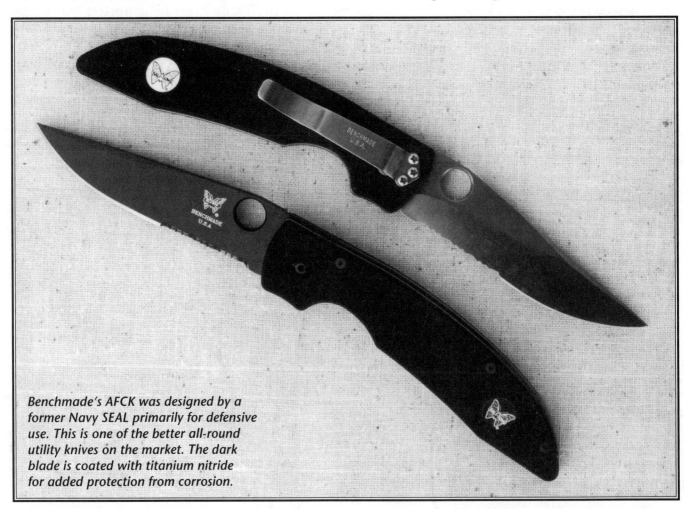

Benchmade's AFCK was designed by a former Navy SEAL primarily for defensive use. This is one of the better all-round utility knives on the market. The dark blade is coated with titanium nitride for added protection from corrosion.

unacceptable play. There is also the matter of adjusting the spring so that it swings to the proper position on the blade tang. Too narrow a swing and the lock may not make enough contact to hold under stress. Too wide a swing and the bar may ride past the blade tang and be difficult to release.

Another problem found on a custom liner-lock folder is that, for some reason, the titanium lock bar flexes when pressure is applied to the blade. The lock bar swings back into the closed position, allowing the blade to fold. The maker has not been able to explain why the spring on this particular knife is so flexible. None of 'this is to say there aren't plenty of knifemakers who have mastered the secrets of making functional and reliable liner-lock folders.

When making a major investment, my recommendation is to shy away from custom liner-lock makers who do not have at least a couple of years' production behind them. Commercially-made folders are less of a monetary risk and the maker will usually replace a defective folder without delay.

BENCHMADE KNIVES

When it comes to factory liner-locks, one company stands out above the crowd: Benchmade Knives. Benchmade was the first major cutlery company to produce the modern liner-lock in large numbers. Because I live relatively close to the factory, I have had an excellent opportunity to watch Benchmade's knife line evolve.

Some time ago, I was asked to evaluate one of the first liner-lock folders off the production line and quickly found several of the inherent design problems mentioned earlier. Upon discussing my evaluation with Benchmade, I found that the design weaknesses had been noted and corrected. Today it's hard to find a knifemaker — custom or production — that does a better job of fitting and finishing the locking mechanism on a liner-lock folder.

Benchmade's Leopards (top) were designed by Pat Crawford, while the Spike is a classic Phil Boguszewski design. The larger Leopard has traveled with me on numerous trips in and out of the country. Although it may seem a little plain at first, this is a design that will grow on you with use over time.

I believe the first liner-lock in Benchmade's catalog was the Panther series of light-weight Zytel-handled, clip carry, right-hand peg opening 4.375-inch closed folders. Some weapons instructors believe the knife to be one of the best-kept secrets on the market. Retailing for around $50, the Panthers feature a steel reinforced handle frame that gives them a significant advantage in strength over some of the similarly sized all-Zytel-handled knives. The blade shape is excellent for a wide variety of uses and, like all Benchmade knives, the Panthers are made entirely in the United States.

From their start with the Panthers, Benchmade began a series of joint design projects with several well-known custom knifemakers. The first was the Walter Brend Combat Talon II, an aluminum framed, stainless steel locking bar, ATS-34 knife with a 3½-inch blade. The knife also featured a stainless steel carry clip and a right-hand opening peg. The recurve cutting edge of the Combat Talon made the knife a highly aggressive cutting tool, and beefy, all-metal construction provided an extra margin of strength for serious users.

Benchmade's Pat Crawford-designed Leopard and Phil Boguszewski's Spike were introduced a short time later. The Leopard is an aluminum framed right-hand peg opener with a spring carry clip offered in a choice of 3¾- and 2⅞-inch blades with or without 50/50 serrations. Premium ATS-34 stainless is used on the acutely pointed blade. The Leopard is one of those folders that doesn't seem particularly special until you have carried it for a while. The handle of the Leopard is very comfortable and the blade shape is highly efficient for most utility needs.

Phil Boguszewski's custom Spikes have had a strong following among Northwest knife users for many years, so it was welcome news that Benchmade had decided to produce a commercial version of this folder. At first glance the narrow, pointed blade might seem suited only to stabbing movements, but it is quite handy for a variety of fine cutting tasks.

Fishermen, in particular, have found the Spike blade useful. Naturally, the blade shape also lends itself well to use as a folding boot knife. Benchmade's version comes in 4- and 3⅛-inch blade versions built on an aluminum frame with a right-hand peg opener and a

Benchmade's Tsunami (top) and Kodiak (bottom) were in-house liner-lock designs. While both were well-received by knife experts, they have been replaced by custom collaboration project knives in the line.

Spyderco's Bob Terzuola model was the company's first attempt at a liner-lock folder.

spring carry clip. The ATS-34 blade is available in a straight or 50/50 edge.

The latest of the Benchmade custom designs is the Ernest Emerson CQC7, a G-10-handled, titanium framed and locking bar folder with a one-sided grind tanto point blade that opens by means of an ambidextrous spine mounted disk. The knife is available in ATS-34 3¼- and 4-inch blade models and in a state-of-the-art 3¼-inch titanium blade with a tungsten carbide tantalum coating on one side of the cutting edge. Benchmade recommends the titanium blade for situations in which high corrosion resistance is desirable. The company claims it's best used for rough cutting in fibrous materials rather than fine work.

From my own testing of the standard 3¼-inch model, I would have to say this is probably the strongest folder for its size on the market. At first the handle seems a little long for the blade, but in use it provides an extremely secure grip.

Benchmade has not been idle with in-house designs. Shortly after the Leopard and the Spike, it introduced the Tsunami and the Kodiak Skinner. Both knives were built on the same aluminum frame with stainless steel liner-locks and right-handed opening pegs. The Tsunami featured a relatively straight 4-inch tanto point blade of G-2 stainless, while the Kodiak had a wide clip point blade of the same material.

The knives were available in either straight edge or 50/50 serrated and each had a stainless steel carry clip on the handle. The Kodiak is better suited to heavy duty outdoor use. The Tsunami is an equally good knife, but the tanto-style point is better suited to defensive use than the clip. Benchmade has since discontinued both models so it could concentrate on the CQC7 and AFCK models. At present, there seems to be a fair number of both the Tsunami and the Kodiak left in the commercial pipeline.

The most recent of the in-house Benchmade designs is the aforementioned AFCK (Advanced Folding Combat Knife). This knife was designed with the help of former-SEAL Chris Caracci and has been designated the official Gun Site Training Center folder. Unlike the previous Benchmade models, the AFCK utilizes the famous ambidextrous

Spyderco's Frank Centofante collaboration knife features an aluminum frame with Kraton inserts and liner-lock.

Spyderco hole in the blade (under license from Spyderco) for an opening system. Like the CQC7, the AFCK features G-10 handle scales, but has a stainless frame and locking

Spyderco's Military is its first effort at a heavy-duty liner-lock folder. The first production also features state-of-the-art CPM 440C stainless blades.

bar. The blade is ATS-34 and is available in both a 3¼- and a 4-inch version, with or without serrations. Despite the aggressive sounding name, the AFCK is one of the better general purpose utility folders on the market, suitable for hunting, fishing, backpacking or any similar outdoor sport.

SPYDERCO

While Spyderco is better known for its rocker-bar lock folders, it does offer a few options in the liner-lock field. The first was the aluminum-framed, stainless locking bar Bob Terzuola model currently available in 2¾- and 3½-inch ATS-34 blade versions. This semi-sheepsfoot blade folder is something most knife users are either very pleased with or simply won't tolerate. Spyderco's second liner-lock was the aluminum framed Frank Centofante-designed model with a 2⅞-inch ATS-34 blade and colored Sanaprene rubber inserts on the handle.

Along the way there was also a state-of-the-art but very expensive carbon fiber-handled Michael Walker design produced on a limited basis. Later a Zytel-handled light-weight

Michael Walker at a lower price was added to better serve knife users.

In late 1995, Spyderco released the Military, a wide 4-inch blade folder in a choice of CPM 440V or ATS-34 stainless steel and G-10 handle scales. Like most Spyderco knives, the Military is available with or without full length serrations, and in this case, with or without a black titanium blade coating. This is one of the largest and lightest heavy-duty folders in the company's line.

CPM 440V has a reputation for being at the head of the pack when it comes to edge holding, but at the same time can be extremely difficult to resharpen. From my own use of the new model, I can say I'm very pleased with the overall design but still have reservations about the 440V option. I had difficulty sharpening my blade until I reprofiled the edge on a ChefChoice Professional model electric diamond knife sharpener. I have since had a chance to work with the ATS-34 model and have been completely satisfied with the knife's performance.

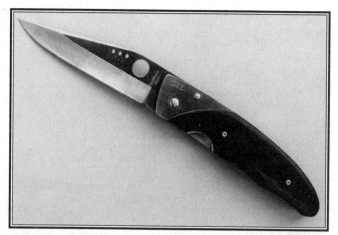

Spyderco's Howard Viele collaboration knife retains the slim, shark-like looks of all Viele designs. The three small holes in the handle are for aesthetics only.

The very latest in liner-locks from Spyderco is its Viele custom collaboration model. This is a 3½-inch clip point AS-8 blade with a thumb opening hole. The handle is stainless steel with black Macerate handle scales and steel carry clip. The model runs around $130 retail, and the workmanship — compared to some factory and custom folders costing much

To meet emergency services and sportsmen's needs, Buck produced the Crosslock in a variety of configurations.

Columbia River Knife and Tool's Cobra Gold is a production liner-lock version of a Jim Hammond custom folder.

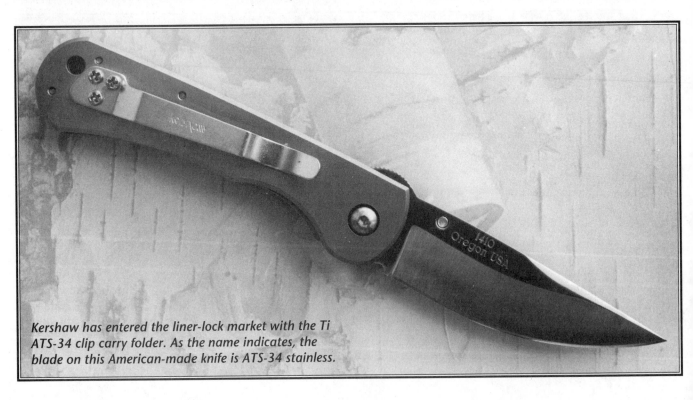

Kershaw has entered the liner-lock market with the Ti ATS-34 clip carry folder. As the name indicates, the blade on this American-made knife is ATS-34 stainless.

Now discontinued, Cold Steel's Ultralocks featured an adjustable liner-lock plus a unique thumb glide system of blade opening. Basically, the thumb was rotated over the end of the blade tang to lever the knife open.

The Zytel-handled liner-lock Spyderco Solo utilizes a flange built into the side of the blade for one-hand opening.

Spyderco's Cricket is another all-metal liner-lock.

more — is surprisingly good. The only real down side to the Viele is that the opening hole is a bit small for large hands.

OTHER FACTORY OPTIONS

Many other commercial cutlery companies are just starting to enter the liner-lock arena. Most have already been mentioned in the one-hand-opening, carry clip section, but Browning, Buck, Columbia River Handcrafted Knives, Schrade, Bear MGC and Kershaw all have entries in the field. Al Mar Knives Quicksilver and Talon models also function on the tang block principal. Gerber has just begun production of its new Applegate/Fairbairn folding combat knife. Other factory-made liner-locks will no doubt follow these companies.

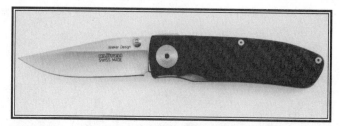

Built like a Swiss watch, the Walker/Klotzki is made in Switzerland on a titanium frame and lock with carbon fiber handles and a 440-C stainless blade.

CUSTOM OPTIONS

A large percentage of the custom folder market is now devoted to the liner-lock system. While it would be difficult to cover every custom maker now making a liner-lock folder, I can recommend several from first-hand field experience.

Columbia River calls these Jim Hammond liner-lock, peg opening folders the Fighting Falcon (top) and Eagle (middle and bottom).

Wayne Clark's all titanium handle, spring carry clip, liner-lock, one-hand disk opener and ATS-34 blade make this folder the perfect example of the modern high-tech knife.

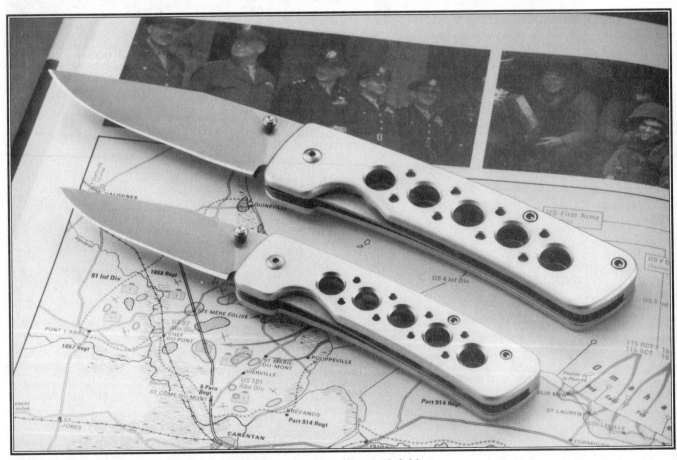

Columbia River's Commander offers a more basic working liner-lock folder.

Ernest Emerson has, without a doubt, been one of the hottest liner-lock folder makers in the last few years with his CQC (Close Quarter Combat) series. This is a 3¼-inch, ATS-34 blade with a one-sided grind, a reinforced tanto point, ambidextrous spine mounted disk one-hand opener, stainless steel spring carry clip, titanium frame and rough finished Micarta handle.

Basically, the CQC6 is a folding boot knife that will also serve a variety of utility functions. Like the Benchmade folders based on Emerson's designs, it would be difficult to find a stronger knife for its size. All of Emerson's designs have found a near cult following in military Special Operations units as they may be counted on when the chips are down. The Navy has made official purchases of a new Emerson model featuring a large, wide clip blade, disk opener and a one-side grind. While the issue model will be restricted to military sales, there will also be a civilian version offered to the public.

While Kit Carson designates his Model 4 a combat folder, I have found my own to be an ideal, heavy-duty field knife. Currently, the Model 4 is offered in 3- and 4-inch blade versions and a variety of handle materials. My own is a 4-inch with a titanium frame and rough surfaced linen Micarta handle scales. Ambidextrous opening pegs are mounted on the wide clip point ATS-34 blade and a stainless carry clip is attached to the blade end of the handle. I have found this to be a super-strong knife capable of handling any chore a folder may reasonably be asked to perform, but at the same time still handy enough for fine work. For those needing something little more compact to carry, the 3-inch version of this same knife is equally useful.

One of the more unique liner-lock designs being offered is Chris Reeve's Sebenza (South African for "work"). Here, the liner-lock bar is an integral part of one side of the titanium handle frame. The massive size of the blocking bar on the Sebenza perhaps makes it the strongest lock of its type. Both left and right hand peg opening versions are offered, as is an optional carry clip. The ATS-34 blade is a modified form of clip point 3½ inches long. Reeve is one of those makers who truly understands how to grind a blade for maximum cutting efficiency. There is also a smaller 2⅞-inch model for those looking for something more pocket size. Either Sebenza will make short work of any task to which it is applied.

An Ernest Emerson CQC6 folder has become something of a status symbol with Special Operations troops.

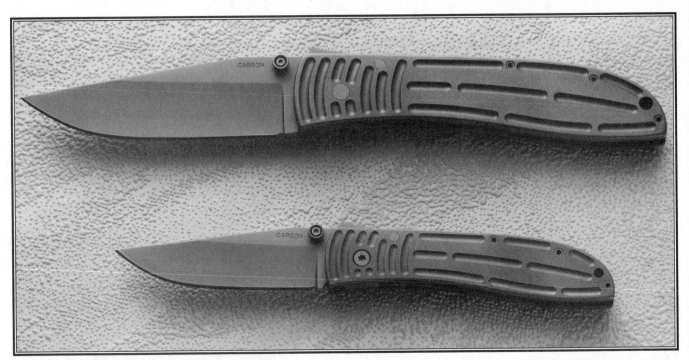

Kit Carson's Model 4 in solid titanium handles. *(PHOTO BY WEYER OF TOLEDO)*

Chris Reeve recently refined his Sebenza into a more trim and efficient package. The top two knives are prototypes of the new model, while the bottom knife is the original.

During a recent hunting season, I had a opportunity to field evaluate the new Blade Tech/Phil Boguszewski folding hunter. This is a special design created by Blade Tech's owner Tim Wegner, with permission from Spyderco to utilize its hump and hole blade opening system. The ATS-34 blade is 3¾ inches long with a dropped point and better-than-average sweep to the edge. Wegner is a dedicated hunter and his blade design was created from first-hand experience. Field dressing and skinning a blacktail deer with the knife removed any doubt I might have had in my mind about the design. It works outstandingly well. The curved design of the Blade Tech handle frame is one of the most comfortable and user-friendly folding hunters available.

For those looking for the largest liner-lock folder practical, there is Northwest Safari's

Entry Team custom made by Butch Vallotton. Butch is better known for his state-of-the-art auto-opening knives, but he does work on a few other projects such as this NWS exclusive and the original custom version of the Gerber Applegate/Fairbairn folder.

The Entry Team is a 4⅝-inch spear point blade with a choice of right- or left-hand opening peg and a Micarta handle with titanium liners and locking bar. Most versions come standard with a short section of serrations at the base of the edge. Originally designed for use by SWAT teams, the ET is well-suited to both utility and defensive weapon use. As massive as the knife appears, the construction keeps the weight down to a very manageable 7½ ounces.

Few makers turn out as many styles and variations of unique folders as Pat Crawford.

The Blade Tech/Phil Boguszewski liner-lock folding hunter is one of the better one-hand opening field knives on the market for outdoors enthusiasts.

Made for Northwest Safari by Butch Vallotton, the 5-inch blade Entry Team is one extremely heavy-duty folder.

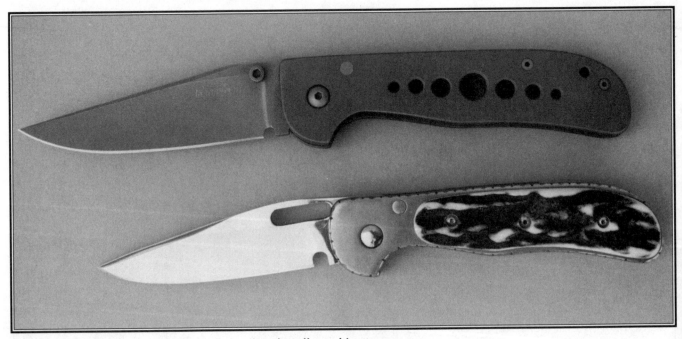

Crawford's Shark line E-lock in an all-titanium handle and in stag.

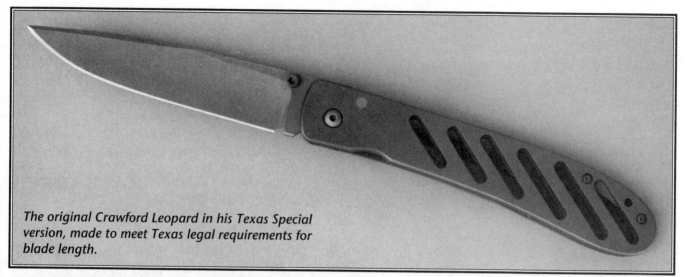

The original Crawford Leopard in his Texas Special version, made to meet Texas legal requirements for blade length.

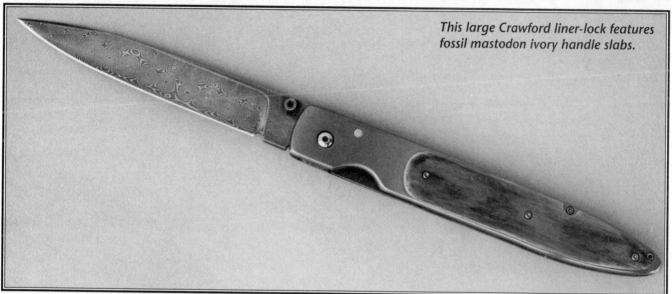

This large Crawford liner-lock features fossil mastodon ivory handle slabs.

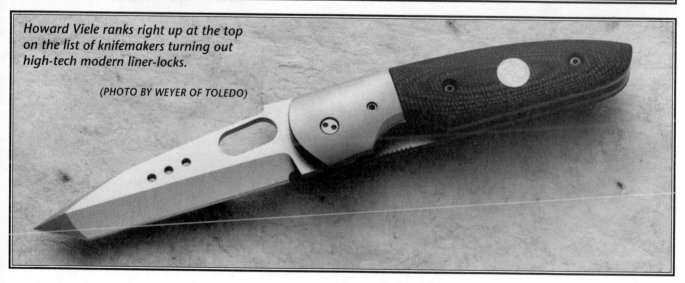

Howard Viele ranks right up at the top on the list of knifemakers turning out high-tech modern liner-locks.

(PHOTO BY WEYER OF TOLEDO)

*Two of Bob Dozier's handy little one-hand opening liner-locks.
The top knife has the seldom-seen green G-10 handle scales.*

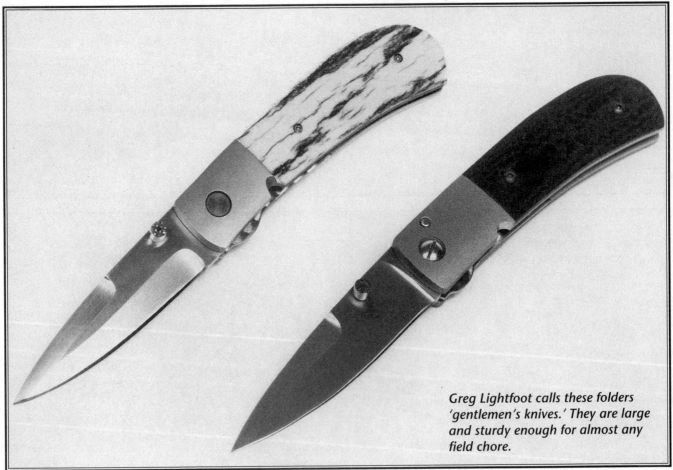

*Greg Lightfoot calls these folders
'gentlemen's knives.' They are large
and sturdy enough for almost any
field chore.*

Along with Leopards in several sizes up to more than five inches in blade length, Pat offers a self-guard liner-lock folder, designated the Shark, as well as two trendy tanto folders with one-sided blade grinds and reinforced chisel points.

One of the real rising stars in the custom arena is Allen Elishewitz. Allen stays on the leading edge of custom folding knife technology with a first class group of liner-lock folders designed to fulfill particular uses. Following the Ernest Emerson school of custom folders, most of Elishewitz's designs are geared for the military and defensive knife carrier market. Among other projects, Allen works with Mission Knives to produce a large utility folder in both 440V stainless and pure titanium bladed versions, and has entered into an agreement with Benchmade knives to work out a custom collaboration with the company.

Howard Viele has been able to take the basic Spyderco opening hole, spring carry clip and liner-lock system and create knife designs that are instantly recognizable as uniquely his own. All are slender and pointed, with the appearance of a cat ready to pounce. At knife shows, Howard usually sells out in the first couple of hours to people who intend to carry and use these knives, possibly the Rolex of the cutlery world. For those on a Timex budget, there is the new Spyderco/Viele collaboration model.

Bob Dozier's little liner-lock folder is one of the few custom knives in the current generation that does not have a spring carry clip or

A selection of Dick Atkinson's custom folders. The top knife is a liner-lock.

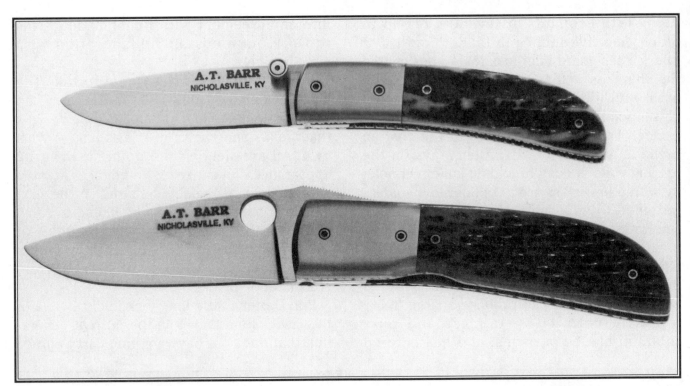

Two A.T. Barr liner-lock folders. The top knife features stag handle slabs while the bottom has jigged bone.
(PHOTO BY WEYER OF TOLEDO)

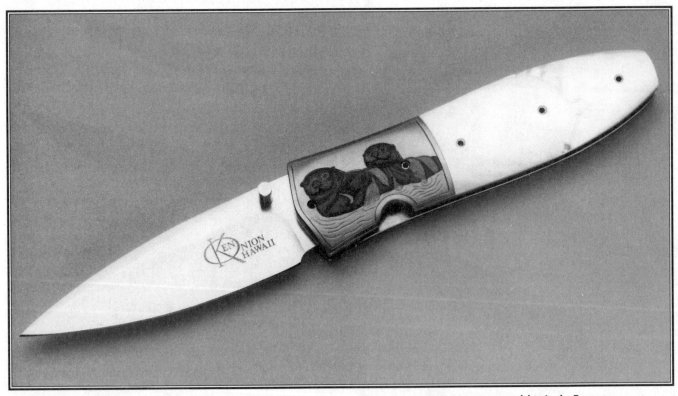

This pearl-handled beauty came from the shop of Ken Onion. The sea otters were engraved by Judy Beaver.
(PHOTO BY WEYER OF TOLEDO)

serrated edge. What it does have is a clean, smooth action that allows the user to push the blade open with little effort. The wide 2¾-inch drop point blade is ground from D-2 steel, a material that may not be as corrosion-resistant as ATS-34, but generally holds a better edge. The handles are light-weight Micarta. This is a first class little cutter with enough size to handle most field game chores without being too large for everyday pocket carry in the city.

In Canada you can find Greg Lightfoot turning out his line of massive folding survival and defensive knives. Greg has loaned me a 4-inch spear point, disk opening, two-sided grind version with a 50/50 edge of his popular Magnum model for field testing.

In keeping with current trends, most Magnums are sold with a one-side grind and a chisel point. I intended to use the evaluation knife as a hunter and have been impressed with the willingness and speed of the maker in providing just the variation needed. I have field dressed two deer with the knife. As an experiment, I tried sawing through the ribs of both deer to open their chests. The serrated edge proved to work quite well for this task. All Greg's folders are as stout as they come. These are knives you may count on when the chips are down.

For those looking for a good buy in a custom liner-lock, Dick Atkinson offers a tang block version of his standard folder for a little more than $100. Dick keeps his knives simple, with straight Micarta handles and no liners. All feature a right-hand peg opener and usually a drop point blade.

I carried an example of his liner-lock around the ranch for several months, using it for all the rough jobs that work knives end up doing. The blade held up with no problems and the handle was exceptionally comfortable.

Allen Elishewitz designed and produced this knife for Navy SEAL contractor Mission Knives.

(PHOTO BY WEYER OF TOLEDO)

Cruising the tables at any major custom knife show will turn up many more makers offering first class liner-lock folders. The one piece of advice I would offer buyers at these shows is to check and see if the knife has any play between the lock and the blade tang when open. If it does, the maker either still has a way to go toward learning his craft or is sloppy in his work. Look elsewhere for a working liner-lock.

Al Polkowski is better known for his tactical fixed blades, but he also turns out a nice folder on occasion.
(PHOTO BY WEYER OF TOLEDO)

8

THE ONE-HAND OPENING, CLIP CARRY, SERRATED EDGE REVOLUTION

In 1982, Spyderco, a company known for its triangular ceramic sharpening rods, introduced a medium-sized, all-metal, rocker-bar locking, folding knife called the Clipit Worker. What made this knife different from the 1,001 other lockbacks on the market were the following features: a strange hump on the back of the blade with a large hole in it that allowed the blade to be pushed open one-handed with the thumb; a serrated blade edge in a two-step pattern common to kitchen knives sold by television ads at the time; and a steel clip mounted on the handle that allowed the knife to be attached conveniently to the top of a pocket, belt, or packstrap.

Anyone who works with a folding knife has been in situations where only one hand was available to open the blade. When one hand is holding a flopping fish, a rope under tension, canoe gunwale in a fast river or a bent tree limb, prying the blade out of many conventional folders with one hand is extremely difficult. Mountain climbers, whitewater rafters and canoers, parachutists and other adventurists may find themselves in a position where their lives depend on one-handed opening. This is why gravity knives (knives that fall out of a hollow handle when a lever or button is pushed without the use of a spring) were issued to the U.S. Navy during the 19th century, and why both the American and the German armies issued switchblades and gravity knives during World War II.

In 1958, however, Congress outlawed the importation or interstate commerce in gravity and spring opening knives as a crime preven-

The Spyderco Worker was the first model in the Clipit family. The bottom knife is a special limited edition Damascus blade Worker made to commemorate the 10th anniversary of the Clipit's introduction.

The Worker was followed by the Mariner, a sheepsfoot of the traditional sailing pattern. The bottom knife is the newer Zytel handle Rescue.

tion measure. While there had been other attempts at producing a legal one-hand opening folder before the Spyderco Worker, none had been successful.

The spring carry clip eliminated having to grope around in a pocket for your knife. If this doesn't seem like a major accomplishment, try carrying any of the clip type knives for a few weeks and then switch back to the pocket carry folder you carried before.

Spyderco did not invent serrated edged folding knives. There have been numerous others in the past, but because of its special two-step serrated edge, they were the first company to successfully market this type of knife.

The serrated edge has the advantage of being about to chew its way through materials — including rope and other fibrous matter — even when it is relatively dull. It doesn't shape wood very well, is not particularly efficient cutting raw meat, and makes a poor skinning blade. When properly sharpened, however, it will cut through just about anything a straight edge will, although not as cleanly.

Sharpening a serrated edge tends to be problematic as a conventional flat hone will not work its way in and out of the teeth. Spyderco's Tri-Angle Sharpmaker does an excellent job honing Clipit teeth. Other tools and gadgets for sharpening serrated knives are appearing on the market, but no one product seems to be more popular than another. Users are simply allowing their blades to go dull and sawtoothed. This is really too bad, as the difference between a well-honed serrated edge and a dull one is quite noticeable.

The 50/50 edge is one attempt at solving the straight edge versus serrated blade controversy. Here, the first half of the blade is serrated while the point half is left with a straight edge. I was skeptical about the 50/50 edge because most whittling and utility chores are done with the base of the blade. While I still try to match the type of edge to the work I expect that day, I have found the 50/50 blade does make a good traveling tool for handling the unexpected. My personal Spyderco Delica 50/50 has now logged thousands of miles. Spyderco has also added a 50/50 Endura to its line.

The original Spyderco Worker Clipit was only a modest success, but Spyderco followed it up with a 3½-inch blade sheepsfoot point model called the Mariner. However, the one-hand opening knife in the traditional sailor's blade pattern appealed to a fairly limited number of knife users. It was the introduction of the Police Model Clipit that really brought Spyderco's concepts to the attention of the general knife-using public. The 5¼-inch closed folder featured a 4¼-inch blade (for legal purposes, 3⅞ inches of cutting edge) with a straight edge and a very pronounced point. As the name indicates, the knife was designed to serve a variety of utility purposes with emergency services personnel and others in need of a heavy-duty one-hand opening blade.

The Police model caught on quickly in professional circles but some felt it was a little heavy for street carry (all early models were made with stainless steel handles), and a relatively serious investment, money-wise. Several other steel and aluminum-handled Clipit models were introduced in the following years, each contributing just a little more to the company's reputation. Spyderco had the fire going but what really made it blaze was the 1990 introduction of the Zytel-handled

The stainless-handled Clipit family evolved into this group of folders. From the top: Police, Mariner, Harpy, Pro-Venator, Hunter, Standard, Worker, Executive and Co-Pilot.

The police model Clipit brought the Spyderco line to the attention of professional knife users.

Part of Spyderco's highly popular Zytel-handled family of Clipit folders include, from the top down, Catcherman, Endura, Delica, Merlin and Ladybug.

Spyderco's line of Wayne Goddard-designed folders, the first Clipits without a hump for the hole.

Delica and Endura models. Now here were practical, light-weight Clipits that most could afford.

Cutlery industry insiders had said that the Spyderco blade hump was ugly, serrations would never catch on, the carry clip was just a gimmick, and that one-hand opening wasn't all that important. Suddenly, they found their sales dropping as Spyderco's shot up like a rocket. The end result was a complete turnaround in the industry's attitude as each company quickly added serrated edges, one-hand opening mechanisms and pocket carry clips to its line as quickly as feasible. It is difficult now to find a major factory or custom folder maker that doesn't include at least one folder with several of these features.

ALTERNATIVE OPENERS

Spyderco had patented the hump and opening hole feature of its Clipits, so the initial problem for many companies was how to avoid copying these distinctive features. The first practical option for knife opening was the thumb peg screwed into the side of the blade. A small company marketed a gadget called the Flicket for a while that allowed the user to

Spyderco's Snap-It model drops the pocket clip for a snap link that allows the knife to be hung from personal equipment.

attach a spring clip thumb stud to the top of any knife; when factory-mounted thumb studs became more common, the Flicket was no longer really needed. The Spyderco peg works fine, but can occasionally snag clothing

For those who don't want a snap link blocking part of their blade, Spyderco offers the remote release.

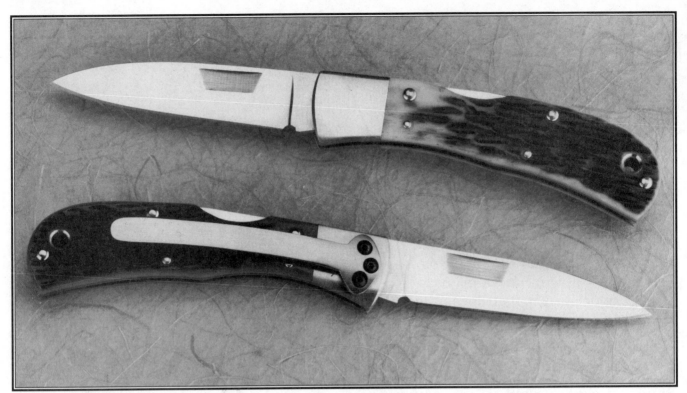

This Jess Horn-designed folder was Spyderco's first model without the blade opening hole. In practice, it proved to be less than successful.

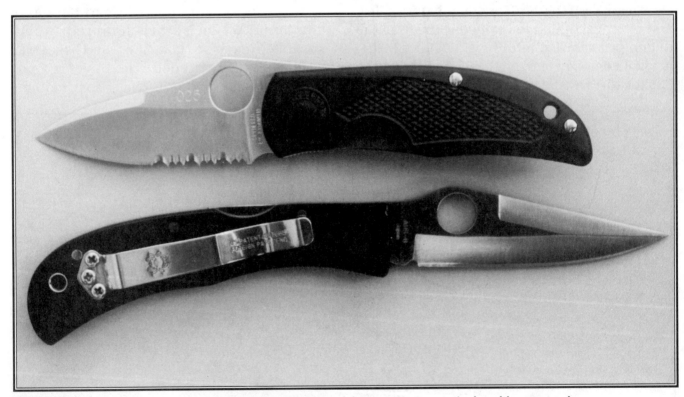

The Jess Horn II (bottom) and the Walker Lightweight models were more practical and less expensive.

The Spyderco Dragon Fly falls between the highly popular Ladybug and the near-cult status Delica in size.

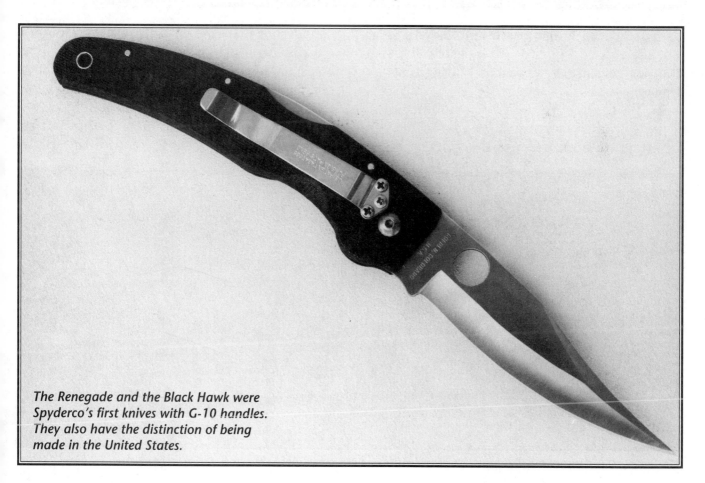

The Renegade and the Black Hawk were Spyderco's first knives with G-10 handles. They also have the distinction of being made in the United States.

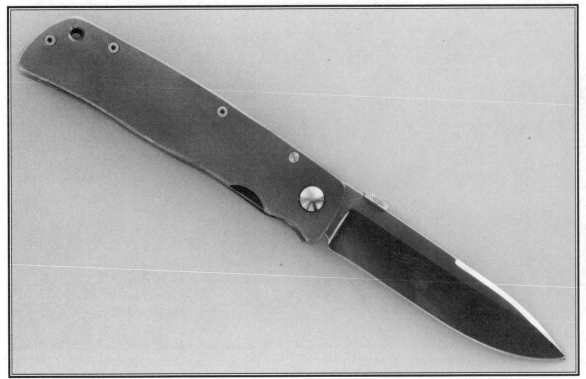

Bob Terzuola was probably the first maker to utilize a flat top mounted disk for opening folders. This particular knife is a left-handed version the author has carried for several years.

as it is drawn. It also has a tendency to wear out the top of a pocket. A few users also feel the peg gets in the way when cutting through thick materials.

To be truly ambidextrous, peg opening knives require either a reversible stud or studs on both sides of the blade. This is usually not possible on side-lock type folders. I mentioned this to custom maker Bob Terzuola a few years ago while handling one of his highly functional tactical folders.

The next time I met him, he handed me a modified version of the same knife with a round disk screwed to the top of the blade.

Gerber's E-Z Outs were the first production knives to be licensed by Spyderco to use its patented opening hole.

The Al Mar Quick Silver offers a compact all-steel option for those looking for a one-hand opening clip carry folder.

With half of the disk projecting on either side of the blade, the folder may be opened easily with both hands. While I have yet to see anyone give Bob credit for the design, spine mounted disks have since become fairly common on custom and factory folders.

In regard to the opening hole, Spyderco has been willing to license its system to custom makers from the start. Gerber Knives also entered into a partnership with Spyderco to produce a hole-in-the-blade opening folder called the E-Z Out. Benchmade Knives followed by receiving official permission to produce its AFCK liner-lock with an opening hole and no hump. Since that agreement, legal departments of several other cutlery companies have concluded that Spyderco's patent only covers the hump and hole combination.

This has not yet been challenged in court, but there are a number of hole opening knives now on the market minus the hump. Simply adding a hole to a conventional blade doesn't always make for convenient one-hand open-

ing, so not all of the new designs unapproved by Spyderco work well.

The Spyderco Endura and Delica have earned a near-cult following among hard core professional knife users. Spyderco quickly followed the pair up with the key chain-sized Ladybug, the mid-sized Dragonfly, a 4¾-inch blade folding filet called the Catcherman, the snap shackle carry Snap-It and a second version of the same knife called the Remote Release, the hawksbill Merlin, a light-weight version of the Pro-Venator (pro-hunter), and a light-weight version of the Mariner called the Rescue, all with Zytel handles.

Taking something of a different tack, Spyderco then began producing a series of custom design collaborations with the C-15 and C-19 Bob Terzuola Clipits. Both these knives were originally aluminum handled, but since have been changed to G-10. These were quickly followed by the first of the humpless Spydercos, the Wayne Goddard-designed C16, 18 and 20 models. The Goddards feature a flat Micarta handle with an integral guard to keep the hand from sliding up on the blade. These are definitely two humpless hole openers that may be recommended as working correctly. (The C-20 Spyderco/Goddard is a bit too small for one-handed use.)

Other custom collaborations include the C-27 Jess Horn with a bone handle and thumb indentation rather than a hole, and the more conventional Jess Horn II; the carbon fiber-handled Michael Walker-designed C-22 and Walker Lightweight; the stark looking aluminum frame C-25 Centofante; and the racy Spyderco/Howard Viele. Several more custom collaborations are in the prototype stages, including a Tim Wegner-designed folding hunter.

Most Spyderco Clipits are made in Japan, but the company has a manufacturing plant in Colorado producing the Bob Terzuola and Frank Centofante models in addition to the 2⅞-inch blade, G-10-handled Blackhawk and the 3⅞-inch bladed Renegade. The most recent addition to the American Clipit line is the Military Police model, a 4-inch blade in a choice of 440V or ATS-34 with a stainless liner-lock and G-10 handle scales.

Spyderco also imports a part of the G. Sakai, Hiro and Moki lines of high quality Japanese knives. The Saki Intrepid is a stout little peg opening folder with a 3-inch blade and a Kraton handle. Hiro's Solo line of folders features a unique integral projection on the back of the blade for one-hand opening. Sizes on the Solo run from a 2½-inch blade to a very pointed 3½-inch version. In the Moki group are the Zytel-handled Elite and Zephyr models

After the Bob Terzuola folders, the Renegade (top) and the Blackhawk were added to Spyderco's American-made line.

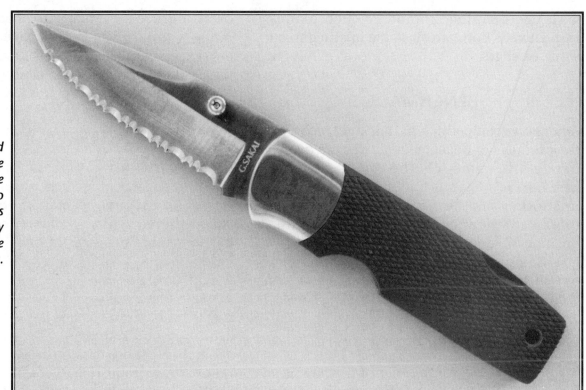

The Intrepid is part of the G. Sakai line the Spyderco imports separately from the Clipit models.

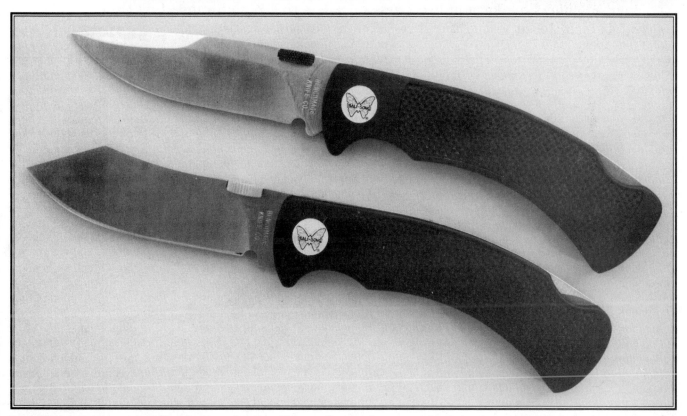

Benchmade's Monarch Utility (top) and Game Skinner (bottom) were some of the first production one-hand openers to utilize the Terzuola disk opener.

with peg opening 2½- and 2¾-inch blades, respectively. Both are available in straight and serrated edges.

BENCHMADE

Among the competition to the Spyderco Clipit, the products of Benchmade Knives are quickly becoming some of the most popular. Benchmade's liner-lock folders are discussed in another chapter, but the company also offers an excellent rocker-bar lock, disk opening folder in its Monarch Utility, Weehawk and Gamesman Skinner. This last model is one of the better folding skinning knives on the market.

GERBER E-Z OUT

Gerber's E-Z Out is another of the humpless hole in the blade openers that actually works. The company offers the knife in two sizes — 3⅛- and 4½-inch closed — and in either 50/50

or straight edge. Handle frames are Zytel. Along with having a fairly conventional looking clip point blade, the E-Z Outs are U.S.-made folders that sell for reasonable prices, often under $30 from mail order sources.

BERETTA

Beretta Firearms has its own line of Zytel-handled peg opening rocker-bar lock folders designed by custom maker Dewey Harris called the Airlights. Available in a choice of handle colors and straight or 50/50 edge, the knives feature a skeletonized blade for added weight savings.

While this would seem to make for a rather fragile tool, Beretta claims it has yet to receive a broken one returned. The largest model, 4¾-inch closed, tips the scales at only 2.5 ounces. Beretta also markets the Lightweight, another rocker-bar, peg opener in a choice of 3⅞- or 4½-inch closed, with a serrated or straight edge.

Beretta offers these unusual skeleton blade one-hand opening folders in several sizes, with or without serrations.

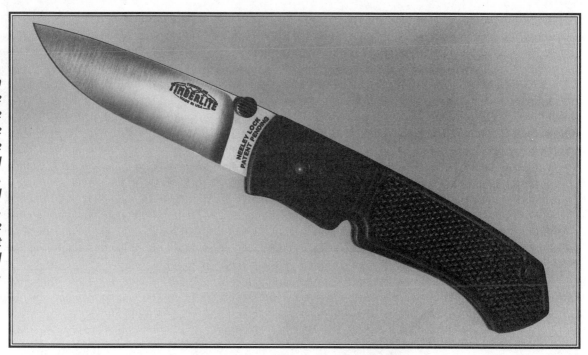

Along with its unique Neeleylock the Timberlite features the now standard carry clip, one-hand opening peg, and a choice of straight or serrated edges.

TIMBERLINE

Timberline Knives departs from the rocker-bar/liner-lock systems by utilizing its own special Neeleylock on its Timberlite folders. Basically, when the blade is thumbed open by means of an ambidextrous peg, it snaps back into the handle frame slightly and locks open. To close, the blade is again pulled out a small distance from the handle and folded. Timberlites are available in several sizes, in a wide variety of handle colors. The 40 percent fiberglass reinforced nylon handle features a built-in spring carry clip at the blade end of the grip.

AL MAR

Al Mar Knives offers several models with various combinations of the serrated edge, one-hand opening peg and carry clip. The Quicksilver Model 2003 provides all three features as do the Back-Ups. Its narrow, 4-inch long, spear point blade and one-hand opening peg has made the Model 1005-BT Eagle a longtime favorite of many professionals. While it lacks the spring carry clip and serrated edge, the peg opening 6105 Elite offers a reasonably priced, 3¾-inch blade, Zytel-handled folder that still provides all of the quality that made Al Mar Knives famous.

One of the most recent additions to the AMK line is the Passport, an aluminum-handled, wide 4-inch spear point blade of AUS-8 stainless with a semi-reversible thumb opener. The first impression of anyone who handles it seems to be, "Boy, this knife is flat!" (The handle frame is right at quarter-inch thickness.) Along with being easy to carry, the goal of the Passport is for AMK to offer a good working blade at less money than some of its standard line.

COLD STEEL

Cold Steel's one-hand opening clip-carry offering is the Zytel-handled Voyager line in 3-, 4- and 5-inch blade lengths. The two smaller blades are offered in either clip or tanto points and all are available in straight or serrated edge. The standard 4-inch straight edge, clip point is a favorite everyday work knife. It does

The Passport (top) and the Micro SERE are two of Al Mar's newest one-hand opening folders.

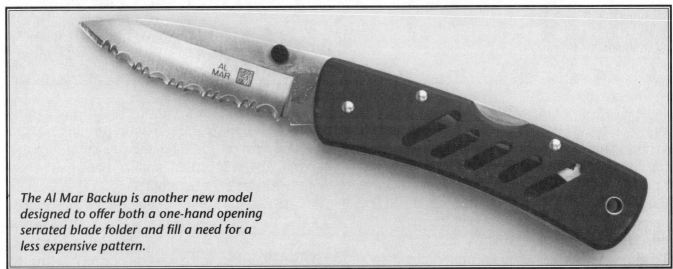

The Al Mar Backup is another new model designed to offer both a one-hand opening serrated blade folder and fill a need for a less expensive pattern.

Cold Steel's Large Voyager and Extra Large Voyager are two of the strongest and most popular clip-carry one-hand opening knives on the market. The Voyager also comes in a 4-inch closed size, in tanto points, with or without serrations.

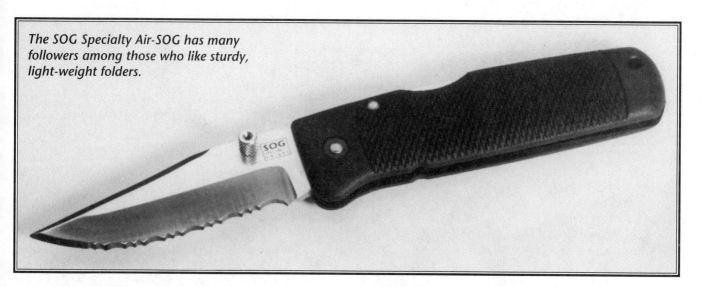

The SOG Specialty Air-SOG has many followers among those who like sturdy, light-weight folders.

an outstanding job of providing a blade large enough for serious outdoor use in an extremely light-weight package. For those looking for a really large folder with the lines of the traditional Spanish Navaja, the 5-inch Voyager is an excellent choice. The largest of the Voyagers serves well as a convenient-to-carry camp kitchen knife, a handy gardening tool and an all-round ranch work blade. Another Navaja-inspired folder is the 6-inch blade Vaquero. While this knife lacks the carry clip, it does feature a Zytel frame, ambidextrous peg opener, and recurved serrated blade.

SOG SPECIALTY

SOG Specialty has introduced a Zytel-handled folder with an adjustable tension carry clip. In situations where added security is required, the thumb screw can be tightened to lock the auto clip in place. The company also offers one-hand opening models in its Magna-Dot, SOG Winder and Air SOG lines. The SOG Winders are heavy-duty folders, while the Air SOG has found favor among those who prefer wide blades of medium length on light-weigh frames.

SCHRADE CUTLERY

The old line knife company, Schrade Cutlery, joined the one-hand opening movement with its innovative Cliphanger folders. Rather than a spring carry-clip, the Cliphangers feature a nylon cord that snaps into the end of the handle. A simple push of the snap's button releas-

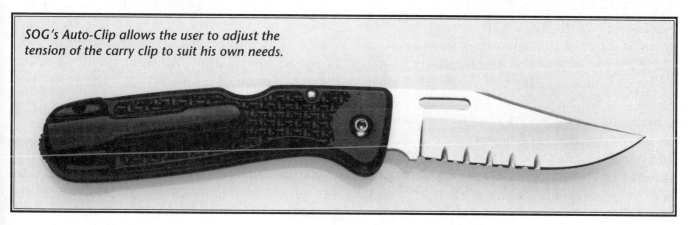

SOG's Auto-Clip allows the user to adjust the tension of the carry clip to suit his own needs.

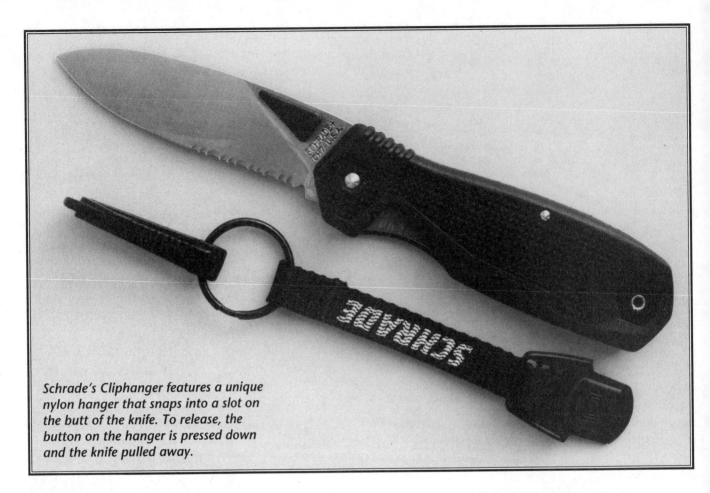

Schrade's Cliphanger features a unique nylon hanger that snaps into a slot on the butt of the knife. To release, the button on the hanger is pressed down and the knife pulled away.

es the knife for use. The knives are available in two sizes, 4½ and 3½ inches closed, and in clip or drop point blade styles. The drop point is a 50/50 edge and the clip is fully serrated.

BUCK KNIVES

Buck Knives spent considerable effort researching the professional law enforcement market before designing its CrossLock. The original model features a 3¼-inch drop point blade on one side of the thermoplastic handle and a combination seat belt cutter and screw driver on the other.

Since its introduction, the CrossLock has grown into a family of folders in both single and double blade versions to include a specialized blade for horse riders to pick hooves. All versions feature pocket carry clips and a choice of straight or serrated edges.

ONTARIO KNIVES

Ontario Knives took a different approach to the one-hand opening problem by designing a group of military-looking folders called the Spec Plus line with large fullers on the blade. The fuller allows the user's thumb to push the blade open in much the same manner a hole or peg would. In keeping with the military theme, the Spec Plus folders are big and plain, with black Zytel handles and 4-inch 1095 carbon steel blades. All offer good value for those in need of a heavy-duty work knife they won't be afraid to use and abuse.

A.G. RUSSELL

A.G. Russell was one of the first companies to enter the one-hand opening market with its One-Hand Opener folder line. These all-steel knives are based on a custom Pat Crawford design that utilizes an integral back spring as part of the handle. The blade opens by means of a thumb peg and closes by pulling up on two projections on the sides of the back spring. While the original models are both relatively flat and light, A.G. has recently added a Zytel-handled version of the knife that is even lighter.

OUTDOOR EDGE

Better known for its T-handled skinning knives, Outdoor Edge introduced a spring

carry, one-hand opening Zytel frame folder called the Field-Lite. This 3½-inch upswept blade is probably better designed for field dressing game than some of its more pointed competitors. The Field-Lite is available in both straight and serrated versions. A spear point version of this same knife should be available soon.

KERSHAW

Rather than the use of Zytel, Kershaw Knives depend on aircraft grade aluminum with Kraton handle inserts and titanium for its

The Buck Crosslock was designed after extensive research with law enforcement personnel.

Recent additions to the Bucklite line include these folders with a removable carry-clip.

Ontario Spec Plus folders depend on a wide fuller that the thumb can press against for one-hand opening.

The Buck CrossLock is being made in limited production runs with aluminum and stainless steel handles.

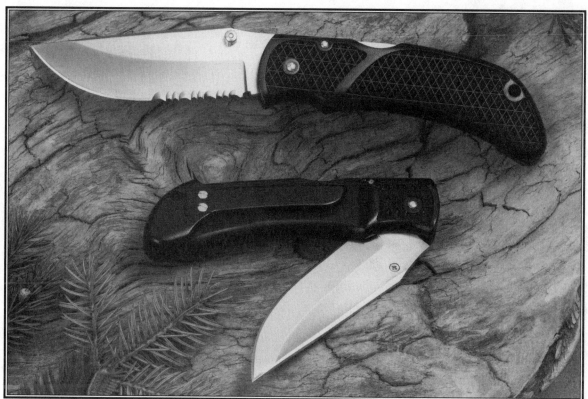

Outdoor Edge's Field-Lite folder offers a bit more edge belly and sweep for skinning than the average one-hand opening clip-carry folder.

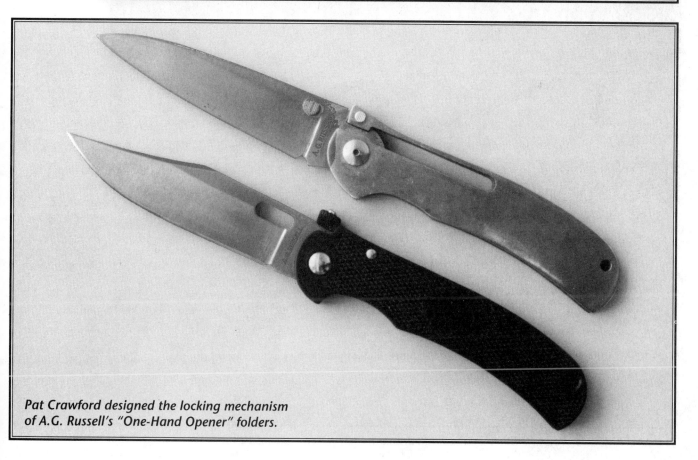

Pat Crawford designed the locking mechanism of A.G. Russell's "One-Hand Opener" folders.

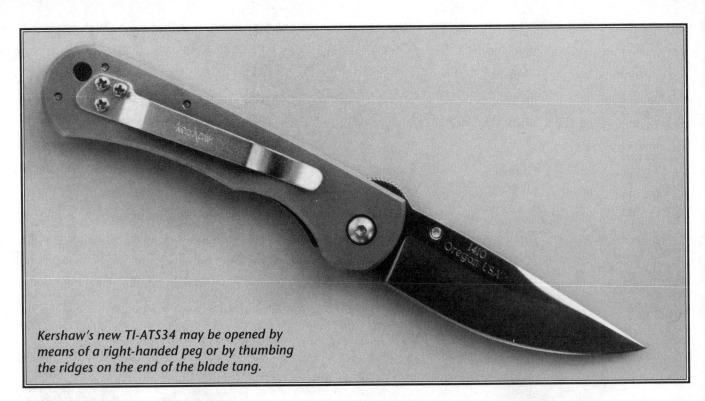

Kershaw's new TI-ATS34 may be opened by means of a right-handed peg or by thumbing the ridges on the end of the blade tang.

Two of Smith and Wesson's basic Zytel-handled, one-hand opening rocker-bar lock folders.

Liner-Action and TI 34 folders. The Liner-Action 3½-inch bladed drop points has gained a good following among working knife users. Unlike most of the Kershaw line, which is imported from Japan, the new 3-inch clip point TI 34 is made in the company's Oregon plant.

DAVID BOYE

David Boye of Dendritic steel fame offers a clip-carry folder with a cast 3-inch blade. Along with providing excellent edge retention, Dendritic steel offers the advantage of allowing the maker to cast just about any design he desires into the blade surface. Boye Knives feature such scenes as a blue whale, an eagle and a primitive bow hunter. Dendritic steel is outstanding material for pure cutting power.

SMITH AND WESSON

Smith and Wesson has licensed its brand name to Taylor Cutlery, which in turn is pro-

ducing a group of medium-sized peg opening folders with Zytel handles and a choice of serrated or straight and drop or clip blades. The S&W 1st Response, a more specialized emergency services tool, has a spring loaded tungsten carbide window breaker and a screwdriver tipped, peg opening serrated cutting blade. This knife utilizes GV6H Grillon, a material some are saying is the next Zytel, for a handle frame and blade lock.

KATZ KNIVES

Katz Knives offers its extra heavy-duty steel framed Cheetah series folders with a spine mounted disk opener and a choice of straight or serrated edge on a drop point blade. The Cheetah is available in 3- and 3¾-inch blade lengths. For those desiring all the modern bells and whistles, there is the Black Kat series of Zytel-handled, clip carry, disk opening folders. Here the buyer has a choice of either a clip or drop point blade in 3- and

Katz Black Kats feature Zytel handle frames and spine mounted disk openers.

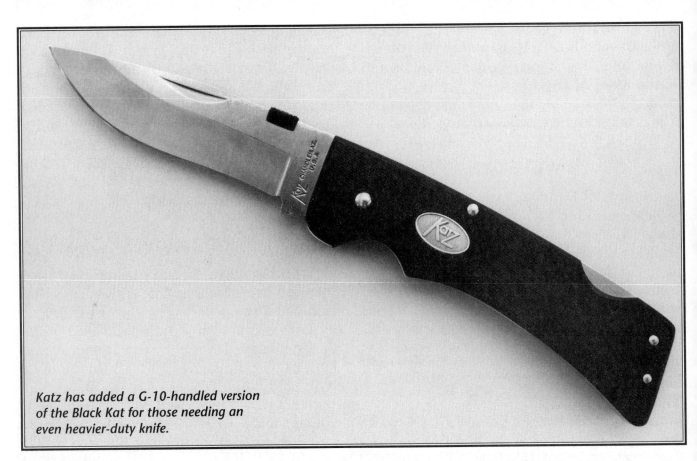

Katz has added a G-10-handled version of the Black Kat for those needing an even heavier-duty knife.

Paragon Cutlery offers several in-house designed models with Zytel handles, carry-clips and a thumb groove rather than a hole for opening the blade.

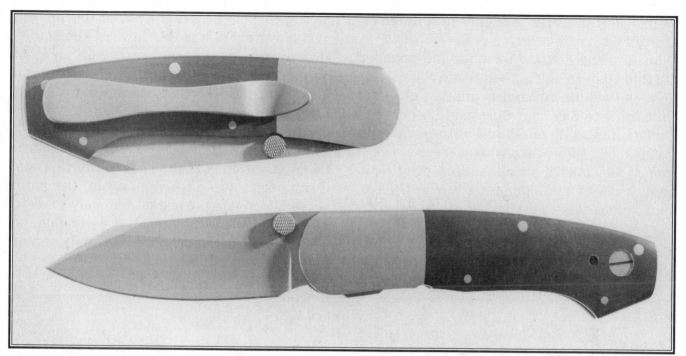

Custom maker Scott Sawby produces this heavy-duty clip-carry knife for the hunter.

Most of Allen Elishewitz's high tech folders include one-hand opening pegs and spring carry-clips.

3¾-inch lengths. All are available in serrated or straight edge.

Most of the demand for one-hand opening custom folders has moved to the liner-lock field and will be covered in another chapter. This isn't to say that outstanding custom rocker-bar lock one-hand folders aren't obtainable. Phil Boguszewski made a Micarta framed 4-inch 440C stainless, drop point with ambidextrous peg openers a few years ago that remains an all-time favorite folding hunter. Another custom maker whose folders are highly regarded is Dick Atkinson. Dick specializes in turning out custom rocker-bar lock one-hand openers at a reasonable price in a wide variety of handle materials and colors. He can provide a spring carry clip on most models as an option. A quick cruise around any major custom knife show will no doubt turn up others who have retained the rocker-bar system on their folders.

Although the one-hand opening, clip-carry folder is currently at the crux of controversial legislation calling for regulation, the knife should dominate the market for many years to come. Its popularity among those who find it a necessity for both everyday work and outdoor chores is unquestioned.

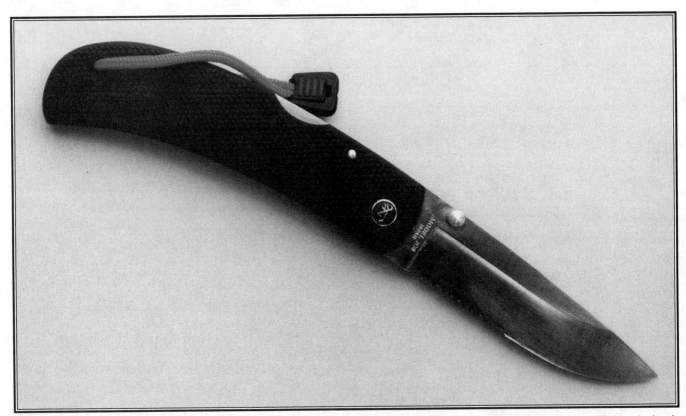

Browning recently entered the field with this Zytel-handled, reversible thumb stud opening, 50/50 edge folder in both 3- and 4-inch blade lengths.

9

MISCELLANEOUS BLADE LOCKING SYSTEMS

In my library is a two-volume set, "Will Hanna's Portfolio of Patents." The books total approximately 400 pages and consist primarily of U.S. patents granted on folding knife mechanisms between 1862 and 1991. This is not a complete list for the period, as such patents as Spyderco's hump and hole are not included.

Scanning the patents, one finds there have been scores of attempts to create a better means of locking a folding knife blade open. While most probably worked, creating an improvement over the rocker-bar and liner-lock systems has been more elusive. A new locking system appears, the maker attempts to market his product for a year or two, and then it disappears. In the end, only a few advanced cutlery collectors even know the design ever existed.

OPINEL

Of the alternative blade locking systems that have established themselves over the years, one of the most famous is probably the French Opinel ring lock. Opinel began producing its folders in the 1890s, but the twisting ring bolster locking system has actually been around for several hundred years.

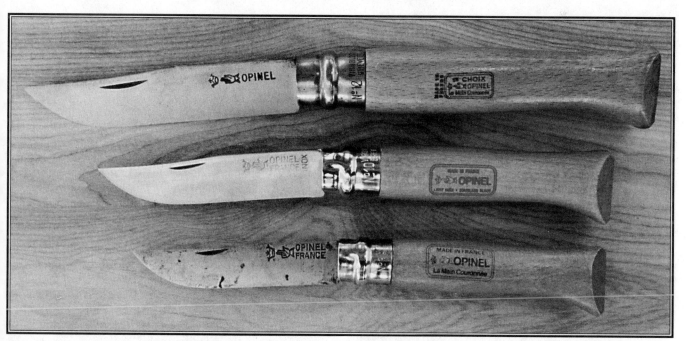

Opinel's twisting bolster lock has been one of the more successful alternative locking systems. The center knife is one of the more recent stainless steel models.

The knife itself is a simple spring-less penny knife. When the knife is open, the bolster may be turned across the tang to block the blade from closing. The primary advantage to this system is that it is extremely simple and cheap to manufacture, making the end product equally inexpensive. You can still buy many models for under $10. While the knife may not cost a large sum, most of Opinel's knives utilize an excellent grade of plain carbon steel ground to a very thin edge that both cuts well and is easy to resharpen. The handles are wood and the only metal consists of the locking ring and blade, making Opinel folders very light in weight, ideal for hikers, mountaineers and backpackers.

The company offers a variety of sizes ranging from a non-locking 1¾-inch key chain knife to a giant 8¾-inch display knife. Most blade patterns are a basic straight back, but spear point and hawksbill models are also available. In recent years, several stainless steel models have appeared, including a line of folding filets ranging from 4⅛-inch closed to 5¾-inch closed. For those not satisfied with natural wood, Opinel also offers brightly colored hardwood handles on some stainless models.

All of these knives are held in the closed position simply by friction between the wood handle and the blade. Under less-than-ideal conditions, this can sometimes make for

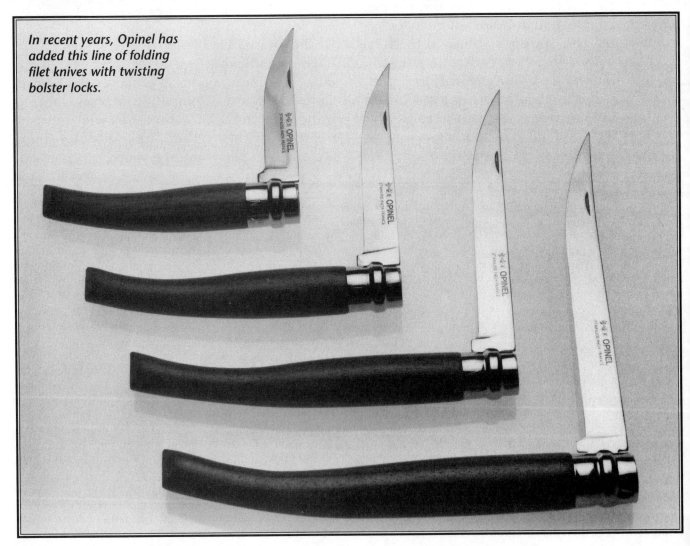

In recent years, Opinel has added this line of folding filet knives with twisting bolster locks.

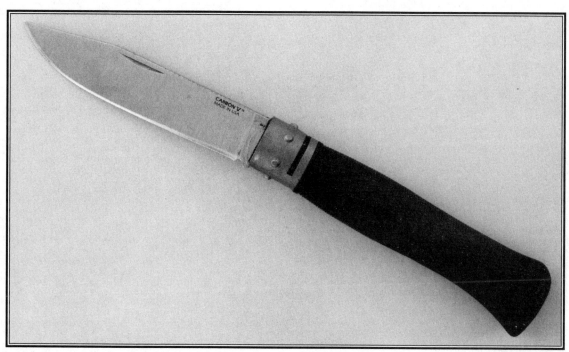

Cold Steel briefly challenged Opinel with its Zytel-handled Twistmaster. While this knife was a bit more expensive than an Opinel, the steel used in the blade was the best available.

difficult opening. One trick offered by Opinel is to tap the butt end of the handle on something hard. This will usually spring the blade just far enough from the handle frame that it may be pulled the rest of the way with the fingers.

The handles on the basic carbon steel Opinel models are made of light colored pearwood. Under wet conditions, this material tends to soak up water and swell. The handle may be soaked in a waterproof wood sealant before use to correct the problem. Harder wood used on the stainless models is less prone to swelling.

COLD STEEL

Cold Steel once offered a line of knives called the Twistmasters that were basically the Opinel pattern with Zytel-handled frames. Since Zytel does not swell and the blade was made of Cold Steel's excellent Carbon V, these were outstanding folders for those who appreciated the simple design. Like the wood-handled French knives, the Zytel frame American folder was extremely light to carry, reasonably priced and very functional. Kershaw followed

up with a little more stylized variation of the twist lock on a medium-sized Japanese-made folder. Unfortunately, neither of these designs caught on and both lines are now discontinued. Some in the industry have suggested that the problem was the two companies simply couldn't compete with the low prices the authentic French items sell for.

RING PULL LOCKS

Another ancient locking system that tends to be a French and Spanish specialty is the ring pull exterior spring system. Here a flat spring with a hole at the blade tang end is bent around the outside of the handle frame. When the blade is opened, a projection on the blade tang snaps into the spring hole.

Some of these knives have a series of projections on the tang that ratchet past the backspring with a very distinctive sound before locking. Legend has it that all a Spanish highwayman had to do was ratchet open his Navaja and travelers would hand over their purses. To unlock the blade, most of these folders have metal rings attached to the back-

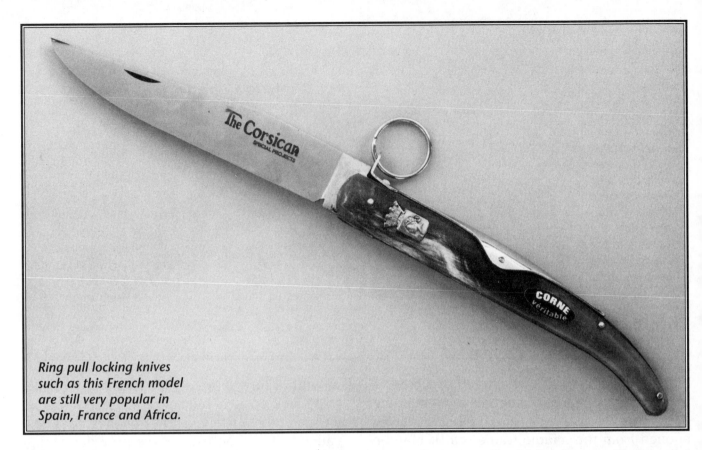

Ring pull locking knives such as this French model are still very popular in Spain, France and Africa.

spring. By pulling up on the ring, the spring is lifted above the tang projection and the blade can be folded.

This type of folder was very popular on the 18th century American frontier, but as the French lost influence in the New World, English pattern folders began to replace the ring pull during the 19th century. Today, the ring pull lock remains popular in France, Spain, the Middle East, Africa and in some former Spanish and French colonies. Outside these areas, this system is practically unknown. One reason ring pulls are still favored in Africa is that they are a very inex-

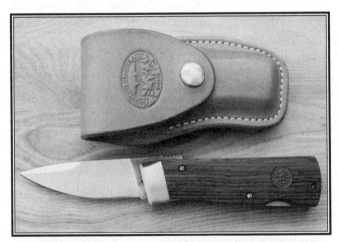

The Blackie Collins-designed Benchmark Rolox is unlike any other lockback on the market in function.

To open, the Rolox blade tang is pressed down and then pushed forward to its locking position.

pensive means of manufacturing a lockback folder of reasonably good quality. From time to time, various companies import French and Spanish ring pull knives, but none seem to stay in business long. A few years ago, Cold Steel imported several sizes of French ring pulls until unreliable deliveries forced it to discontinue these models. This was unfortunate as the knives were ideal for those involved with fur trade reenactment. If you see a ring pull you like, buy it — as you can't count on the importer being around next week.

BENCHMARK ROLOX

Blackie Collins designed the Rolox system for Benchmark knives. It is hard to describe how the Rolox works, but in some ways it is a rocker-bar lock turned upside down. When the base of the blade is pushed down, the point

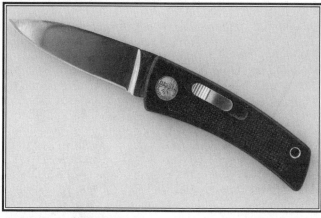

The author carried this Gerber Bolt Action Utility knife of outstanding design for a number of years on the job as a forester. Along with the usual field chores, it has dressed out several deer and a wide variety of small game and fish.

springs slightly out of the handle frame. The user then pushes the blade straight forward, one-handed, into the locking position. The

Gerber also makes an exchange blade version of the Bolt Action that makes an even more versatile package for the hunter.

The Gerber Parabellum, now discontinued, was an attempt to make a survival knife out of the Bolt Action locking system.

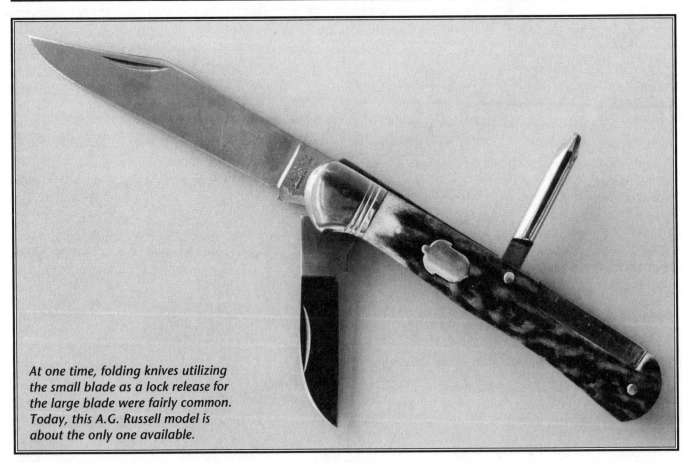

At one time, folding knives utilizing the small blade as a lock release for the large blade were fairly common. Today, this A.G. Russell model is about the only one available.

lock release is on the underside of the handle frame and functions much the same as any other rocker-bar. Since the introduction of hole and peg openers, the design has become semi-obsolete.

GERBER BOLT ACTION

A more modern and successful locking system is Gerber's Blackie Collins-designed Bolt Action. On this knife, a spring loaded internal bolt snaps into place when the blade is opened, thus locking it. To unlock, a button on the side of the handle is pulled toward the rear of the knife and the blade is folded in the conventional manner. Gerber claims this is a much stronger mechanism than the conventional rocker-bar lock.

Since Gerber and Collins hold the patent on the design, Gerber is currently the only company utilizing the mechanism. Gerber catalogs five Bolt Action models: Utility, Hunter, Skinner, Exchange Blade and Filet. The first four are all basically the same Zytel frame with different shaped 3½-inch blades. As the name indicates, the Exchange Blade offers a choice of two knife blades and a saw that interchange on the same frame. The Filet is a flexible 5-inch blade.

Gerber once offered a folding Bolt Action survival knife called the Parabellum with a wide 4¼-inch blade and a trick scabbard for carrying the knife in the open or closed position. Light and strong, this was once one of the author's favorite medium-sized factory lockback. The Parabellum is an outstanding heavy-duty lockback folder that has been discontinued. If you find one on the shelves of a store or at a knife show, snap it up.

Different internally, retracting button lock releases similar to Gerber's Bolt-Action have been fairly common on folding knives. Victorinox utilizes it on its 4⅜-inch series of lockback multi-blade Swiss Army utility knives. Its primary Swiss competition, Wenger,

has a similar button release to unlock what is basically a liner-lock mechanism. Both of these knives are discussed in more detail in the chapter on Swiss Army knives.

PEN BLADE LOCK RELEASE

During the late 19th and early 20th centuries, many European lockback knives utilized a system where the main blade was unlocked by pressing on the spine of a second smaller blade in the folded position. While these knives are relatively uncommon today, A.G. Russell imports a high quality 4⅜-inch long closed with stag handles replica from Japan. The main blade is a 3½-inch clip point with the secondary a 2⅛-inch sheepsfoot. There is also a Phillips screwdriver folded into the back of the handle.

This folder is impressive for several reasons. First, the workmanship is outstanding. Second, a large clip and small sheepsfoot combination is one of the best possible options for a folder. Third, the knife has an excellent handle to blade length ratio. Finally, the entire knife is both compact and built for strength and hard use.

BUTTON RELEASES

Then there are all the push-button lock releases. Most seem to be covered by separate patents, so it may be assumed that they vary with their internal mechanisms. Queen has offered two models of its own design for several years; one a 3¾-inch closed and the other a 5¼-inch. Both have been field tested and were found to function well. The larger of the two seems to have an especially good grade of stainless steel in the blade as it remains razor sharp through field dressing and skinning a blacktail buck.

Boker recently released an interesting button lock called the Model 707 Toplock. This German-made aluminum frame 3⅜-inch drop

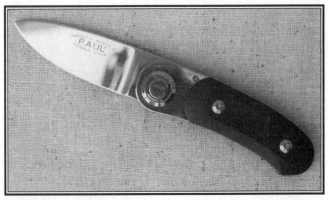

After having been out of production for several years, Gerber recently brought back the Paul Knife button lock.

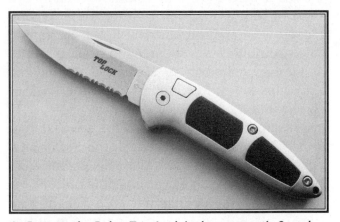

In Europe, the Boker Top-Lock is the automatic Speed-Lock. In the United States, it is simply another button lock release.

point blade folder is actually an auto-opener in Europe. The spring open version has found considerable favor with German paratroopers and Special Operations units. In the United States, the button simply locks the blade both open and closed.

GT Knives also turns out an American-made button lock that seems similar to the Boker internally. It is reported to be very well made and overall appears to be a functional design.

Several knives have utilized buttons that push down and twist to both open and lock the blade. The Paul lock, created by custom knifemaker Paul Poehlmann, is perhaps the most well known. The custom versions of this knife are finely tuned works of art that should be compared to a Rolex watch or Mercedes auto, with prices to match. Gerber once offered a factory version of the Paul knife that was more reasonably priced, but still expensive for a production folder. Unfortunately, the knife was discontinued from lack of sufficient demand.

In early 1995, Gerber announced that it was reintroducing the Paul knife to its line. The new knife seems to be more refined than the original production model. The overall design

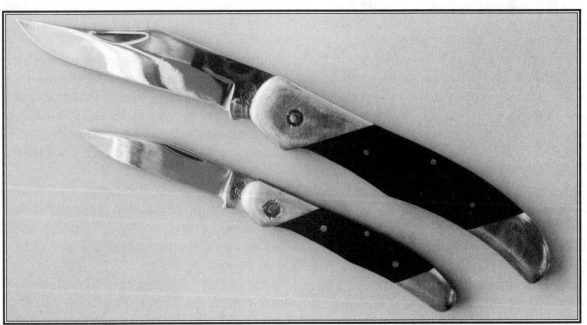

Queen Cutlery offers these two button release locks in its line of folders.

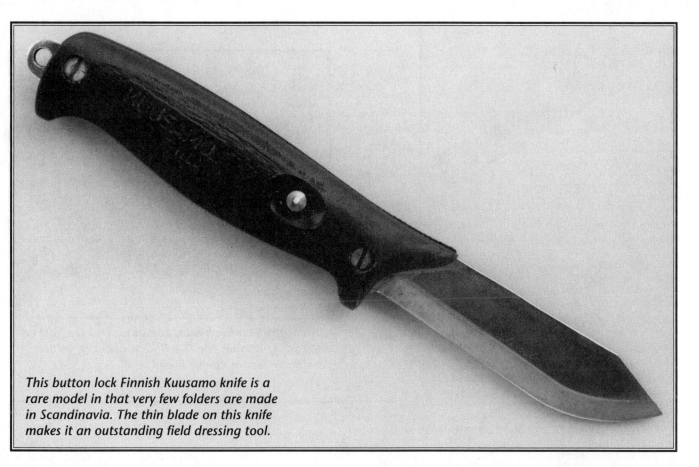

This button lock Finnish Kuusamo knife is a rare model in that very few folders are made in Scandinavia. The thin blade on this knife makes it an outstanding field dressing tool.

appears to be outstanding for outdoor use and field dressing game in the deer range.

The obvious disadvantage to many button lock systems is that the button may be accidentally depressed, unlocking the blade at the least opportune time. When buying this type of knife, check to make certain that the button is recessed into the handle. As a general rule, these mechanisms — such as the Paul — that require pushing and twisting are safer to use.

EXECUTIVE EDGE

B&D Trading brings in the Executive Edgeline of Brazilian folders with its unique Deadlock. As the blade swings, a projection on the end of the tang snaps into the hole on one side of the handle. To close, the handle scale is lifted off the tang with the thumb. All Executive Edge knives come with a sheepsfoot point blade. While this type of blade has many uses,

some type of clip or drop point would be more utilitarian for the average user. Several of the smaller Executive Edge folders come with carry clips and a general outline of an ink pen for easy, low key pocket carry. The larger models are serious working tools capable of standing up to considerably more abuse than a conventional folder. With a bit of practice, the Executive Edge system may be opened one-handed. Another unique feature of the Deadlock is that the blade may be folded past the locking point for use as a scribe or pattern cutter.

COLD STEEL ER1

To open Cold Steel's ER1, a button at the bottom of the handle frame is pushed to the opposite end of the knife, thus sliding the blade into position. Once extended, the button snaps into a locking notch and the knife

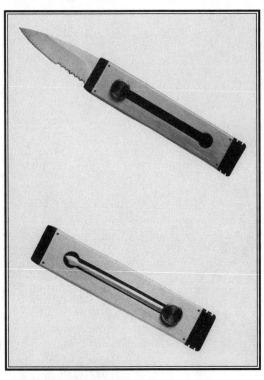

This knife from Zelco works somewhat like the Cold Steel ER1 with a button that must be pushed the length of the handle.

Once the pin on the blade tang snaps into the hole on the spring/ handle, the Deadlock is about as secure a locking system as can be found.

Executive Edge's Deadlock folders come in a variety of sizes and colors to fit every taste.

Cold Steel's ER1 along with the now discontinued MR1 and SR1.

is ready to use. This may be done one-handed with practice, but is not as easy as some of the other common opening systems. The serrated, sheepsfoot blade of the ER1 is an aggressive cutter and makes a handy tool around the garden and for anyone working with webbing or rope.

BOKER-MATIC

Boker's Boker-Matic opens in a similar manner to the ER1, except that one handle scale must be pushed to the side before the button will slide forward. The special feature of Boker's knife is that when the handle scale is pushed again, the spring-loaded blade snaps closed. Some call this a reverse switch-blade system.

Boker had many problems with customs over importing this 2⅞-inch bladed knife. Authorities were worried that someone would either figure out a way to reverse the spring action or take it out altogether and convert the knife into a gravity opener. Boker was initially told it would be allowed to import the Boker-Matic, but then the company's shipments were impounded. Eventually, an

agreement was reached in which the knife's handle scales would no longer be assembled with screws. Like the ER1, this system has no great advantage over other one-hand openers.

CASE TRI-FOLD

Case's Blackie Collins-designed Tri-Fold bears a certain amount of resemblance to an old Marble's knife design. The Zytel folds out into two sections, the blade is then swung open and the lower handle section folds down over

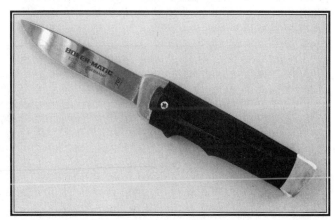

The Boker-Matic is often called a switchblade in reverse because the blade closes at the push of a button.

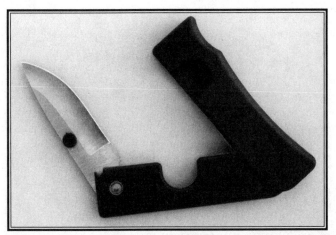

The Zytel-framed Case Tri-Fold offers an inexpensive but slow method of creating a locking blade folder.

BALISONGS

The butterfly or balisong knife has a bit of an image problem as folding knife locking systems go. First, the origin of the design has been lost. It is known that the French used the system at least 200 years ago and that an American patented a balisong design in 1890. Some Filipino knife buffs are equally certain the butterfly originated in their homeland. It is an established fact the balisong found its greatest acceptance in the Philippines. Some have theorized that an American G.I. may have brought a knife to the Philippines and that it quickly caught on because its no-spring design was easy to manufacture with primitive equipment. By the end of World War II, the balisong was well established in Filipino culture and many of these knives were brought home by returning servicemen.

the upper section thus locking the blade in place. The primary advantage is that the Tri-Fold doesn't require springs or rivets, thus keeping the cost down. Prices usually run under $15, a bargain for a real Case knife.

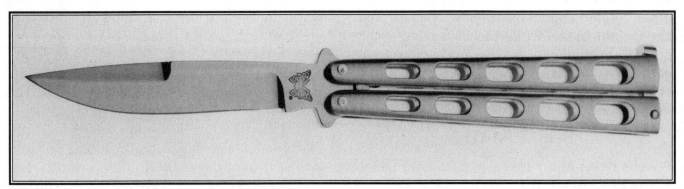

Benchmade has made this style of balisong synonymous with the butterfly knife. Not only is it of far better quality than the old Filipino models, it is still in legal production. (PHOTO BY DAN FITZGERALD)

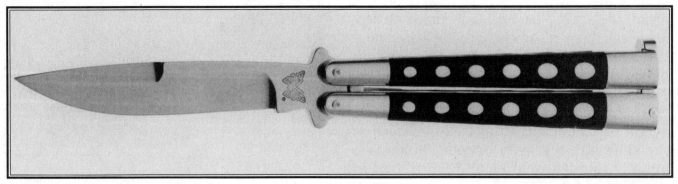

A fancier version of the balisong. Benchmade has a special shop producing a true custom version of its Bali-Songs. (PHOTO BY DAN FITZGERALD)

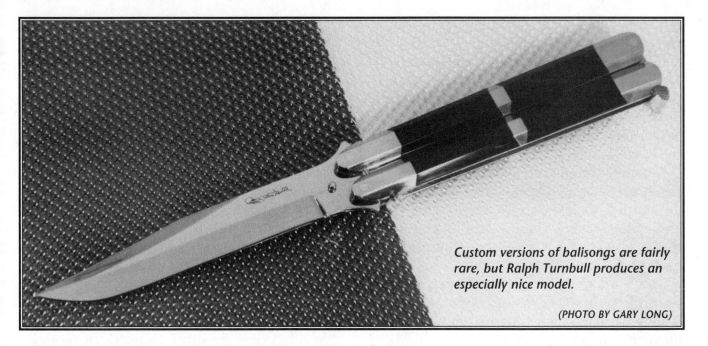

Custom versions of balisongs are fairly rare, but Ralph Turnbull produces an especially nice model.

(PHOTO BY GARY LONG)

As to how the basic balisong functions, the handle is formed by two hollow bars that fold around the blade top and bottom. On most designs, the two sides are held closed by a cross bar at the butt end of the knife. To open, the bar is lifted and the two handle halves are swung completely around, 180 degrees. With practice and a certain amount of skill on the part of the user, this may be done one-handed very quickly. The true masters of the balisong have developed all manners of trick openings and closings but most are for show rather than practical use.

After World War II, a small number of Filipino balisongs were imported into the United States each year until the early 1970s, when U.S. customs declared the knives to be illegal gravity openers. This did not ban the knives in the United States, but the importation of foreign-made balisongs. Seeing a marketing opportunity, Les de Asis started a company, known as Pacific Cutlery, to manufacture American-made balisongs. (Balisong is a Filipino word for this type of knife. Bali-Song is a registered trademark owned by Benchmade Knives.) Unlike most of the Filipino knives, Pacific Cutlery's butterflies were very high quality, semi-custom pieces made from state-of-the-art materials. Pacific Cutlery also developed a skeletonized metal handle and a clip point blade pattern, the Weehawk, that was instantly recognizable. The PC balisong quickly became popular in martial arts circles and outdoor users.

During this same period, an importer approached U.S. Customs with a request to bring Hackman Camp knives in from Finland. The Camp knife was basically an inexpensive

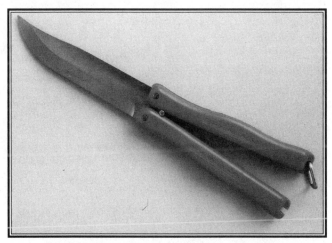

The Finnish Hackman Camp knife was once issued to the CIA. Many consider this one of the finest field knives available, but it can no longer be imported.

modern version of the butterfly with two nylon plastic handles, a 4-inch stainless blade and a wire bail to hold the grip section together. Unlike most butterflies, the Hackman fit together relatively tightly, making one-hand opening very difficult. Customs reversed its earlier position and allowed the importation of the Finnish knife.

An interesting aside in reference to the Hackman Camp folder was that the CIA bought a quantity for issue to its agents. While the knife was not much of a weapon, as a utility tool it served as a "sterile" item, not traceable back to the United States.

The Finnish knife only achieved modest popularity, but the rising demand for the Pacific Cutlery knives in martial arts action movies — combined with the reversal of the Customs decision — opened the flood gates for a tidal wave of imported butterflies. Most were made in Japan as inexpensive copies of Pacific Cutlery's modern designs rather than traditional Filipino patterns.

The tremendous competition from cheap imported balisongs soon had Pacific Cutlery on the rocks financially. Customs also used negative media attention to violence to again ban the importation of butterflies. One importer challenged the ruling in court and won, but Customs appealed the ruling. Each appeal was, in turn, challenged and defeated, only to be appealed again. Given the unlimited legal resources on which the government draws compared to the modest means of the importer, the pro-butterfly advocates soon had to give up the fight. Balisongs remain banned from importation to this day.

The Customs ruling had nothing to do with the legality of balisongs; only their importation. Eventually, Les de Asis was able to raise Pacific Cutlery from the ashes as Benchmade Knives. Currently, Benchmade offers two separate lines of its trademarked Bali-Song folders. One group is an all metal-handled selection of mass produced butterflies in a choice of 3- or 4-inch blades and either a

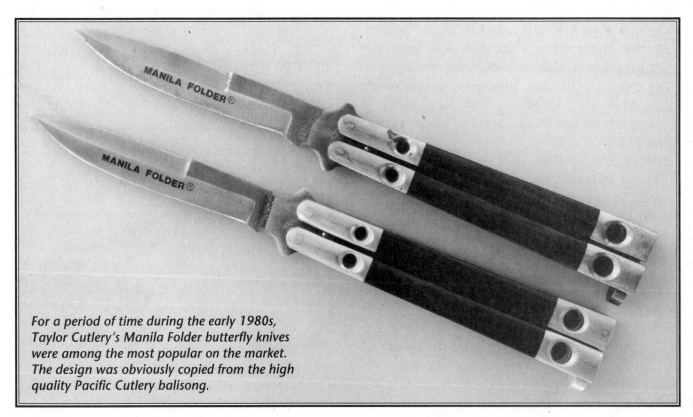

For a period of time during the early 1980s, Taylor Cutlery's Manila Folder butterfly knives were among the most popular on the market. The design was obviously copied from the high quality Pacific Cutlery balisong.

The Wood locking system works something like a butterfly knife. In practice, it is a little complicated and slow but very secure and attractive.

(PHOTO BY WEYER OF TOLEDO)

Weehawk or Utility clip point. Prices range from $45 to $125 (1996 list). The other group of Bali-Songs are handmade customs in a choice 4-, 5- or 6-inch blades in a wide variety of point styles and handle materials. Again using 1996 prices, these start at $400 and go up sharply. While this may seem expensive, these are perhaps the finest butterflies made, and well suited to serious use.

BEAR MGC

The only other U.S. commercial butterfly manufacturer is Bear MGC, which produces four variations of the basic Pacific Cutlery-style skeleton handle in 3- and 4-inch blade lengths. While perhaps not up to Benchmade standards, quality is adequate on Bear's butterflies. All make good introductory trainers for those just learning the ins and outs of manipulating a balisong. Suggested prices range from $30 to $40 with heavy discounts offered by mail-order companies.

Custom butterfly knives are not overly common, but now and again someone tries their hand at what would seem like a simple project for a skilled maker. Three hand-makers of butterflies are Walter Erickson, Ralph Turnbull and Ken Largin. All produce good, basic knives of modern materials and style. Others are certainly out there for those who diligently search the custom knife shows and catalogs.

Although it depends on the blade pattern to some degree, once open a butterfly is no different than any other knife of the same size. Most of the standard clip and Weehawk bladed versions are excellent outdoor tools. Proficient one-hand opening of a balisong requires considerable practice and really isn't any faster than the standard hole and peg openers. Extreme care is suggested for learning to open a balisong one-handed as almost everyone cuts himself at least once, and sometimes these cuts are fairly serious.

Mechanically, the balisong system provides a blade lock that can't fail as long as the hand remains wrapped around the handle sections. Martial artists like to argue whether the handle latch should be on the edge or the spine side section of the handle. A few even prefer the handle sans latch for quicker opening, but none of this is of concern to those simply looking to use the knife as a cutting tool. The one weakness found in some of the older Filipino knives is that the pin through the tang that holds the blade in place between the handles section may wear and fall out. If this happens, the blade will fold back on the hand of the user.

WOOD KNIVES

A blade opening and locking system that bears some resemblance to the butterfly, but lacks the one-hand opening speed, is that popularized by custom maker Barry Wood. Usually known as a Wood knife, the two handle sections turn away from the flat side of the blade rather than the edge and spine. A detent in the handle holds the two sections together in the open position.

Wood entered into a business agreement with Colt Firearms during the 1970s and produced an outstanding folding hunter based on his design that is now highly sought after by collectors. Since then, several factory and custom versions of the Wood knife have appeared without really catching on. Barry Wood continues to produce handmade folders of this design. While the Wood folder is not particularly fast to open, it is a strong, functional and good-looking outdoor knife.

TIMBERLINE TIMBERLITES

The Timberline Timberlites have a number of favorable features, including light-weight Zytel handles, ambidextrous one-hand opening pegs, a choice of serrated or straight edge, many handle colors, and several sizes along with the unusual Neeleylock blade locking system. While they have been fairly popular, there are a few bugs in the system. The blade may unlock during heavy cutting, is difficult to clean and can fail if sand or dirt gets into the spring mechanism. However, the knives seem suitable for everyday office use and other light duty.

There are many other blade locking systems out there as someone is always trying to build the better mousetrap and additional designs are inevitable. While many work after a fashion, most seldom offer any real advantage over the more established systems. This is not to say that some of these new designs won't turn out to make significant advancement in cutlery design.

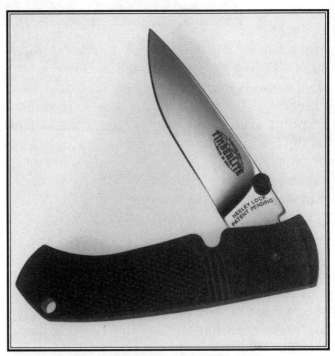

The Timberline Timberlite folder's Neeleylock is another unique system. When opened, the tang of the blade snaps back into the handle slightly. To unlock, the blade is pulled forward and folded. The only problem has been that occasionally the blade will drag in a cut and unlock itself.

10

THE SWISS ARMY KNIFE AND OTHER POCKET TOOL KITS

In May of 1968, I was traveling through O'Hare Airport in Chicago on my way to Vietnam. Although it's hard to believe today, at that time it was common for airport gift shops to sell a wide variety of knives. I had a custom Ruana bowie, a Buck 110 folding hunter and a carbon steel, three-blade Western stockman in my duffel, but a red-handled multi-blade folder in one of the airport shops caught my eye. The certainty of being in combat within a short time gave me a strong desire to seek out anything

that might improve my chances of survival. The two screwdrivers and the can and bottle openers seemed worthwhile additions to my gear, so I quickly laid my money down.

The knife I bought was a contract-made, Hoffritz-stamped version of the Victorinox Spartan. During my first week in Vietnam, I carried the Western stockman in one pocket and the Swiss Army in the other, only to find the carbon steel knife was turning into a rusted mess from my body moisture. The stainless

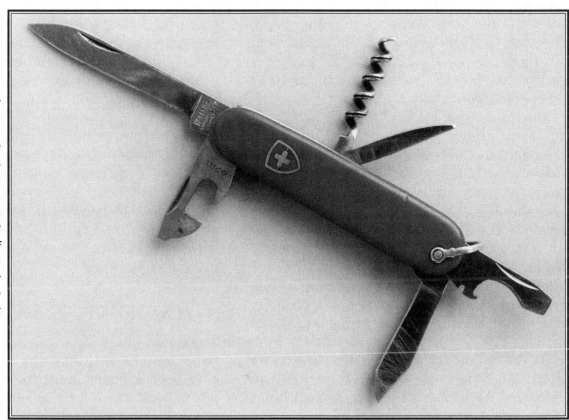

The author carried this heavily worn and scarred Swiss Army Victorinox Spartan through Vietnam and four years of college, plus several summer jobs with the U.S. Forest Service.

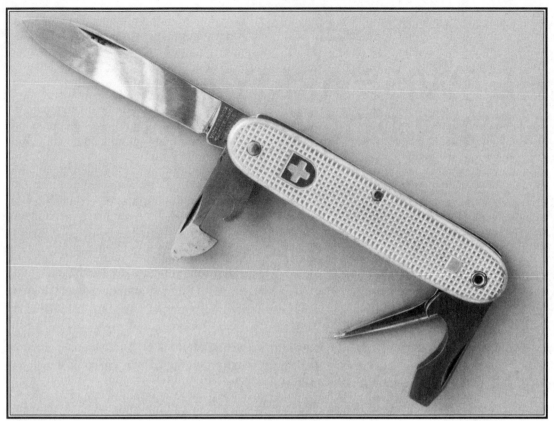

The actual issue pocketknife in the Swiss Army is a fairly basic model very similar to the one issued to U.S. troops. The author has carried this particular knife for more than 10 years and has found the more rounded handle profile of the Swiss model easier on pockets and hands than the U.S. folder.

blades of the Swiss Army, on the other hand, were still as bright as new. The stockman went back into my stored baggage for the remainder of my tour and the Swiss Army became my inseparable companion.

Much has been made of the unreliability of the M-16 rifle in Vietnam. Like any weapon, it needed to be kept properly cleaned and lubricated. The correct cleaning gear was frequently not available, so my Swiss Army was in constant use cutting bore patches from old T-shirts, pushing pins in and out, and scraping carbon off bolt parts. I give my Swiss Army much of the credit for the fact that my rifle never failed me a single time under fire. The Swiss Army also saw far more use in the field than my large fighting Bowie or Buck 110.

By the time I left the service I had become a dedicated Swiss Army carrier and have remained one ever since. No matter what other knives I have on me, you can always count on finding a Swiss Army or similar tool knife down at the bottom of my pocket.

Time and again it has been proven that practically anything can be repaired with a Swiss Army knife and a little ingenuity. This is why even U.S. space shuttles and manned spacecraft are equipped with the little red-handled folders. Autos, computers, radios, firearms — you name it — Swiss Armies have made them function when people's lives were on the line. The late Peter Capstick, an African pro-hunter, liked to say, "If you can't fix it with a Swiss Army you can use the knife to make a tool that will."

HISTORY OF THE SWISS ARMY

The Swiss didn't invent the multi-blade tool knife. Knives with various folding gadgets have been in common use for several hundred years. Most tended to be relatively bulky in size and high in price.

Karl Elsener, founder of Victorinox, first received a contract to produce pocketknives for the Swiss Army in 1891. Previous issue folders had been purchased from German firms. The original Swiss Army knife was a wood-handled swell-end jack with clip, screwdriver, can opener and leather punch blades. In 1897 the company introduced a red fiber-handled six-bladed equal-end folder that functioned off only two springs. Called the Officer's Knife, it featured a spear and screwdriver blade at one end, a small clip and can opener blade at the other, plus a cork screw and a leather punch that folded from the back of the handle. In basic form and function, this model is what is today universally known as a Swiss Army.

Rather than allow one company to monopolize production of the issue knives, the Swiss government granted a second contract to produce official issue folders to Wenger. Both companies are Swiss and both produce folders for that country's military. After years of disagreement, a settlement was reached whereby Victorinox calls its knives Original Swiss Armies and Wenger designates its as Genuine Swiss Armies. Today both companies produce approximately 40,000 each for the Swiss Army a year. While both companies are famous for red plastic-handled knives, in 1961 the Swiss Army switched to a red aluminum handle on the official issue model. In 1965 the aluminum handle was changed from red to silver in color. The metal handle has an advantage in durability under extremely hard use.

BOY SCOUTS

Not too many years after the Swiss Army knife was created, American cutlery companies started producing an equal end folder commonly called the Camp Utility or Boy Scout. (While the Boy Scouts do use this type of knife, only officially sanctioned brands may

The top knife, a Camp Utility or Boy Scout, has long been the American answer to the Swiss Army. At one time companies such as Remington made models with five or more blades, but these have pretty much disappeared. The knife shown on the bottom is a recent Remington reproduction.

use the phrase 'Boy Scout Knife' in their advertising.)

The American knife was an obvious spin-off of the Swiss model, but with some distinct differences. Where the classic Swiss Army had six blades, the American normally utilized only four: a spear, combination bottle and screwdriver, can opener, and leather punch. Occasionally, the leather punch was replaced with a small blade. Can opener styles also evolved as more efficient designs were created. The standard frame size was a 3⅜-inch closed with a heavy metal bolster on either end of the frame and a metal bail for carrying the knife on a lanyard or chain.

Compare the Boy Scout to the Swiss Army and you find that the American folder is noticeably heavier and gives the appearance of being more durable. A few companies, such as Remington, did occasionally offer 6-bladed, cork screw and leather punch on the back

versions of the Camp Utility, but these were always premium items that sold in limited numbers.

CAMPER'S KNIFE

Pre-World War II, a few American cutlery companies also offered a large 4¾-inch closed multi-tool folder called a Camper's Knife. In its standard form, the knife had a large clip point master blade, sheepsfoot secondary, leather punch and can opener. As a backcountry folder, the Camper's Knife was probably a better knife than most Boy Scouts or Swiss Armies, but a less practical multipurpose tool.

During the early 1990s, Remington brought its Camper's Knife back as a limited edition Bullet Knife. These still seem to be fairly common on the collector market, but no other company is known to be producing the pattern.

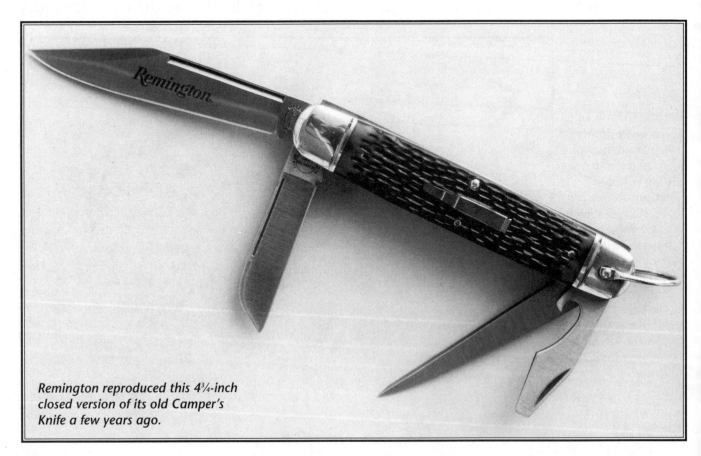

Remington reproduced this 4¾-inch closed version of its old Camper's Knife a few years ago.

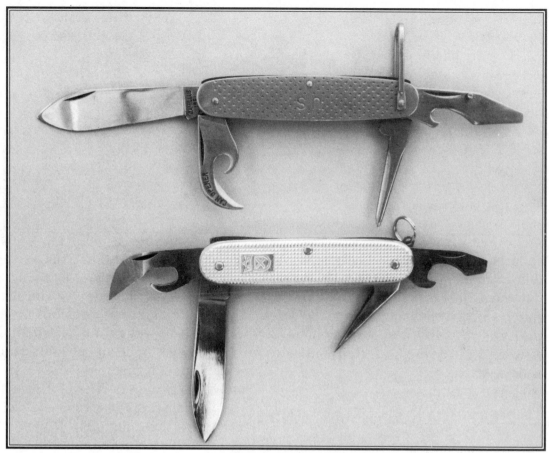

The top knife has been the official issue folder of the U.S. military for approximately 50 years. Basically, it is a Boy Scout with an all-steel handle. The bottom knife is an aluminum-handled multi-blade made by the Spanish firm of Aitor for the Dutch military. It seems to be a direct copy of the official issue Swiss model.

U.S. MILITARY MODELS

Genuine Swiss Armies did not reach American shores in any great numbers until the 1950s. Given the numbers of Boy and Girl scouts, plus the basic utility of the Camp folder, the American pattern quickly became one of the more common pocketknife patterns in the United States. During World War II, the military bought large numbers of the standard Camp Utility and created a new pattern issue folder based on the civilian knife.

The issue knife featured a stainless steel handle with the standard large spear, combination bottle opener and screwdriver, can opener, leather punch and carry bail. Early models utilized carbon steel blades, but this was soon changed to stainless. The Utility Pocket is still standard issue to all branches of the service. Special Forces troops, the most common users of the Utility Pocket, usually refer to the pattern as a Demo Knife as it is issued with their demolition gear.

SHELL BOLSTERS

There is one group of Camp Utility folders that should be avoided under most conditions – the inexpensive shell bolster models one commonly finds in drug stores and other discount markets. Shell bolster refers to the fact that the knife handle is made from light sheet metal bent around a thin inner frame to give the appearance of a conventional solid bolster knife.

Imperial and Colonial have long specialized in this type of budget cutlery, but others have used it from time to time. While shell bolster knives have long been the accepted first knife for youth, under the assumption they would

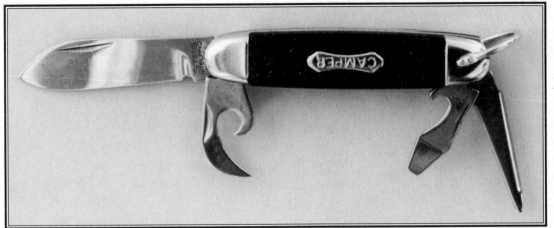

The Shell Bolster Camp Utility, such as this one made in Ireland, is one of the most common pocket knives around. Despite its appearance, it will not stand up to heavy use like a solid bolster knife.

soon be lost or broken, this type of construction cannot be depended on for serious use. Low cost has assured huge numbers being sold over the years and the shell bolster Camp Utility is probably the most common folder you will find around flea markets and antique stores.

PICKING A SWISS ARMY KNIFE

Both the civilian Camp Utility and the military Utility Pocket are strong, basic tools that have their fans. In general, though, the Swiss Army style folder has captured the majority of the market for multi-purpose tool pocketknives. The Swiss Army's tools seem more refined and sophisticated than the average Scout folder. In the basic four to six blade models, the Swiss Army is lighter in weight than the competition, although that does not necessarily mean it is weaker than an American Camp Utility. The Swiss have been quick to create many new special purpose blades and tools to add to their folders. There are now dozens of models including the Victorinox Swiss Champ with 29 features and tools.

Which brand, Victorinox or Wenger, is best? Both make excellent knives, but each has its own special models and blade/tool combinations. For instance, Wenger is the only one that produces left-hand Swiss Armies, an optional locking blade on its standard size

This basic Wenger Swiss Army includes scissors and a nail file instead of a pen blade.

The Victorinox Spartan is always a good starting point when trying to select a Swiss Army Knife. With this basic selection of tools you can then decide if and what other specialized blade you require.

knives, and screw driver points that lock when pressure is applied. Victorinox's can opener/screwdriver combination is generally considered superior to the one on Wenger's standard models. The Swiss Army actually requires that Wenger use the Victorinox can opener on issue knives.

The logical place to start when deciding on a Swiss Army is with what might be called the two basic models. For Victorinox, this would be the Spartan and the Tinker. For Wenger, the Viking and the Trailblazer would be considered basic. All these knives feature a large spear blade, small pen or clip blade, can opener, bottle opener, screwdriver (the Spartan has a screwdriver point on both the can opener and the screwdriver) and a leather punch. The Spartan and Viking each have a cork screw, while the Tinker and Trailblazer replace this option with a Phillips screwdriver. These are the most time proven and frequently used tools by most users.

For additional tools, the next blade should be a wood saw. Victorinox's model would be the Hiker; Wenger's is the Backpacker. Swiss Army sawblades are far more efficient than their small size would indicate. Additional blade/tools pretty much depend on individual needs. Scissors are highly popular on many models and several versions now feature small sets of pliers folded into the handle. From a survival prospective, with patience one can start fires with the magnifying glass on a Victorinox model.

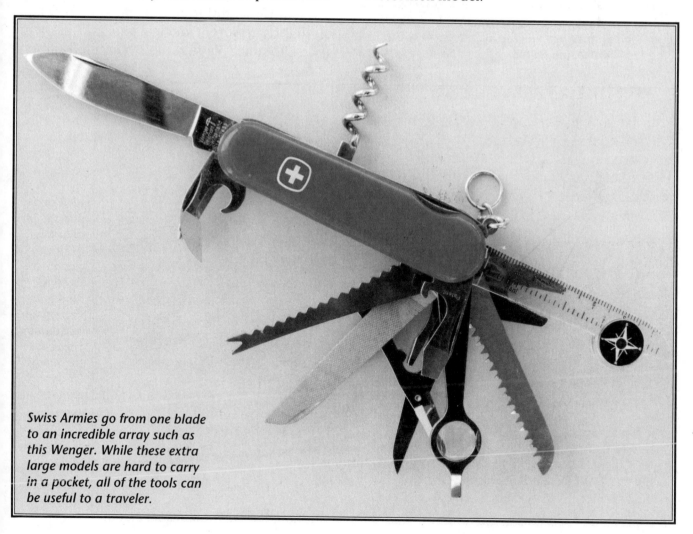

Swiss Armies go from one blade to an incredible array such as this Wenger. While these extra large models are hard to carry in a pocket, all of the tools can be useful to a traveler.

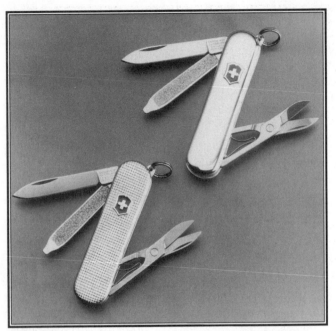

Even though these two Swiss Army Knives have solid silver handles, they remain functional tools — which is more than can be said for many dress knives.

LARGER MODEL SWISS ARMY KNIVES

In recent years, both companies have added a second line of larger, locking main blade outdoor folders to their lines. All seem to be outstanding tools. The 3¼-inch sawblade option found on several of these larger models will outcut all but the most efficient of the hollow handle, sawback Rambo knives popular a few years ago.

SWISSBUCKS

A few years back Wenger entered into a marketing agreement with Buck knives to produce SwissBucks. These are standard Wenger models with the addition of a black plastic handle of slightly different design and an American style clip point blade rather than the tradition-

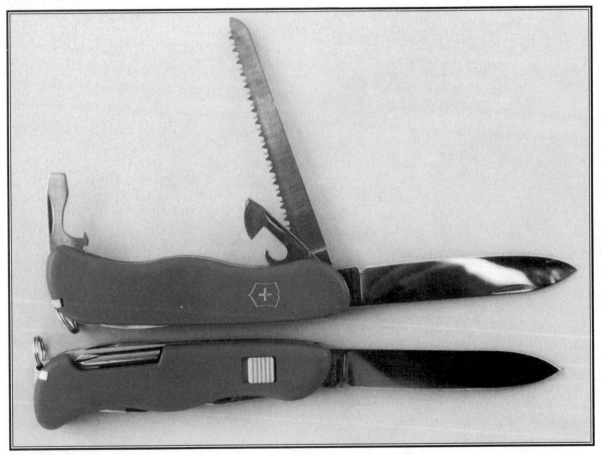

Victorinox offers a line of large 4⅜-inch closed lockback models that make outstanding knives for the survival kit or camper.

Buck's large locking blade Swiss Armies are made for the company by Wenger. The blade locking system is a liner-lock that is released by sliding the bar on the side of the handle.

This SwissBuck Trekker model is actually made for the company by Wenger. Unlike the traditional European model, Buck's knives feature a clip-point master blade.

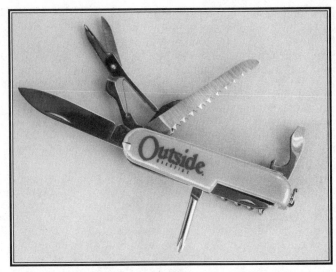

Chinese Swiss Army-style knives such as this promotional model may look good at a glance but the workmanship and materials are generally poor.

Buck and Wenger offer a variety of small multi-tool folders such as these Attaché dress knives.

A multi-blade folder is said to be issue to Russian Army troops.

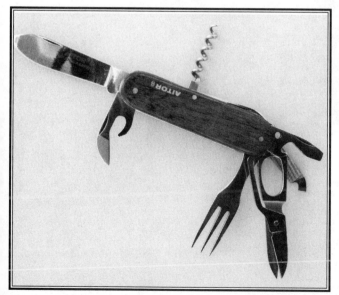

A 4¼-inch Aitor multi-blade folder would make a good camp knife.

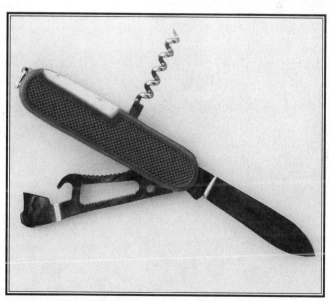

A 4¼-inch closed Aitor model is said to be issue to the Spanish Army.

al European spear. There are also two 4⅞-inch closed lockbacks, one a simple clip and Phillips screwdriver combination; the other a multi-blade that includes pliers, can and bottle openers, screwdrivers, cork screw, leather punch, 3⅞-inch clip point blade and wood saw. The main blade locks on the liner-lock principle. These larger knives are also available from Wenger in Swiss versions without the Buck logo. The large multi-blade in either the Wenger or Buck version is probably one of the best folders around for the one-knife-does-it-all backpacker or traveler.

SWISS ARMY "STYLE"

From the real "made in Switzerland" folders one can move to all the imitations. There are Swiss "style" knives from makers in Spain, England, France, Italy, Germany, Taiwan, Hong Kong, Japan, Bulgaria, Russia, the Peoples Republic of China and the United

Aitor's Al-Ligator provides a large size multi-tool knife with a pair of useful pliers that fold from the same handle.

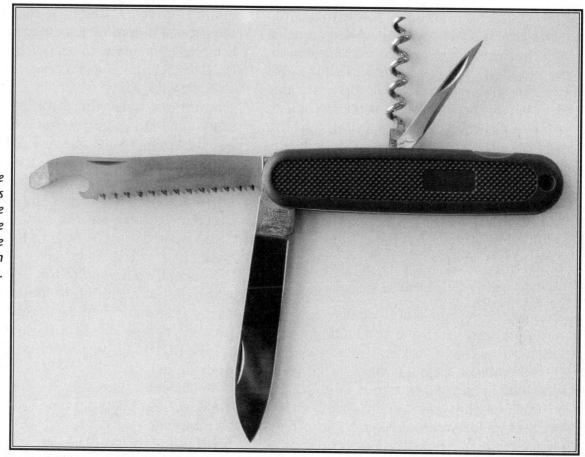

This large size Swiss Army-style knife is issue lin the German Army.

States. Most of these knives aren't meant to deceive but simply to fill a demand for an established pattern of folding knife. A few, particularly those from the PRC, are shoddy knockoffs intended to be sold at the lowest possible prices.

As for the others, quality is a case by case matter. Good multi-blade tool knives are made in Spain, France, Italy, Japan and Germany. Schrade Cutlery imports a line of red-handled folders made in a factory located in the former East Germany. These are close copies of Swiss knives and seem to be of very good quality.

AITOR

The Spanish brand of Aitor warrants a close look. Not only do they produce several red-handled standard size knives (3½-inch closed), they also have a second line of 4¼-inch closed folders. This second group comes with green plastic handles and several models are actually issue in the Spanish military. The 3¼-inch spear point main blade on these beefy multi-purpose folders offers some advantages over the standard size frame Swiss Army and is large enough to make a fairly good hunting knife.

GERMAN ISSUE SWISS ARMY KNIVES

Another of the "larger than standard" tool knives is the 4¼-inch closed German Army issue model. This folder features a non-locking 3¼-inch spear blade, a combination saw, can opener, bottle opener, screw driver blade, leather punch and cork screw. Early models were all made by Victorinox on contract for the Germans, but the contract went to the

Italian company of MKM. While either knife meets German Army specs, the Swiss model is a little better made — when it can be found. Even though a seemingly huge variety of Swiss Armies are imported, this is not the entire line. Swiss Armies are the one pocketknife you can purchase in practically any country in the world. Should you find yourself outside the United States, take a close look a the Swiss Army Knife display in any cutlery shops you come across. You may find a model not imported that is exactly what you have been looking for.

COLONIAL

For some reason, possibly because the Boy Scout style was already in production, Swiss Army copies have never been common with U.S. makers. Colonial makes a group of low-priced, stamped-out tool knives with red handles that are acceptable as first pocketknives for youth and others who need an expendable folder. In the Camp Utility/Boy Scout line, Camillus, Case and Remington (actually made by Camillus) all turn out

quality products. Camillus also continues to offer the standard military issue Utility Pocket Knife to civilians with a choice of USMC, US, USN, or USAF handle markings.

The Swiss Army or Camp Utility folder is one cutlery field where the buyer is pretty much limited to factory products. Multi-blade custom folding knives in any pattern are still not common simply because they are extremely difficult to make well. While custom knifemakers might not have too many problems turning out the cutting blades for a Swiss Army type folder, the various tools would be a nightmare.

Now and again one of the better craftsman will turn out a multi-tool folder, but in most cases these seem to be simply projects to prove it can be done. In the end you have a folder that may be attractive but probably doesn't perform the various tool functions quite as well as a real Swiss Army. In all likelihood, it also costs 20 times as much as the factory knife.

No matter what other knife or knives you carry, there is always room for a Swiss Army or similar tool knife in your pocket.

At one time, Victorinox produced this model on the German Army knife frame for Mauser. It may still be available in Europe.

11

MORE TOOL KIT KNIVES

In the late 1970s, a would-be knife designer by the name of Tim Leatherman was working on a prototype of a new design. The idea was a pair of folding pliers with a number of tools and blades stored in both sections of the handle. Combining pliers, scissors and wrenches with folding knives was nothing new as there have been many such designs created over the last 100 years.

During the 1960s, a cheap set of pliers with a knife blade, bottle opener and fish scaler folded into the handle was imported from Japan as a fisherman's tool. None of these combination tools had ever become particularly popular or common. Even though Leatherman's design was well made, he was told it would never sell in any great numbers. Wrong!

Today, Leatherman produces literally millions of his Leatherman Tools each year in a modern Portland, Ore. factory. Not only has Leatherman been wildly successful, one

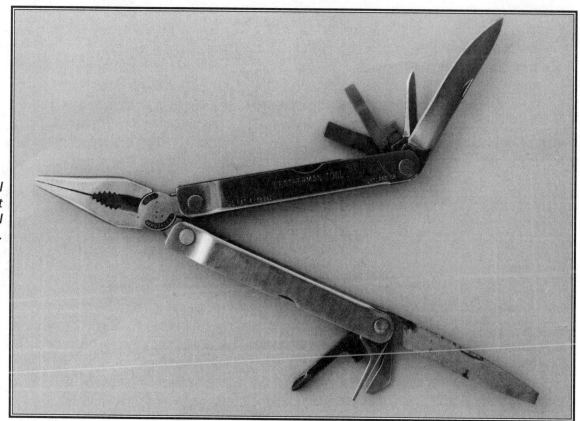

This is the tool that started it all, the original Leatherman.

cutlery company after another has introduced pliers/tool knives of their own.

In hindsight, the reasons why this particular combination tool has made such a hit when previous tools flopped are easy to see. First, the Leatherman system of folding the pliers made it much more compact and easy to carry than many of the earlier tool designs. Combined with a neat carry pouch (during a period when carrying a knife in a belt pouch is an accepted manner of dress), the Leatherman is an extremely handy item for any working person to add to his belt or tool kit.

Second, where some of the tools before it were not much better than novelties, the Leatherman is a quality piece of equipment made to last under hard use. The individual tools are well thought out and improvements are added whenever a problem is identified. The computer age probably didn't hurt the Leatherman as it has become popular among those working on electrical equipment. The Leatherman also is seen as a non-threatening way to carry a knife in an urban environment.

A basic fact of modern life is that there is a far larger potential market for a compact general purpose fix-it kit than there is for a more specialized cutting tool. Vast numbers of people who did not carry pocket knives in the

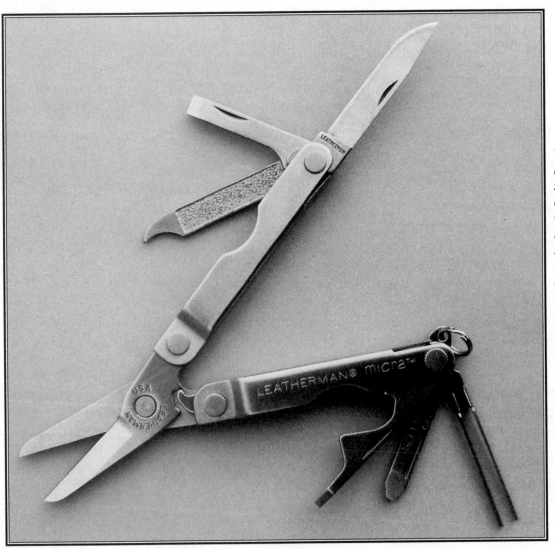

The Leatherman Micra replaces the standard pliers with a pair of scissors. Other tool options include several screwdriver points, tweezers, bottle opener, knife blade and nail file. The Micra is small enough to fit in a watch pocket and will serve most of the same functions as a Swiss Army.

Not only is the Leatherman Super Tool larger than the original, all of the various blade and tool options lock when open.

past now carry Leathermans or similar pliers/tool folders.

LEATHERMAN LINE

The Leatherman line currently consists of five basic models: the Original tool, the Mini-Tool, the Super Leatherman, the PST II and the new Micra. The Original Tool consists of pliers, wire cutters, knife blade, ruler, can and bottle opener, large screwdriver, small screwdriver, Phillips screwdriver, medium screwdriver, file and leather punch. Because these tools have become practically mandatory equipment for those in Special Forces military units, the Leatherman may also be purchased with a blasting cap crimper built into the pliers' head.

The Mini-Tool features handles that fold twice and pliers, wire cutters, knife, ruler, can opener, bottle opener, screwdriver and metal file blades. Both the can and bottle openers are built into the handle frames rather than as separate tools as on the Original. The Super Tool has expanded the 4-inch frame of the Original to 4½ inches and added a second serrated blade plus a combination wood and bone sawblade. All 10 tools and blade lock open.

Geared toward fishermen, the PST added a serrated blade, scissors, diamond surfaced file and fish hook sharpener to the Original. Leatherman's latest addition, the Micra, substitutes a compact pair of scissors for the pliers, along with a knife blade, medium screwdriver, small screwdriver, Phillips screw-

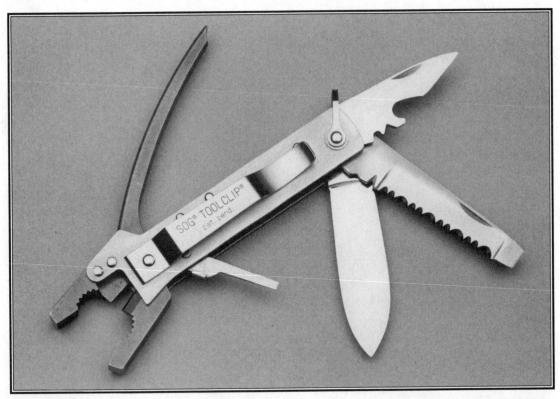

SOG Specialty's first entry into the tool/knife market was the Toolclip.

SOG's next effort was the Micro Toolclip, a light duty but handy little folder.

driver, bottle opener, nail file and tweezers. A small and light tool, the Micra seems to be a popular substitution for a Swiss Army in a lot of pockets. All of the Leatherman Tools are stainless steel and, except for the Micra, come in a choice of a leather or nylon pouch.

AL MAR 4X4

Once Leatherman proved there was a market for combination pliers/tool knives, competing designs started to appear. One of the first was probably Al Mar's reproduction of the so-called World War II OSS Escape Knife. The original Escape Knife, of British design, was created as a demo tool for agents sabotaging enemy structures or equipment. The originals were also very similar to tool knives made for gardeners and handymen before the war.

Al Mar's 4x4 is a fairly conventional folder with a pair of pliers, 3-inch spear point knife blade, 2-inch sheepsfoot, file, screwdriver, pliers and Phillips screwdriver working off a stainless steel frame. For those not needing the full range of tools, AMK offers the Quickclip, a tool knife with a pair of pliers at one end and a 3⁷⁄₁₆-inch serrated spear point blade at the other. The stainless steel handle frame includes a spring carry clip.

SOG

The next entry in the tool knife parade was the SOG Toolclip, another semi-conventional folding knife with a pair of pliers/wirecutter, several screwdriver tips, a large spear point blade, a combination serrated edge, screwdriver, wire stripper blade, bottle opener and light pry bar. As the name indicates, the Toolclip also features a stainless steel spring carry clip on the side of the handle.

The full-size Toolclip was quickly followed by the Micro Toolclip, a Zytel-handled folder with pliers/wirecutter, screwdriver, spear point blade and serrated sheepsfoot. While

the Micro might not be up to the really big jobs, at 3 ounces, it makes a handy item to carry on an everyday basis.

The success of the first two SOG tools caused the company to rethink its entire marketing program. SOG's company name derives from its first product, a replica of the sterile combat knife issued to Special Operations teams in Vietnam. For the first few years, all SOG products had some link to this combat knife. SOG soon added the Paratool, a set of pliers that — like the Leatherman — features tools folding out of the two separate handle sections. The unique way the pliers head folds back into the center of the handle also allows the pliers to be used at various angles. Blades and tools include a

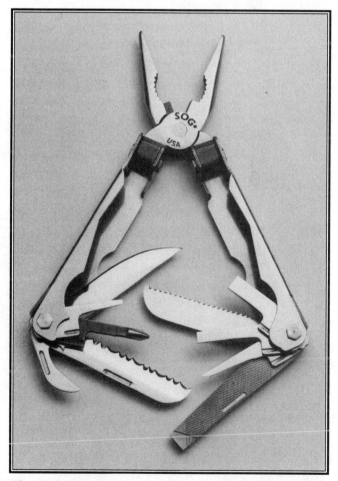

The SOG Paratool was a more conventional Pliers/knife combination.

spear point knife, sheepsfoot serrated knife, file, awl, several screwdriver tips, ruler and a combination can and bottle opener. A double-tooth woodsaw and a serrated line and seatbelt cutter are optional. Tools may be added or replaced with the assistance of a special optional wrench.

In 1995, SOG introduced the Power Pliers, a folding pliers/tool kit with a gear-driven head for extra leverage and power when cutting wire or gripping objects. The tool section remains basically the same as that offered on the Paratool. The introduction of a slightly smaller version of the Power Pliers, called the Pocket Power Pliers, came in 1996 for those needing a more compact tool. While SOG continues to offer its fixed blade combat and survival models, it is obvious the main thrust has become specialty pliers/tool knives.

GERBER

At the same time SOG introduced its Paratool, Gerber threw its hat into the ring with the Multi-Plier. Rather than fold into the handle, a button is depressed and the head slides straight in and out of the frame. With a little practice, opening may be accomplished with a flick of the wrist and the help of gravity. People always like toys so this has been a major selling point for the Multi-Plier.

Current tools include several screwdriver points, a clip point blade, a serrated sheepsfoot, leather punch, can opener, wire stripper,

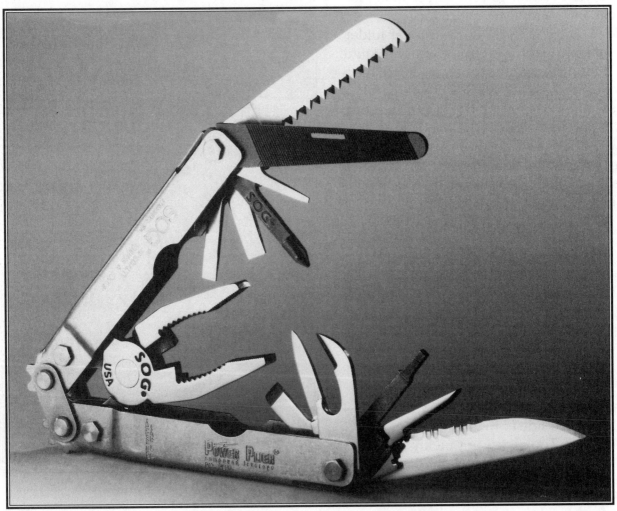

The SOG Power Pliers added the leverage of a gear action to the pliers, but pretty much retained the standard tool options.

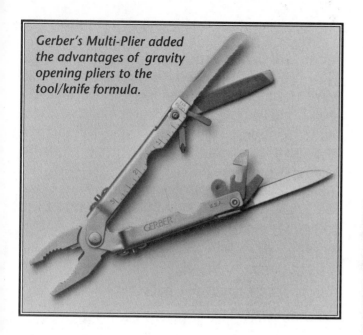

Gerber's Multi-Plier added the advantages of gravity opening pliers to the tool/knife formula.

The new tool is a 180-degree folder like the Leatherman with needle nose pliers head, wirecutter, clip point knife blade, leather punch, can opener, bottle opener, several screwdriver tips, file, wood saw and ruler. Similar to the Multi-Plier, the MBT comes in a black non-reflective military finish as well as flat gray stainless steel.

bottle opener, ruler, pliers and wire cutter. The pliers head is available in a choice of square or needle nose. An optional kit comes with an adapter and nine additional screwdriver bits. Early Multi-Pliers had a design flaw that cause many users more than a little pain. The handle sections closed completely together and tended to pinch the palm of the unwary user. This was quickly corrected, and eventually the Multi-Plier became a far greater success than even Gerber expected. Today, the tool is produced in hundreds of thousands of units each year.

In late 1995, Gerber added a second pliers/tool knife to its line called the MBT (Military Provisional Tool). According to Gerber literature, the MBT was designed to government specifications and deployed by U.S. military personnel worldwide.

The government had been purchasing large numbers of Leatherman Tools for various military units. At some point, GSA drew up a set of specifications designed around the original Leatherman tool and put the package out to bid. Gerber then created the MBT to win the contract and had been supplying the tool to GSA for nearly two years before they released it to the public.

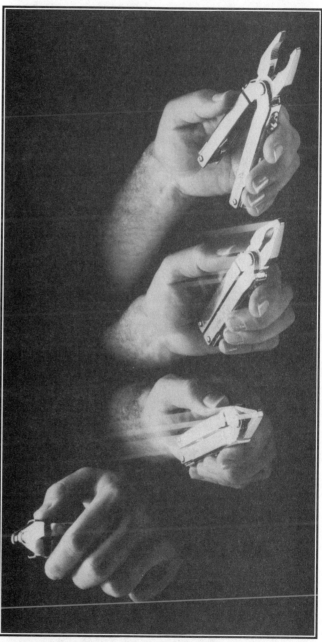

The Multi-Plier is opened by pressing down on two buttons and snapping the wrist.

BUCKTOOL

Buck Knives introduced the BuckTool as its own version of the pliers/knife family with a system "designed by popular complaint," according to its promotional literature. Buck Knives researched what users liked and disliked about existing tools and tried to correct the problem areas.

One feature in particular stands out: Each handle section has a lock button that functions all of the tools in that half of the tool. Can Buck take this new locking mechanism and utilize it in a conventional multi-blade folding knife, say a standard trapper? The company is looking into this possibility. The tool selection includes needle nose pliers, wire cutters, two knife blades, two Phillips screwdrivers, can and bottle opener and three slotted screwdrivers. Icons engraved on the side of the handle allow the user to locate each tool without opening the blades.

KUTMASTER

The old line cutlery company Utica (Kutmaster) introduced its Multimaster tool in early 1996. This tool follows the Al Mar 4X4 and SOG Toolclip systems of having a set of pliers built into one end of a conventional folding knife frame. Tool options include plier/wirecutter, clip point blade, serrated sheepsfoot blade, can and bottle opener, saw, and coarse and fine sided file. The end of the pliers handle is slotted to accept several sizes of screwdriver bits.

BEAR MGC

Still another 1996 addition to the pliers/tool knife family is the Bear MGC Bear Jaws. At first this appears to be another copy of the Leatherman, but closer inspection reveals one rather unique feature. Instead of the tools folding on the inside of the handle when the

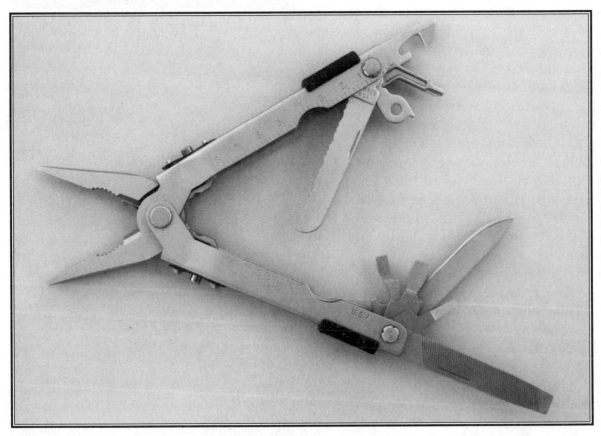

Gerber updated the Multi-Plier into an all-locking blade version.

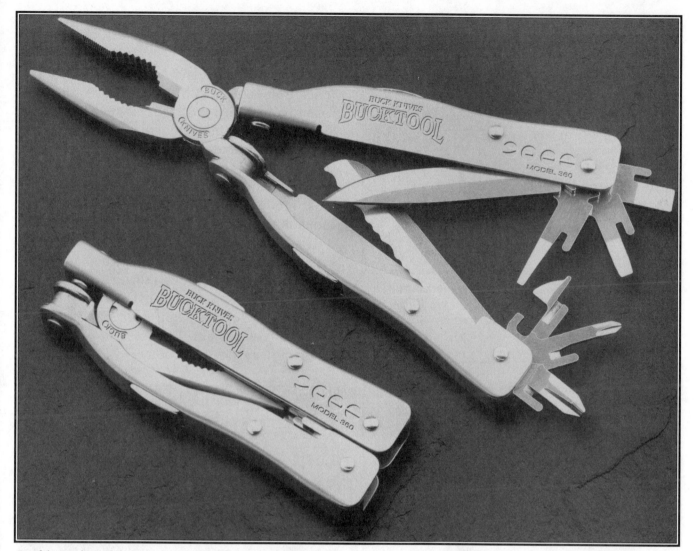

Buck's BuckTool features locking blades and tools that function off a single lock release in each of the handle halves.

tool is closed, the various blades are set on the outside of the Bear Jaw frame. Thus, any of the tools may be used without having to unfold the pliers. Tools include clip and serrated sheepsfoot blades, various screwdriver tips, double sided file, can and bottle opener, and a ruler along the handle frame.

KNOCK-OFFS

There are a number of imported knock-offs of several of these pliers/tool knives. People who have used the copies say they are poorly

made and seldom hold up to much hard use. In other words, you get what you pay for.

VICTORINOX, WENGER AND AITOR

For light-duty situations, both Victorinox and Wenger offer Swiss Army models with small pliers included as tool options. Aitor offers the Al-Ligator, a large Swiss Army pattern folder with a set of pliers built into one end of the handle. The knife falls somewhere in between the light-duty Swiss Army pliers and the full size Leatherman-type items for field use.

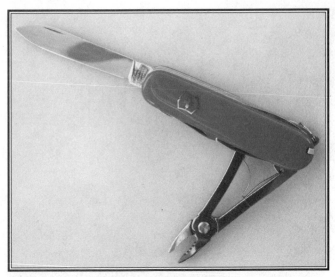

Many of the more elaborate Swiss Army models have a small pair of pliers as one of its tool options. While these are not especially heavy-duty, they are work well for small jobs.

Coast Cutlery's Pocket Mechanic has become one of the best-selling tool knives on the lower end of the price scale.

Wenger also introduced a similar large Swiss Army with pliers built into the end of the handle in early 1996.

Pliers/tool knives should not be accepted as true replacements for the more traditional forms of folding knife for several reasons. First, on most models, opening the knife blade is a much more difficult procedure than thumbing into place the cutting edge of any one of the many one-hand openers. Second, on most models, the knife blade is a rather small tool suitable only for fine work.

The primary market for the pliers/knives seems to be the technician and or handyman who needs the various screwdriver tips and pliers functions with only an infrequent requirement for a cutting edge. However, the pliers/knives remain the fastest growing field in the cutlery industry today.

Along with the standard pliers and tool options, Kutmaster's Multimaster offers a recessed handle that accepts universal slotted and Phillips screwdriver bits.

12

THE MODERN AUTO-OPENER AND GRAVITY KNIFE

Shortly after I joined an Army Ranger Long Range Patrol company in Vietnam during 1968, I was given a pass into the central highlands city of Pleiku. Being a country kid from the Midwest, this was the first time I had ever been turned loose in a culture outside the borders of home. I knew exactly what my first goal was going to be: to find a switchblade knife.

Even then I was a knife buff and had heard most countries did not restrict auto-opening knives the way the United States did. After much searching through the shops and hard-ware stores of the Vietnamese city, I discovered a display of folding guard push-button knives with plastic handles and four-inch spear point blades. None had any blade markings besides "stainless," but I suspect they had been made in Japan. After a certain amount of haggling with the shop owner, I paid $15 for one of the knives. I was probably taken since the same model seldom sells for much more today, but I had my first auto-opener.

For the first day or two I was satisfied with pushing the button and watching the blade

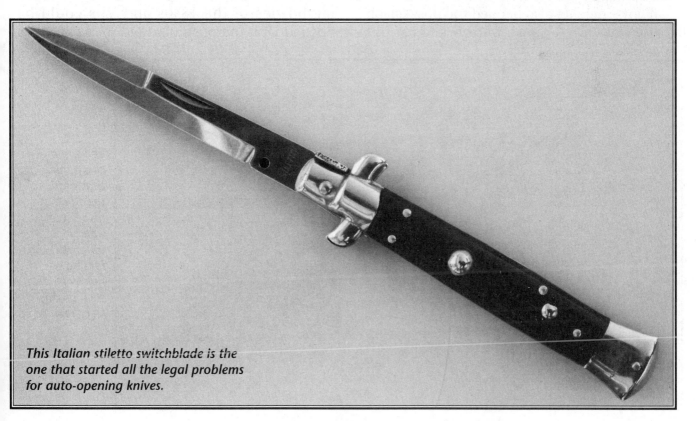

This Italian stiletto switchblade is the one that started all the legal problems for auto-opening knives.

spring open, but I was soon to learn a basic fact about switchblades. Once they are open, they are aren't any different than any other folding knife. The fact that the blade opened by spring power didn't offset the fact that this was a weakly constructed, poor quality knife. I don't remember ever carrying the switchblade to the field and eventually I traded it to another team member for something useful — a C ration can of peaches. Nevertheless, the lesson stuck with me: There is nothing magical about a knife opening at the press of a button; it's still just a cutting tool.

In 1958, the federal government banned the interstate sale and shipment of spring activated and gravity opening knives. Supposedly, the sole civilian function of the push-button knife was as a weapon of juvenile delinquents. Movies such as "Rebel Without A Cause" and "West Side Story" reinforced the concept that switchblades were a social problem that needed to be cured with a federal ban. During the same period, many state and local governments also banned the possession and/or carrying of push-button knives, but failed to consider the basic folding hunting, fishing and gardening knives that also opened with the push of a button.

A switchblade — or auto-opening knife — is a blade that opens automatically under spring pressure when some type of release is moved. In the classic sense, a gravity knife falls from the handle without the aid of spring pressure when a blade release is moved. The logic behind both designs is very simple: There are many times when a knife user only has one hand available to open his folding knife. Many people also have trouble simply opening a stiff backspringed conventional slip-joint folder with their fingers. Adding a spring and a button solved this problem. Tiny push-button knives were once marketed as tools for the lady's sewing kit so she didn't have to risk breaking a nail opening the blade. Obviously, the speed of opening increases its appeal as does the mechanical toy aspect.

Spring opening knives have been around for at least 150 years. Many of the Sheffield folding bowies of the 1840s and '50s could be opened with the push of a button. As early as

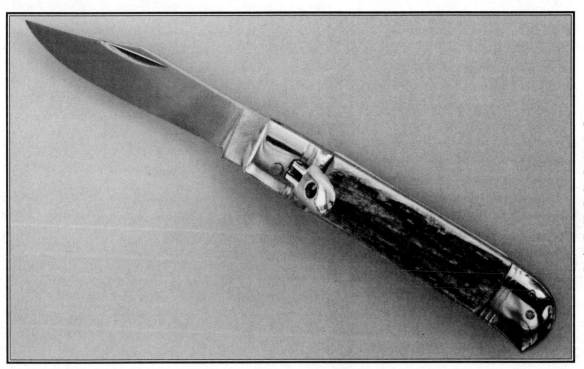

The same companies that produce the stilettos also produce handy auto-opening folding hunters such as this lever-release.

Auto-openers such as this Schrade Mk-2 were issue to U.S. Army paratroopers from World War II through the early days of the Vietnam conflict.

1886, Miller Brothers was cataloging a simple gravity knife as ideal for both hunters and sailors working with "one hand for the ship and one for yourself." The U.S. Navy issued a Miller Brothers gravity knife with a sheepsfoot point to sailors during the Spanish-American War. In the later part of the 19th century, there was a great surge in spring opening knife designs both here and in Europe. As with blade locks, the basic concept of a spring activated blade allowed for dozens of different ways to accomplish the task.

GEORGE SCHRADE

In 1893, George Schrade started the Push-button Knife Company, the beginning of several generations of Schrade leadership in auto-knife production in the United States. Soon practically all major cutlery companies offered several automatically opening folders in their lines. Remington, W.R. Case, Ka-Bar, Imperial, Colonial and Camillus offered push-button knives as standard items. Most of these lines were directed toward the fishing, hunting, camping, gardening and upscale pen knife market.

Both George Schrade and Schrade Cutlery (two separate companies) produced dozens of basic one-hand opening folder models for everyday knife users. Most were a simple, single blade, clip point design with a button release and a sliding safety on the side. When World War II began, the United States chose to issue its newly-formed Airborne units George Schrade and Schrade Cutlery push-button knives as a means to free themselves from their parachute harnesses. That these were not intended to be fighting weapons is evidenced in the number of other serious combat knives also issued at the same time to paratroopers.

GRAVITY KNIVES

Gravity knives were not unknown in the United States before World War II, but they were never common. During the war, the German army issued a massive gravity knife to its aircrews and paratroopers. After the war, a

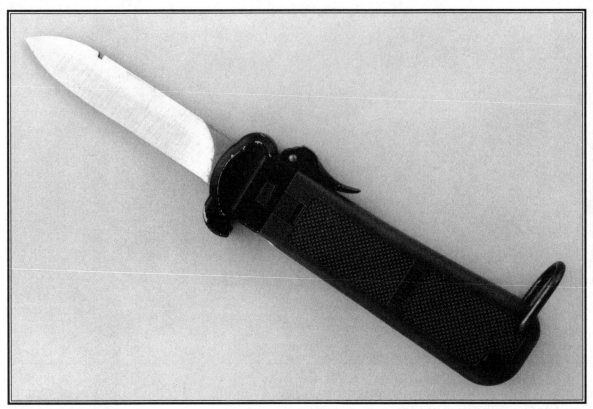

German paratroopers are still issued this heavy-duty gravity knife for jumping. Gravity knives tend to have poor handle-to-blade length ratios.

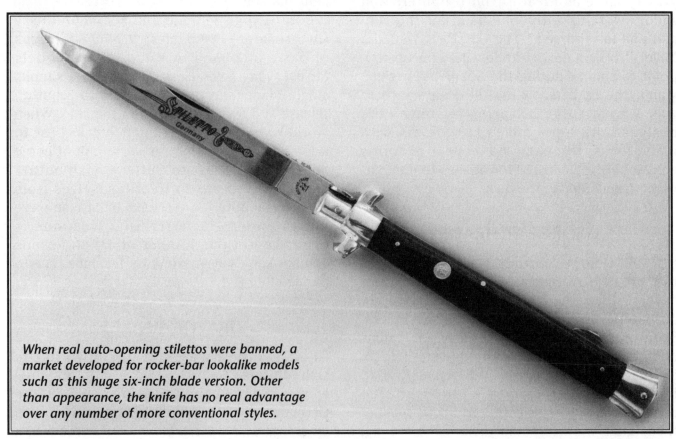

When real auto-opening stilettos were banned, a market developed for rocker-bar lookalike models such as this huge six-inch blade version. Other than appearance, the knife has no real advantage over any number of more conventional styles.

few German companies tried to get back on their feet by exporting civilian versions of their wartime products, but they had overly large handles, heavy weight and poor blade-to-handle ratios. They were banned in 1958 along with spring activated folders.

Shortly after World War II, large numbers of Italian stiletto switchblades were also being imported, perhaps as a result of a demand created by G.I.s bringing the knives home from Europe. After the war, a devastated Italian cutlery industry was only too happy to supply any type of cutlery the American market desired, including the stiletto.

The classic Italian switchblade is a folding dagger with a small cross guard. Blade lengths vary from one inch up to as much as two feet, but most tend to be an inch or two longer than the average folder. The spear point blade is not a true dagger as it is not double edged, and a real stiletto utilizes a three or more sided blade with no cutting edges. Most of these knives are of reasonably good steel and, once honed, can perform any function a long narrow blade is suited to.

During the late 1950s to the 1970s, the only new switchblades on the market were those smuggled in each year by tourists. (In many other countries where firearms are difficult to obtain, auto-opening knives remain legal.)

Push-button knives also remained legal for military issue and a certain number of Army Mk-2 and the newer Air Force MC-1 models found their way into civilian hands. On rare occasions, a custom knifemaker tried his hand at making an auto-opening folder, but folders in general had not yet caught on with handmakers.

Given their 'forbidden fruit' nature, auto-knives gained a near-cult status with a sub-culture of knife collectors. In general, the legal system had better things to do than chase down eccentric cutlery buffs, so few auto-knife collectors ever got into trouble over their hobby.

During the 1980s, two events took place that reinstated the market for auto-opening folders. The first was a court ruling in Oregon that push-button knives were covered under the state's law as a right to keep and bear arms, and that mere possession could not be banned. The judge in the case voiced the opinion that simply adding a spring to a folder did not make it a dangerous weapon. Oregon became the Mecca for the legal switchblade, with both commercial and custom makers adding models to their lines.

The second event is not quite so simply explained. Basically, an importer discovered he could legally bring foreign knives into this

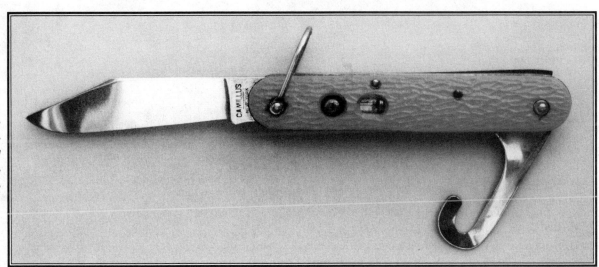

The MC-1 has been issue as an Air Force parachute survival knife since the late 1950s.

country if the springs were removed. These same knives could then be shipped interstate to buyers sans springs. The buyer was allowed to install the spring himself and bore the brunt of any local legal problems.

Soon the country was awash in cheap, imported auto-openers. At Oregon gun and knife shows, prices for push-button folders that once went for $50 to $100 on the collector market dropped to below $10 (thus reflecting the real value of most of these imported toys). This went on for several years before Customs found a way to shut down the bulk of the imported springless auto-knife business. However, knife dealers had discovered that shipping auto-knives interstate without the spring was not a crime. Custom knifemaker were also quick to note that collectors paid high premiums for good examples of this cutlery art form, and many took a second look at this concept.

The first custom auto-opener to hit it big was the now-famous Black Knife, created by Charles Ochs and two other custom knifemakers. From the beginning, this large aluminum-handled, drop point folder was intended for use by military special operations, law enforcement and other emergency services personnel. The name derives from the overall black coating (several different types were used) and when collectors started associating the knife with covert or "black" military units.

As auto-openers go, the Black Knife was a basic cutting tool of practical design and first-class construction. Given the added benefits of one-hand opening, the Black Knife was ideal for many official duty uses. The 1958 law exempted the military from its ban, but recent legal interpretations have enabled police and other government agencies to legally purchase the knife. The Black Knife quickly became a fad item of personal gear in many military and law enforcement circles. The U.S. Navy SEALs bought a handful of these knives and some were field tested in combat during the Gulf War.

BENCHMADE

While the Black Knife was turned out in relatively small numbers, it proved there was a

Two variations of the legendary Black Knife. A small number of these auto-knives were actually issued to the SEALs.

legitimate user market as well a great deal of collector interest in auto-opening folders. The next auto-opener to appear on the market was the short-lived joint effort between Al Mar and Benchmade Knives called the GPA (General Purpose Automatic). In many ways, this is a more refined version of the Black Knife with a contoured aluminum handle and a 3½-inch drop point blade of ATS-34 stainless. Many traditional spring opening knives have inherent problems with the blade hitting the end of the opening arch and bouncing back before the lock is set. Both the Black Knife and GPA use a non-rebounding coil spring system that correct this problem. Neither knife has a safety to prevent accidental pressing of the handle button, so both are better suited to pouch — not pocket — carry.

The Al Mar/Benchmade partnership only lasted a short time and the GPA was soon renamed the Benchmade AFO (Armed Forces Only). Its success quickly spurred Benchmade to expand its line of auto-opener models for sale to military and law enforcement only. The company is now the leader in legal sales of spring-activated knives to government agencies.

Benchmade's second auto-opener effort was a push-button version of the Phil Boguszewski-designed Spike, an extremely pointed 3.6-inch spear blade with a straight taper to the rear aluminum handle. The Spike was followed by the Mel Pardue #3000, one of the more modern looking and utilitarian auto-openers to come along in recent years. Sleek and useful, the Pardue is a 3.9-inch clip point blade with a 50/50 serrated edge, aluminum handle frame with Kraton inserts, and pocket carry clip.

The Reflex and Mini-Reflex are similar to the AFO, but with a single built-in finger groove on the handle. Blade lengths run 4 and 3.2 inches. Both knives are available with 50/50 serrated edges and the Mini has a pocket carry clip. The Mini-Reflex in particular seems to have caught on with law enforcement personnel.

Benchmade's Reflex auto-opening folders are highly popular in law enforcement circles.

From the top, the Benchmade Auto Spike, Benchmade/ Pardue, and the Benchmade AFO (Armed Forces Only).

To keep up with the demand for tanto style blades, Benchmade brought out the four-inch Model 7500 in a choice of straight or 50/50 serrated edge. In 1996, the company began producing a four-inch blade auto-opening version of the Emerson Model 975 with G-10 handle scales. No doubt once their new factory comes fully on line, more auto-opening models will become available to qualified purchasers.

C&C SPECIALS

The success of Benchmade and Ox Enterprises brought a considerable number of black market C&C-made auto-openers out of the woodwork. Most of these are exact copies of the first two companies' models, but the actual makers keep a very low profile, making it difficult to ascertain who produces them.

STRAIGHT-OUT-THE-FRONTS

One facet of auto knives that seems to have never-ending fascination for some people is the straight-out blade. Straight-out openers are highly sought after among auto-knife buffs. (During the hey-day of the European kit switchblade, a common straight-out model was sold as the NATO, with the insinuation that it was issue to our military allies.) An interesting feature of this knife is that the blade has spring tension upon both opening and closing so that a press of the button per-

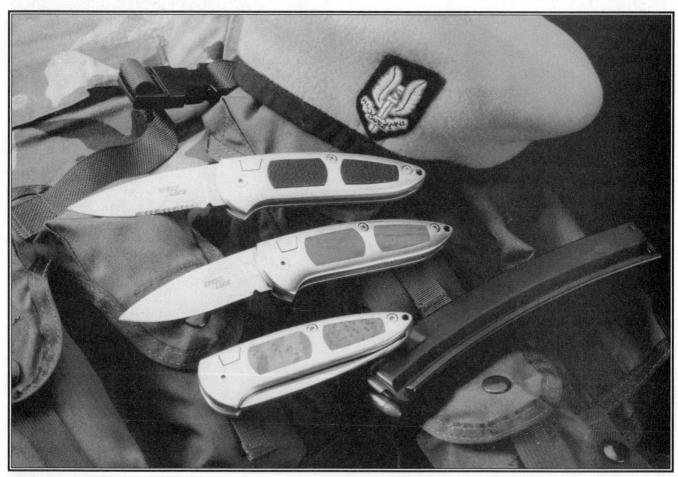

What is known as the Boker Top-Lock in this country is the auto-opening Speed-Lock in Europe. Several European military units have bought this folder for issue to Special Operations units.

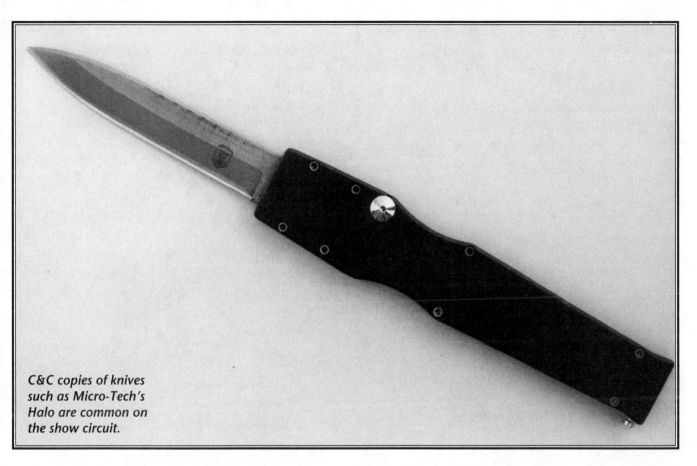

C&C copies of knives such as Micro-Tech's Halo are common on the show circuit.

forms both functions. Judging from Spanish cutlery catalogs, the dual action in-out auto-opener seems to be popular in that country.

MICRO-TECH

The Florida firm of Micro-Tech has made a name for itself producing a large (and expensive) straight-out opener with an aluminum handle frame. On this model, a cocking bar at the base of the handle must be pulled back to reset the blade. The company also offers two sizes of a folder based on the old Black Knife design and a new double action auto-opener. "Double action" is collector jargon for an auto-opener that can be opened in the conventional manner by hand or by the push of a button.

Barrell Industries is another commercial producer of swing-out auto-opening knives of the modern coil spring variety. The current DB-1 standard model features a 3¼-inch drop point blade of S7 carbon steel, shaped aluminum handle and spring carry clip. The handle on DB-1 is one of the more comfortable designs around in the field and is available with and without a titanium coated blade, straight and 50/50 serrated edge, and with or without the spring carry clip.

There are several other auto-opener prototypes that various handgun companies are considering for addition to their law enforcement equipment lines. Whether any of these will actually go into production remains to be seen, but it does show there is considerable interest in the legal sales end of the auto-knife market.

Among custom makers, the name that most stands out is the Vallotton family — Butch, Arey and their sons Rainy and Shawn. No other custom makers have experimented with as many opening mechanisms and few can

White Wolf uses a variety of custom-made blades on their own handles and opening mechanism for this interesting line of auto-openers. All are very practical utility knives. The author has field dressed a deer with a model like the Walter Brend blade, second from the top.

match the Vallottons for functional one-hand opening cutting tools. Several commercial designs have had the assistance of the Vallottons in their concept to include the stud-opening Gerber Applegate/Fairbairn folder. The Vallottons have made everything from copies of the classic Italian stiletto and folding hunters to limited edition push-button combat knives for the Soldier of Fortune show. Most of their designs are shipped without the spring installed and will function as normal peg opening lockbacks in this form.

Other custom auto-knife makers who can be recommended include Darrel Ralph, Dewey Harris, Pat Crawford, Kit Carson, Charles Dake, Bill Wolf, Steve Hill, Bill McHenry and Bob Brothers. Be forewarned: Custom auto-openers are considered the ultimate challenge by many makers and their prices reflect this accordingly.

Micro-Tech's version of the SEAL Black Knife.

The Micro-Tech SOCOM auto-opener.

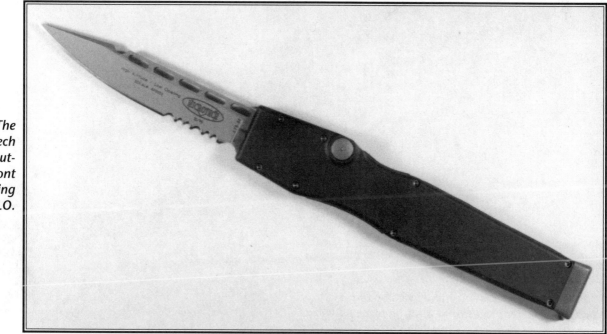

The Micro-Tech straight-out-the-front opening HALO.

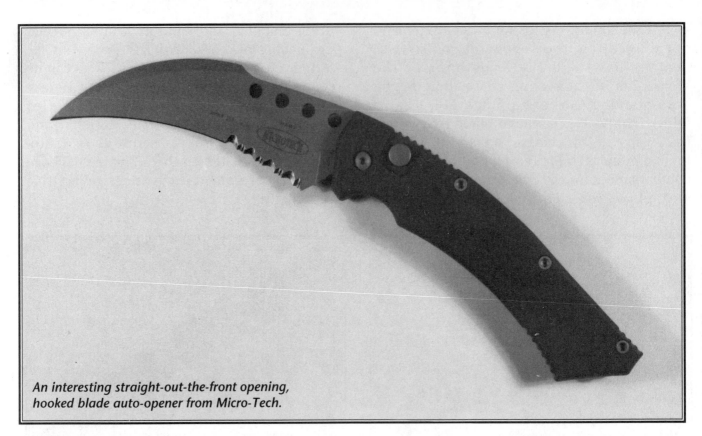

An interesting straight-out-the-front opening, hooked blade auto-opener from Micro-Tech.

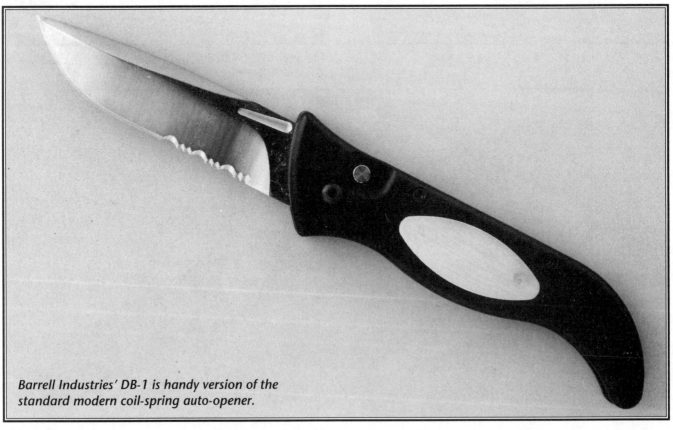

Barrell Industries' DB-1 is handy version of the standard modern coil-spring auto-opener.

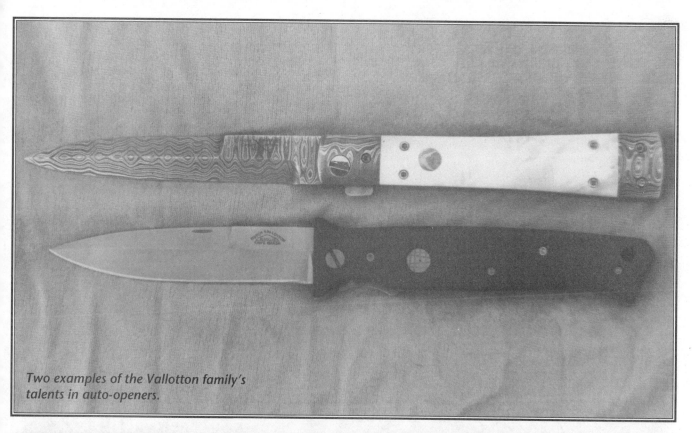

Two examples of the Vallotton family's talents in auto-openers.

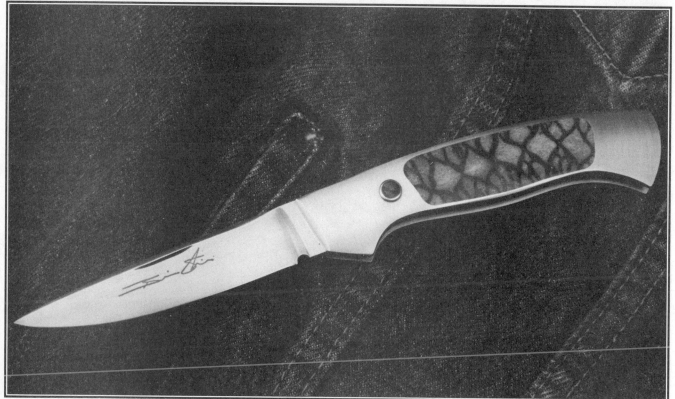

A button release auto from Brian Tighe.

Steve Hill calls this auto the Deguello.

(PHOTO BY WEYER OF TOLEDO)

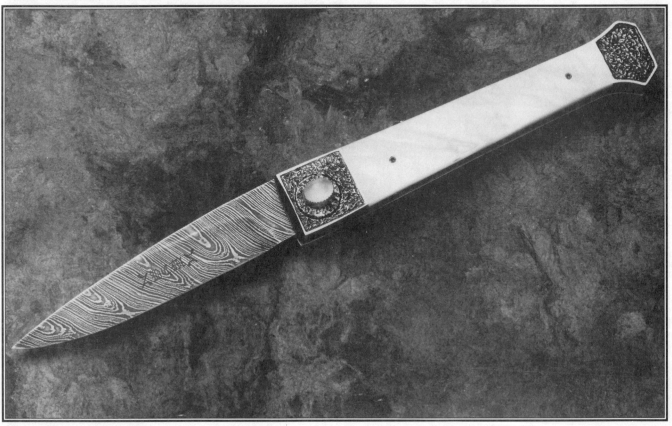

Darrel Ralph's Bat in Damascus steel and pearl.   *(PHOTO BY WEYER OF TOLEDO)*

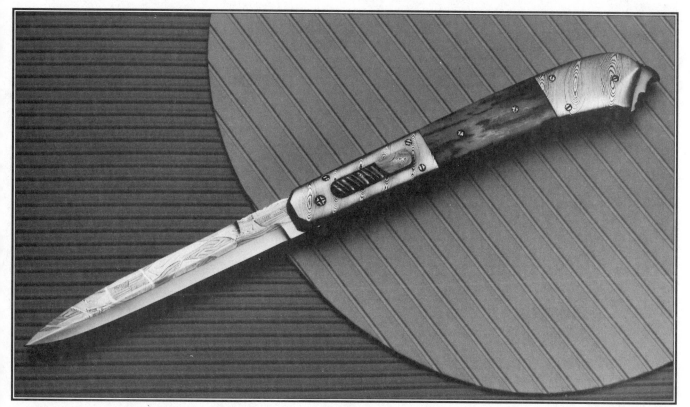

Ralph Selvidio handled this Damascus auto in fossil mammoth ivory. (PHOTO BY WEYER OF TOLEDO)

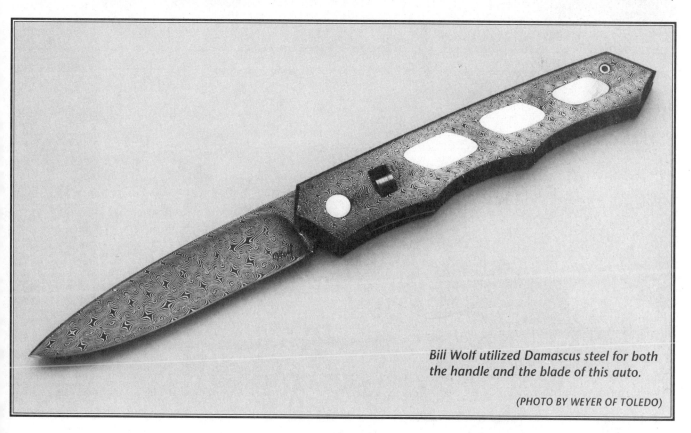

Bill Wolf utilized Damascus steel for both the handle and the blade of this auto.

(PHOTO BY WEYER OF TOLEDO)

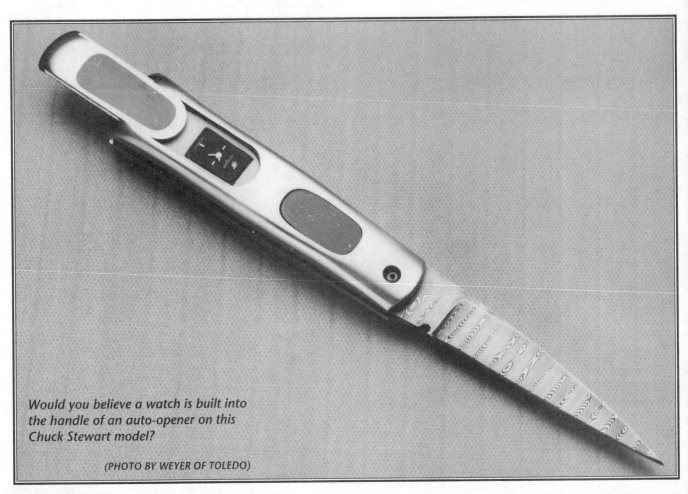

Would you believe a watch is built into the handle of an auto-opener on this Chuck Stewart model?

(PHOTO BY WEYER OF TOLEDO)

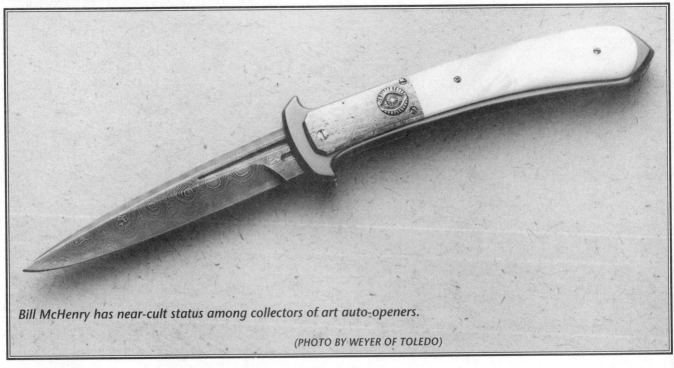

Bill McHenry has near-cult status among collectors of art auto-openers.

(PHOTO BY WEYER OF TOLEDO)

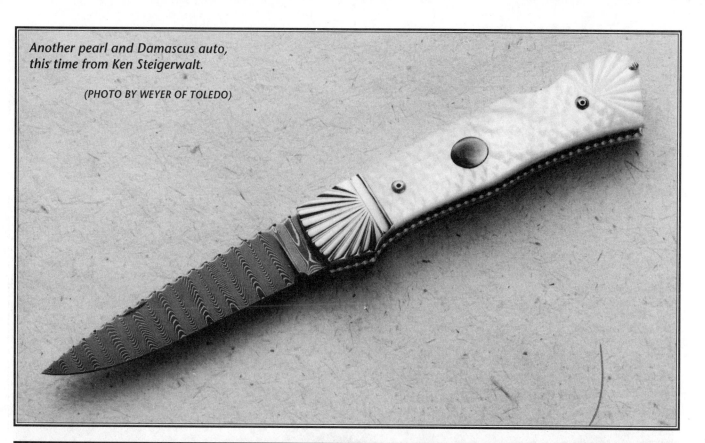

Another pearl and Damascus auto, this time from Ken Steigerwalt.

(PHOTO BY WEYER OF TOLEDO)

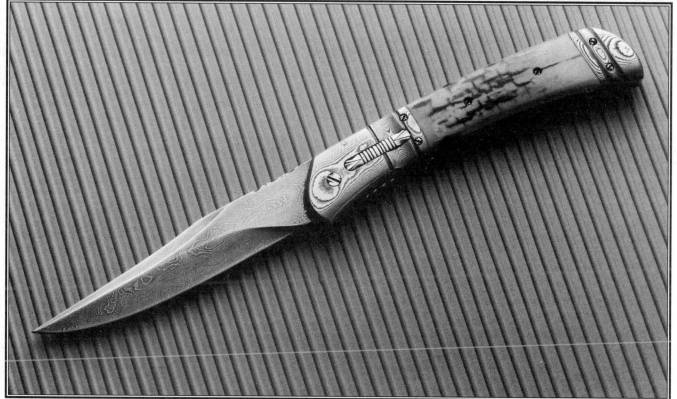

A protégé of Bill McHenry, Jason Williams also turns out a nice art auto-opener.   (PHOTO BY WEYER OF TOLEDO)

Ken Onion has a knack for combining highly functional designs with good looks in his modern auto-openers.

(PHOTO BY WEYER OF TOLEDO)

13

FOLDING KNIVES AS DEFENSIVE WEAPONS

Bare hand self-defense against an armed adversary requires years of training, constant practice and better-than-average physical conditioning. A short club or baton might be a better option but they are both difficult to carry and illegal in most areas. Enter the folding knife. With a relatively small amount of training and practice, a person armed with a knife can keep uncommitted opponents at bay, break holds, and disarm attackers. There may be no guarantee you will be able to defend yourself successfully with a folder, but submitting to someone bent on murder leaves you with few options.

Probably the most important advantage of a folding knife as a defensive weapon is that it has many legitimate uses besides self-defense. Most will find they use their knives a dozen times a day for ordinary utility tasks without anyone around them objecting. Modern folding knives tend to be light in weight and may be easily forgotten until needed. They may be purchased legally in practically any area of the world and will usually pass through Customs without incident. Outside the larger cities, a heavy-duty folder carried in a belt pouch seldom causes much legal comment.

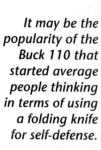

It may be the popularity of the Buck 110 that started average people thinking in terms of using a folding knife for self-defense.

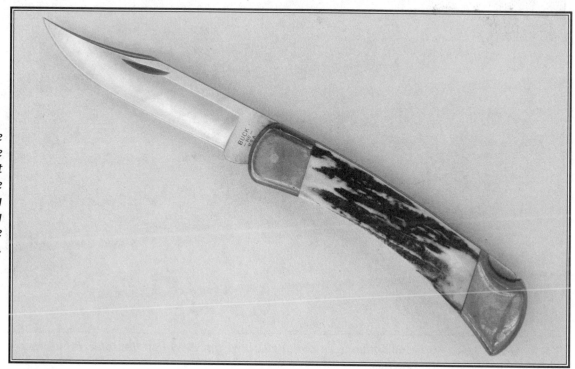

A knife might allow the user to do just enough damage to escape without taking a life, but there are both pros and cons to this theory. It is important to understand that from a legal standpoint, a knife remains a deadly weapon, the same as a handgun. In most United States jurisdictions, one is not allowed to use, or even threaten to use, any weapon against another person without a "reasonable" fear of death or serious bodily injury. The bottom line is to expect to be arrested on charges of assault and/or attempted murder if you start waving a blade around without a very good reason. If you actually use the knife, you will most likely still have to go in front of a Grand Jury, which may or may not decide to charge you with a crime — depending on the circumstances of the altercation.

Even in cases where a death is legally justified, it is still far better to wound and flee an attacker than to take his life. For many years the only knife combative training around was based on military methods. Normally, this meant using a large fixed blade with the intended goal of taking out your opponent in the most ruthless manner possible. The average folding knife with a blade under four inches in length is not a particularly good weapon for these tactics as its stopping power is something like using a .25 auto for self-defense. A chest wound from either may halt the attacker but the odds are just as good that it will not.

In recent years, martial artists have developed a new school of more practical knife combatives centered on using the folding knife. The theory now is that a knife should be used to disarm and/or disable the attacker with cuts and thrusts to his hands, arms and legs. In many cases, these tactics allow the use of a knife small enough to be carried legally in most areas. Cuts to non-vital areas will make a plea of self-defense easier to establish.

The Spyderco Delica (top) and Endura (bottom) are lightweight Zytel-handled folders that have become extremely popular with self-defense experts.

Should these defensive cuts not halt an attack, the better instructors — such as those of Northwest Safari's Defensive Clip-It Class tailored for the use of the Spyderco Delica — may also provide more lethal targets suited to the small, folding knife blades. Much of this instruction is intended to allow the defender to break away from an attacker who has already seized the victim. Other classes are offered at various seminars by instructors such as Bob Kasper, Bob Taylor, and the team of Chris Caracci and Ernest Emerson.

If there is one maker's products that can be given credit for inspiring the modern school of defensive folding knife combatives, it would have to be Spyderco's Clipits. For years, there have been a number of tricks around to open a folder lacking the Spyderco blade hole or thumb peg, but for most people they remained just that — tricks. Spyderco created a practical system for one-handed opening and, in turn, opened the door for a flood of other similar systems. Not only is the one-hand opener well suited to defensive knife use, the pocket carry-clip places the knife within easy reach of the hand in an emergency.

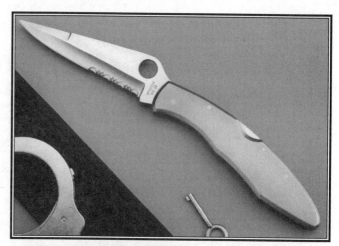

Spyderco's Police Model was one of the first modern one-hand opening knives that was practical for self-defense.

SPYDERCO

Spyderco's first and still highly popular folder suited to self-defense was the Police Model. This 4¼-inch blade one-hand opener comes with a straight, serrated or 50/50 edge, left or right hand, and stainless steel, aluminum or titanium frames. This range of options makes it one of the more versatile knives in the company's line. The Police Model is highly suitable for daily carry. Its handle is relatively flat, making it suitable to wear inside the waistband or top of the pocket positioning. The metal frame makes it extremely strong and the blade is large enough for most utility or defensive needs. Some complain the Police is too heavy for pocket carry, but the aluminum-framed versions are lighter.

A few years after the Police was introduced, Spyderco added several Zytel-handled Clipits to give knife buyers a more economical option to the metal frame folders. The first of these models were the Delica (four-inch closed) and the Endura (4¾-inch closed) in straight, serrated or 50/50 edge, but only right hand handles. These practical folders quickly gained something of a cult status with both serious knife users and those interested in self-defense cutlery.

The 50/50 edge Delica may be carried through numerous airports both in and out of the United States without any major problems. Often at many security gates, the knife is laid across the palm of a guard to check the blade length. This is a quick check used by many in law enforcement to determine blade length. However, it is not an entirely accurate method since it relies somewhat on size of the hand doing the measuring and the local blade length limit. At a hair under three inches, the Delica will pass the test in most areas.

Another advantage of the Delica and other one-hand openers of similar size is that it may be carried in the hand closed without being obvious to the casual observer. Several defensive knife trainers advocate this ready-to-go position when one finds himself

Spyderco's heavy-duty military makes an excellent all-round tool and potential weapon.

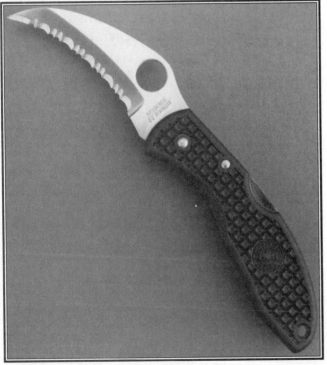

Spyderco's Merlin is popular with martial artists looking for a hooked blade folder.

in dangerous environments such as dark deserted streets, isolated parking lots, or when leaving buildings late at night.

Spyderco's new Military model may be the best defense folder yet from the company. Offered in a choice of 440V stainless or ATS-34, the Military's titanium frame, liner-lock and G-10 handle scales are made for hard use. At the same time, the wide four-inch blade knife is light to carry. Probably the only down side is that it may be too large for urban carry in some areas. For those looking for something a little more upscale, the medium and large sizes of the Spyderco Wayne Goddard are excellent knives. Both are offered in straight and serrated edges.

There is an evolving martial arts school of knife combatives based on the hooked — or hawk's bill — blade. The Spyderco Harpy, originally created for use by commercial fishermen to mend nets and cut lines, is a good example of this. Spyderco also has a more

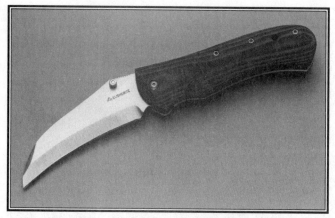

Allen Elishewitz's Parrot Beak folding defense knife.
(PHOTO BY WEYER OF TOLEDO)

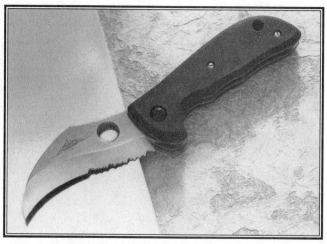

The Emerson Eagle is popular with Special Operations troops.

extremely hooked blade folder called the Civilian that is well suited to this use. Custom knifemakers such as Pat Crawford, Allen Elishewitz, Kit Carson and Ernest Emerson have all added hooked blade folders to their own lines recently. It's hard to be convinced that the hooked blade offers any real advantages in self-defense over a more conventional straight blade, although the Harpy and Civilian have proven to be excellent garden knives around the homestead.

BENCHMADE

Gaining quickly on Spyderco's popularity in this specialized field of folding cutlery is Benchmade Knives. One early design in the Benchmade's line — the Panther — remains a sleeper among suitable defensive folders. With its Zytel handle, one-hand opening peg and G-2 stainless 3¼-inch blade and spring carry-clip, it falls into the same general category as the

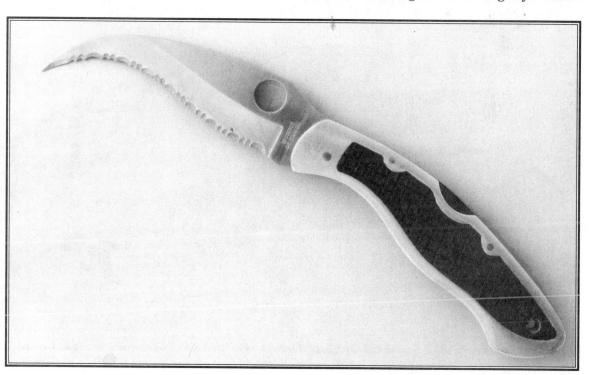

The Spyderco Civilian appears quite menacing but requires special training to be effectively used.

Benchmade's Emerson-designed CQC7 series are some of the fastest selling knives on the market today. From the top, four-inch CQC7, titanium bladed 3¼-inch and the original ATS-34 3¼-inch.

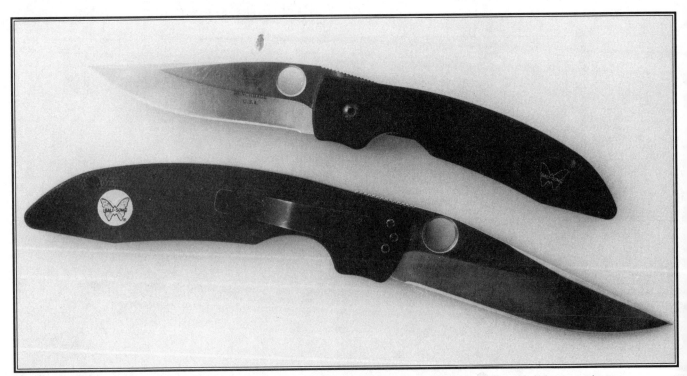

The Benchmade AFCK in both sizes is another knife that has become very popular with self-defense trainers.

Spyderco Delica. Its main advantage can't be seen without dissembling the knife, but the Zytel handles are actually reinforced with aluminum liners, giving the knife a useful increase in strength.

All of Benchmade's custom designed folders — Crawford, Boguszewski, Pardue and Emerson — are highly suited to self-defense carry. The Benchmade/Crawford Leopard is a favorite and very useful both as a tool and a potential weapon, although the knife is not made with a left hand as well as right opening peg.

For those looking for ease of penetration, it is hard to beat the pointed blade of the Benchmade/Boguszewski Spike. This aluminum-handled model is available in either 4.1 or 3.125-inch blade lengths. For those with the proper legal credentials, there is also the auto-opening version of this knife.

Benchmade's 3.9-inch blade AFCK and 3.25-inch blade Mini AFCK (Advanced Folding Combat Knife) were designed with the assistance of ex-SEAL and well-known close combat trainer Chris Caracci. Despite the moniker, the long, sweeping edge of the AFCK is an excellent everyday working tool that doesn't look particularly menacing. Caracci was particularly concerned the handle/blade angle on the AFCK would work in the reverse-grip for defensive situations, but this requires a bit of special training.

After the AFCK, probably the hottest selling models in the Benchmade defensive folder line are the Emerson 975, 970 and 970ST. All feature the one-sided grind and chisel point made popular by custom knifemaker Ernest Emerson. The original 3.375-inch blade 970 has become extremely popular with self-defense users. The larger 975 hasn't been around long enough to be compared adequately to the 970 in popularity, but indications are that it will do well.

The titanium-bladed 970ST is something of a

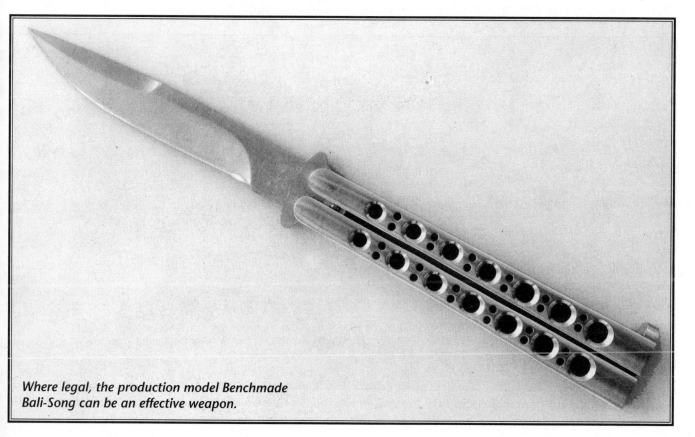

Where legal, the production model Benchmade Bali-Song can be an effective weapon.

specialty item. Benchmade claims that this tungsten carbide-coated edge is better suited to rough work — such as cutting sand impregnated rope — than for fine tasks requiring a razor-keen blade. Titanium is also rust proof, making it a good knife for divers, sailors and others who work around salt water.

Benchmade's Bali-Songs remain the best on the market, the custom versions being especially interesting. Currently, these are available in four-, five-, and six-inch blade lengths and come in a choice of 10 different blade styles. The only problem with the butterflies is that they carry a certain amount of stigma and are illegal to possess in some areas. This same problem exists for the company's fine line of auto-openers.

COLD STEEL

Cold Steel's Voyager series is another excellent choice for defensive users. The three-inch Medium Voyager is probably best for everyday urban carry but it is also available in a four-inch Large model, which has a wide blade and an excellent cutting edge geometry on the clip point. The thumb opening stud may be reversed for left hand use but the tiny screw is Loctited with something that makes this a bit difficult. For those who require point strength, there are tanto point Voyagers in medium and large sizes.

The next size up, the five-inch blade Extra Large Voyager, moves toward the strictly field knife category. Given its light weight and carry clip, it really isn't all that hard a knife to carry in a front jeans pocket. Cold Steel's new super large S-curved edge serrated six-inch blade Vaquero Grande may be pushing the envelope a bit too far.

This knife would make an outstanding defensive weapon, but with a 7¼-inch folded length, it might be time to consider carrying a fixed blade. On the plus side, the Zytel frame of the Vaquero makes the knife much lighter than it would appear.

Although the Vaquero (top) may be pushing the limit in size, any of Cold Steel's lockback folders are excellent for defensive purposes.

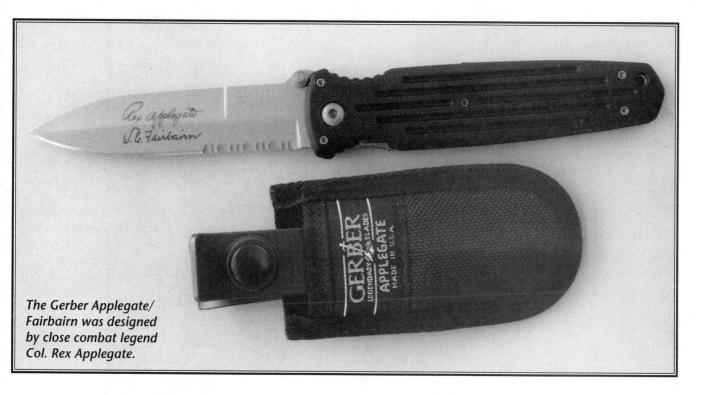

The Gerber Applegate/Fairbairn was designed by close combat legend Col. Rex Applegate.

GERBER

Gerber's new Applegate/Fairbairn Combat Folder and its Harsey/Vallotton custom counter parts are all well thought out defensive knives. The 4½-inch blade is large enough to perform some fairly heavy field chores, but at the same time may be too long for urban carry in many areas. A smaller version better

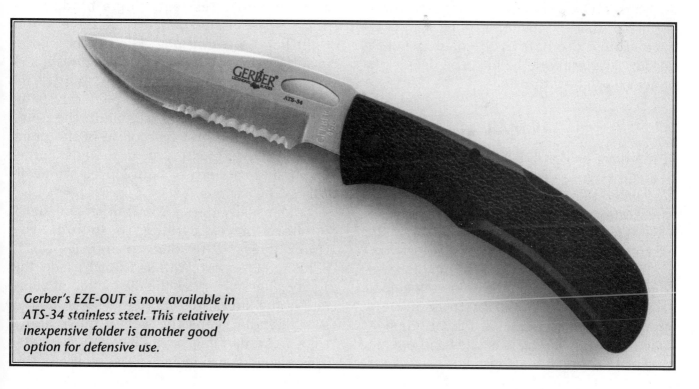

Gerber's EZE-OUT is now available in ATS-34 stainless steel. This relatively inexpensive folder is another good option for defensive use.

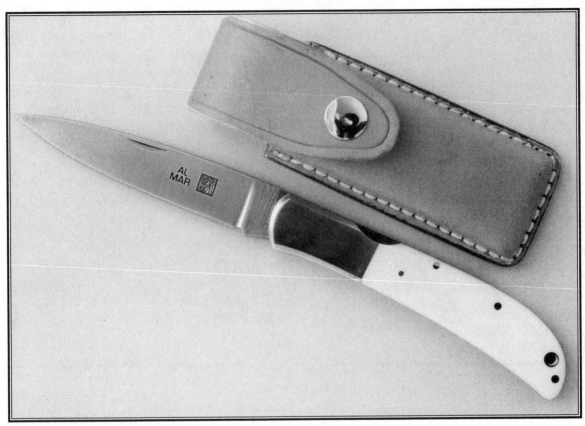

In the days before thumb studs and holes, the AMK Eagle was very popular with professionals.

suited to street use exists in a custom version and may be added to the Gerber line in the near future. One good feature on the A/F folder is the fact that the thumb opening stud is set back against the base of the blade where it doesn't interfere with the blade on deep slices or act as a stop on thrusts.

AL MAR

In the days before one-hand opening folders became vogue, the Al Mar Eagle series — designated the 1005WM — was highly popular in certain military and intelligence circles. The original version of this knife was a narrow four-inch drop point blade with a white Micarta handle. Given the simple single edge grind of the blade, the spine remained a relatively thick ³⁄₃₂ inches with good point strength. The Eagle remains a favorite among knife users, but the various one-hand opening system has made it semi-obsolete.

Several variations of the Eagle have appeared over the years with some of the more recent ones featuring a blade with dagger-like unsharpened false edge and a right hand opening peg. The peg is a good idea but the double edge style grind results in an extremely thin point area. While the newer version may look more effective, the difference won't be noticeable in the field. Breaking off the first inch or so of the point would be a serious problem, though. Three-inch blade versions of both knives are available as the Falcons.

Al Mar also offers several other one-hand openers in its catalog to include the Quicksilvers, Elite, Backup, Interceptor 1, SERE and Passport. With its 5⅞-inch blade, the Jumbo Quicksilver has the distinction of being one of the largest defensive folders around. A Zytel handle keeps the weight down and a right hand opening peg allows quick access. This a good travel knife for tossing in the suit

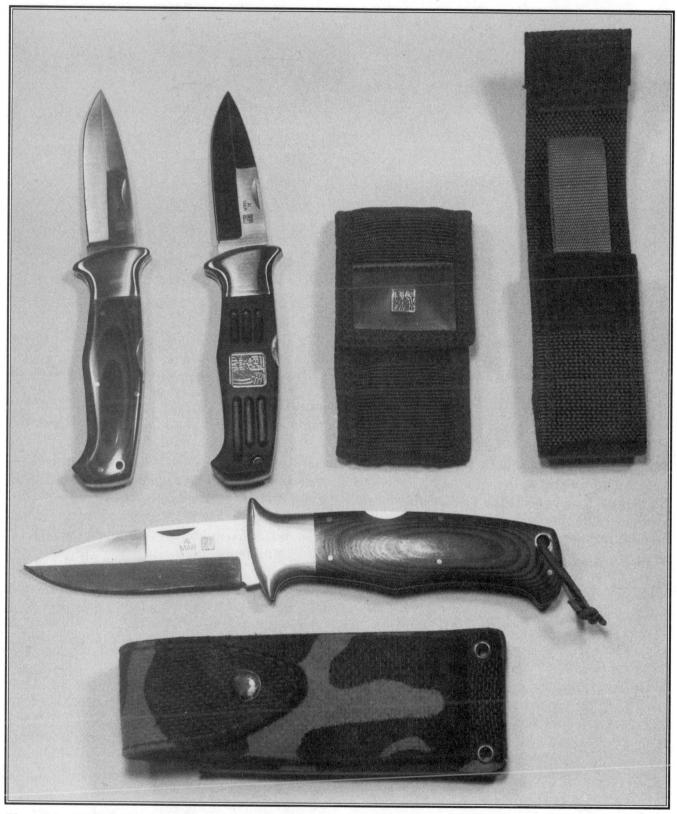

The original SERE folder (bottom) was designed as an Army survival knife. The smaller 3½-inch blade SERE II makes a good street knife.

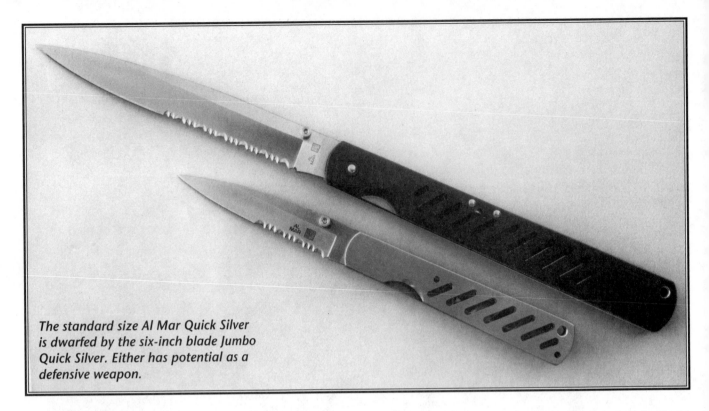

The standard size Al Mar Quick Silver is dwarfed by the six-inch blade Jumbo Quick Silver. Either has potential as a defensive weapon.

case, but don't try to carry it any place other than your checked luggage on a plane. The aluminum frame Back-Ups are meant to be more economical one-hand opening clip carry folders than some of the other knives in the AMK line. Either version's three-inch blade makes a good everyday urban carry knife.

AMK once worked with Army Special Forces to develop the SERE folding survival knife. In its original version, this 4⅜-inch bladed knife is massive. Few other folding knives can match it for pure brute strength, but it requires a belt pouch to carry comfortably and lacks a one-hand opening capability. The SERE is available in two smaller sizes: 2⅞-inch and 3⅜-inch blade lengths. Both retain the strong-as-a-bull construction of the original version.

AMK's Passport features a wide 3⅞-inch

SOG Specialty's SOGWinders are extremely sturdy one-hand opening folders well suited to defensive use.

The Air-SOG is very popular with people looking for light weight and medium size.

spear point blade and flat aluminum frame. This combination provides a very strong blade in an extremely flat, durable package. Like the Back-Ups, the SERE Passport is meant to be a lower priced option for those still wanting the famous AMK quality. The same may be said for the Interceptor 1 and its

four-inch spear point blade, aluminum frame and spring carry-clip.

SOG SPECIALTY

As with the AMK's Eagle, SOG Specialty introduced the Tomcat in the days before

The SOG Specialty also occasionally dresses up knives, such as their Stingrays, with Coco bolo and stag grips.

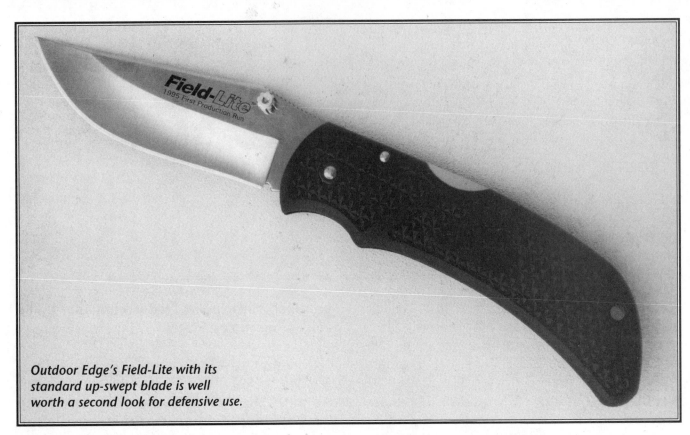

Outdoor Edge's Field-Lite with its standard up-swept blade is well worth a second look for defensive use.

Outdoor Edge's spear point Field-Lites offer good strength and light weight.

industry focus turned to one-hand opening folders. Although it loses something in the conversion, the Tomcat was intended to be a folding version of the Vietnam Special Forces Studies and Observation combat knife. This 3⅝-inch blade folder is massively built and pure hell for stout, but does take two hands to open. The more recent SogWinder 2 features the same heavy stainless frame but with a spear point blade and a right hand thumb stud opener. For those looking for something a little more suited to pocket carry, SOG offers the Zytel-handled Air-SOG and Magna Dot. The three-inch blade Air-SOG seems to have an especially strong following with law enforcement and emergency service personnel.

OUTDOOR EDGE

Outdoor Edge's 3⅝-inch clip point Field Lite was originally intended to serve as a hunter's knife, but its up-swept blade, one-hand opening peg and pocket carry clip also make it useful for self-defense. In early 1996, the company added a spear point version of the same knife to the line that is even more suited to this type of use.

PAT CRAWFORD

In the custom knife field, one of the first names that comes to mind is Pat Crawford. Pat turns out an incredible variety of folding knives suited to self-defense with most coming in multiple blade lengths. One of the first was a unique frame-lock folder that utilized a section on the back of the all-steel handle for a rocker-bar spring and notch. A projection on this bar automatically snaps into a cut-out on the blade tang when the knife is opened. To unlock, the spring is pulled back from the tang cut-out.

Crawford offers the strong, simple system on a number of different blade styles and sizes. A.G. Russell also has permission to use the system on his popular One-Hand folders. The plain, handle-less scale construction of these knives keeps them very flat and easy to carry. Some of Crawford's frame locks range

Two of Pat Crawford's ever popular tanto pointed, chisel edged, liner-lock folders.

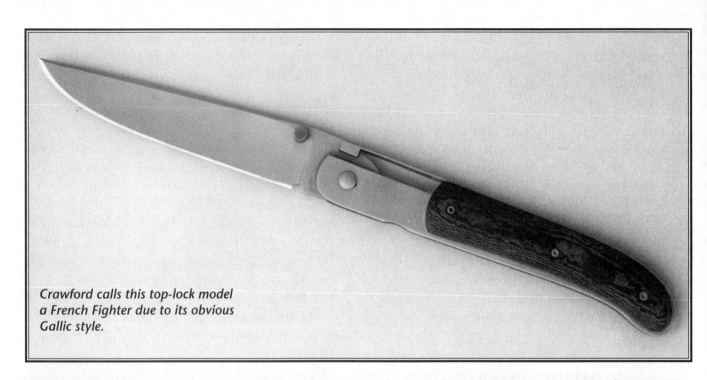

Crawford calls this top-lock model a French Fighter due to its obvious Gallic style.

Crawford's Leopard comes in a wide variety of sizes ranging from 2¾ to five inches to meet every need.

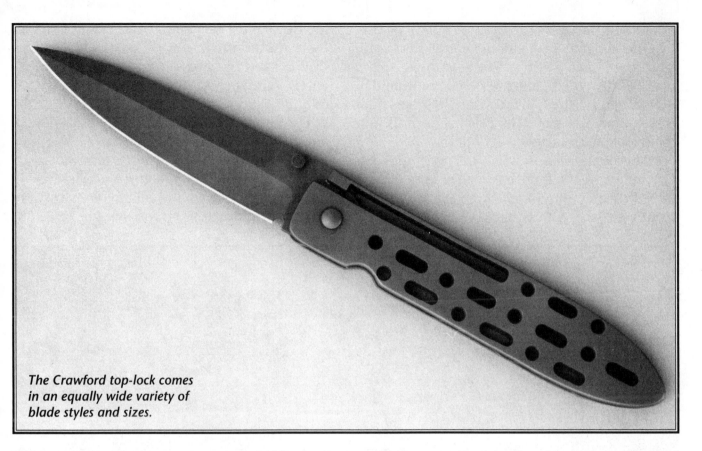

The Crawford top-lock comes in an equally wide variety of blade styles and sizes.

up to six inches in blade length, making them potentially more effective than the average pocketknife.

When the liner-lock became the "in" system for defensive folders, Pat quickly added an equally large variety of these to his line. Most are all steel or a combination of steel and titanium. As mentioned, the popular Benchmade Leopard has its origins in a custom Crawford design. Unlike Benchmade, Crawford can provide titanium frames, left hand opening and blade lengths more than four inches. One particularly interesting version is the Texas Special, which has a blade length slightly larger than five inches. This is the maximum legal blade length legal one may carry in that state.

Crawford has also been quick to add the popular one-sided grind, chisel point style of folder to his offerings. One big plus for this maker is that he can often provide a knife directly off the shelf when other popular craftsmen have waiting lists of several years.

ERNEST EMERSON

One of the hottest names in the custom defensive folder business has been Ernest Emerson. A skilled knifemaker, Ernest is also a highly qualified martial artist, which is reflected in his specialized designs. Most of the credit for the current popularity of the one-sided grind, chisel point blade can be traced back to Emerson designs. The CQC6 (Close Quarters Combat) proved to be the knife that really put the maker on the map.

Emerson said he felt too much emphasis had been put on large military fixed blade fighters that, while effective, were impractical for everyday carry. He saw a need for a compact, easy-to-carry folder that was reliable and massively stout as well. With proper training, the knife would still be capable of defending its user. The 3¼-inch blade of the CQC6 is roughly an eighth of an inch thick and features an ambidextrous top-mounted opening disk. The frame and liner-lock are titanium with rough finished Micarta handle scales and a steel spring carry clip. Both right and left hand locking mechanism are offered.

The popularity of Emerson knives may be attributed to the fact that many Navy SEALs have privately purchased the maker's folders. However, two common misconceptions about the CQC6 must be pointed out. The first is that the knife is official SEAL issue. All Emerson CQC6s used by those in the service were privately purchased. The second fallacy is that only SEALs are allowed to purchase CQC6s. While the maker has a long backorder list, all his knives are for sale to the public.

Usually, the easiest way to purchase one quickly is to find a large custom knife dealer, but be ready to pay a premium. For many, an Emerson folder is a status symbol on a par

This is Emerson's Banana, a folding fighter specially designed for both saber and reverse grip techniques.

(PHOTO BY WEYER OF TOLEDO)

The bottom Emerson knife is a special design for the Navy SEALs. The top knife is a prototype of a civilian version of the same knife. The hole opener has now been replaced with a spine mounted disk.

Both these folders are left-handed versions of standard models. Top, Allen Elishewitz; bottom, the legendary Emerson CQC6.

Emerson entered the production knife field with the Raven E1-A and E1-B. Both are made in the U.S.A. and show a lot of promise.

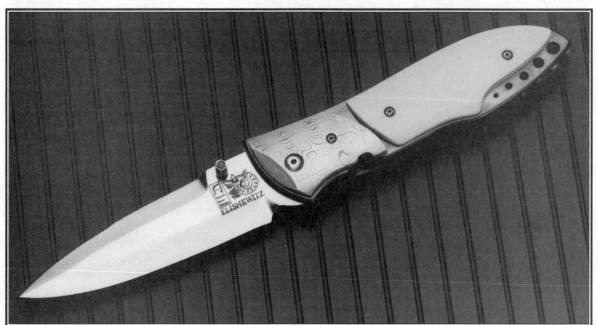

The Elishewitz Phantom will be made as a production knife by Benchmade.

(PHOTO BY WEYER OF TOLEDO)

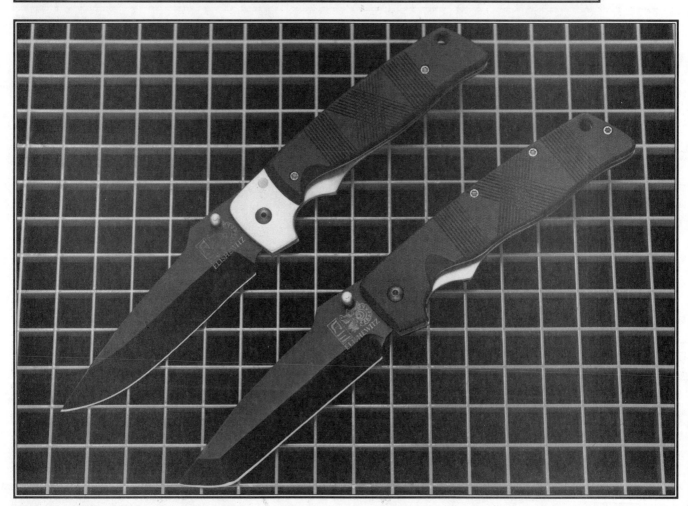

Two more typical Elishewitz tactical folders.

with a Rolex watch. Other popular Emerson models include the CQC7, chosen by Benchmade for mass production, the hawk's bill Eagle, the Banana and the SEAL issue ES1-M and ES1-C.

Having been officially purchased by the Navy, the ES1 stands to be one of the more sought-after knives. This is a 4¼-inch clip point, one-sided grind folder with a titanium liner-lock and G-10 handle scales. There are two versions of this knife: one official issue (ES1-M); the other a civilian model (ES1-C). The difference is that the official SEAL model utilizes a special trick blade opener along with the spine mounted disk. The all-round utility of both these folders would make great outdoor knives.

ALLEN ELISHEWITZ

One of the fast risers in the field of custom defensive folders is Allen Elishewitz. Like Emerson, this maker specializes in titanium framed, liner-lock folders with Micarta or G-10 handle scales, but with a choice of right or left hand side mounted opening peg. Many of Elishewitz's models also feature a one-sided blade grind and a modified chisel point. All have a distinct look that instantly identifies the maker to the experienced knife buff.

Unlike many south paw folders, Allen gave this one a left-handed (bevel on left side) one-sided blade grind. For those who have tried to make do with the right-handed grinds, it does make a difference. This knife has proved to be an excellent tool and a ready companion, but resharpening is more difficult with the one-sided grind than with a double grind.

Another Elishewitz model favored by experience users in the field is the Tung Pan Allen produced in partnership with Bud Nealy. This

The Elishewitz Tung-Pan is an ideal size for urban street carry: small enough to meet most areas' legal requirements but large enough to be useful in trained hands.

is a 3½-inch double edge grind spear point of ATS-34 stainless with a right hand peg opener, titanium liner-lock, spring carry clip and G-10 handle scales. This is a good mid-sized knife with a blade that is useful for a variety tasks and legal in most areas.

KIT CARSON

Retired Army Armor First Sergeant Kit Carson uses his 20 years of combat arms experience in his folder designs. All offer heavy-duty titanium frames, liner-locks, spring carry clips and ambidextrous peg openers. Most models are built around his Model 4 Combat folder, a straight clip point currently available in four- and three-inch blade versions. Handle options include G-10 with titanium bolsters, straight G-10 and solid titanium grips. The four-inch Model 4 is an outstanding everyday work knife for life around the ranch. For those who feel it's a little too large for urban carry, the three-inch version is about as strong a compact cutter as you will find. Unfortunately, Carson discontinued his 3½-inch versions of the Model 4, which were probably the ideal compromise for those seeking an urban self-defense folder. Kit has made a small number of auto-opening Model 4's that are ideal for those in the military or law enforcement.

BOB TERZUOLA

After having made his name producing fixed blade combat knives for Special Operations troops, Bob Terzuola switched over to producing state-of-the-art folders. Bob was perhaps the first to offer the top mounted ambidextrous disk blade opener.

Most Terzuola folders feature either titani-

Kit Carson offers his Model 4 in a variety of sizes. Here are the 4- and 3½-inch versions.

Two of Bob Terzuola's most popular models are the Century StarFighter (top) and the Advanced Technology Combat folder (ATCF) bottom.

um or G-10 handle frames with spring carry clips and ATS-34 blades. One of his more plain models with a left hand lock and carry clip is a particularly good urban carry knife. The ratio of the 3½-inch blade to a 4⁵⁄₁₆-inch titanium handle is outstanding. Folded, the knife looks much smaller than it really is. The unadorned metal handle and the plain spear point blade give it a relatively non-threatening appearance when going through airport security checks or passing through Custom inspections. It is as good for everyday utility as it is for urban defensive use.

CHRIS REEVE

The massive titanium spring liner bar of the Chris Reeve Sebenza makes this among the strongest locking mechanism used on any of the folders suitable for defensive use. Newer models of the Sebenza feature a spring carry clip and a trimmed down and round handled-frame for more comfortable use. The older model Sebenzas are of excellent design, and the thin, hollow ground edge profile on this folder is an extremely aggressive cutter. Some users claim this makes for a weak edge that will not stand up to heavy abuse, but seldom does anyone ever define what comprises "heavy abuse." No folder can truthfully be called a "sharpened pry bar" and anyone who uses a pocketknife in this manner will be disappointed in its durability. Use the Sebenza as a cutting tool and you will have no complaints.

Currently, the Sebenza comes in two sizes: 3½- and 2⁷⁄₈-inch blade lengths. The 3½-inch is recommended for normal, everyday carry but if this size is a legal liability, the 2⁷⁄₈-inch model will get the job done in trained hands.

BUTCH VALLOTTON

Although Butch Vallotton and his sons are best known for auto-opening knives, practically all of their models are available in liner-lock

The top knife is Chris Reeve's highly popular and super strong Sebenza side-lock folder. The bottom knife is a Bob Terzuola Utility folder.

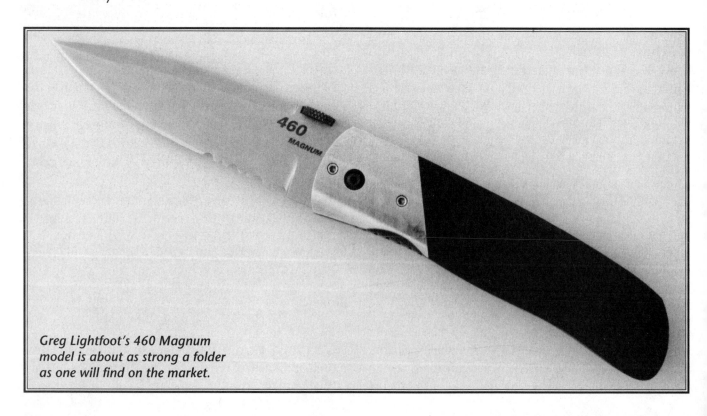

Greg Lightfoot's 460 Magnum model is about as strong a folder as one will find on the market.

versions. The Vallottons are especially good at designing defensive folders with blades larger than four inches in length without creating handles too large for comfortable use. Northwest Safari's exclusive Vallotton Entry Team is an excellent example of this with a 4¾-inch blade enclosed in a slim six-inch Micarta handle. This particular one-hand opening liner-lock is very popular with Northwest SWAT teams and military users.

In the more urban-friendly size range is the 3½-inch blade Vallotton Chameleon in both the auto-opening version and the conventional ambidextrous peg opener. Like the Applegate/Fairbairn folder designed for Gerber by Vallotton and Harsey, the Chameleon set the opening peg as far back on the blade as possible so that it doesn't interfere with actual cutting or penetration.

GREG LIGHTFOOT

A test version of a very heavy-duty folder called the 460 Magnum comes from a Canadian maker named Greg Lightfoot. Greg produces a wide variety of practical liner-lock designs. The test knife features a very heavy four-inch spear point blade with a double sided edge grind, a short section of serration at the base of the edge, and ambidextrous disk opener. The handle is titanium with G-10 scales and a spring carry clip. At six ounces, the knife is a bit on the hefty side, but the blade holds an excellent edge and this maker deserves high recommendation.

Other respected names in the field of custom folding defense knives include Phil Boguszewski, Roy Helton, Howard Viele, Jim Hammond, J.J. McGovern, Walter Brend and Darrel Ralph. A visit to any large custom knife show will turn up many more makers who have yet to make their names in the cutlery media but are hand-crafting excellent folders for various users. The best advice is to read the various cutlery magazines and attend a few shows to see

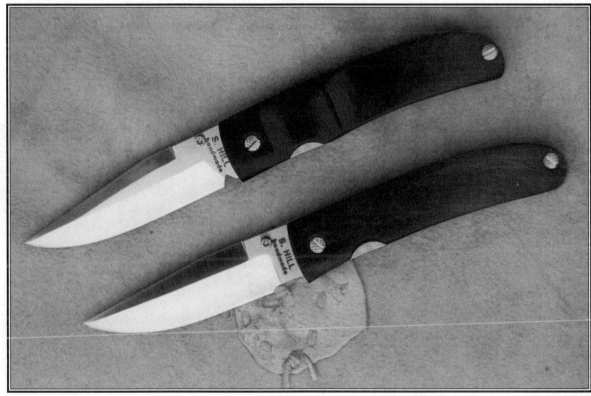

Two liner-lock folders from Steve Hill.

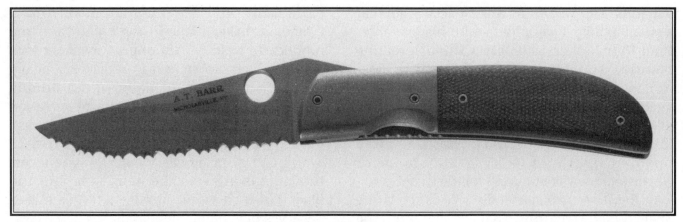

An aggressive looking one-hand opening liner-lock from A.T. Barr.   (PHOTO BY WEYER OF TOLEDO)

A classic Howard Viele urban tactical folder.   (PHOTO BY WEYER OF TOLEDO)

Bill Levengood produces this 3½-blade liner-lock.   (PHOTO BY WEYER OF TOLEDO)

Two spring carry clip, one-hand opening folders from Roy Helton, designer of the Buck Crosslock.

(PHOTO BY WEYER OF TOLEDO)

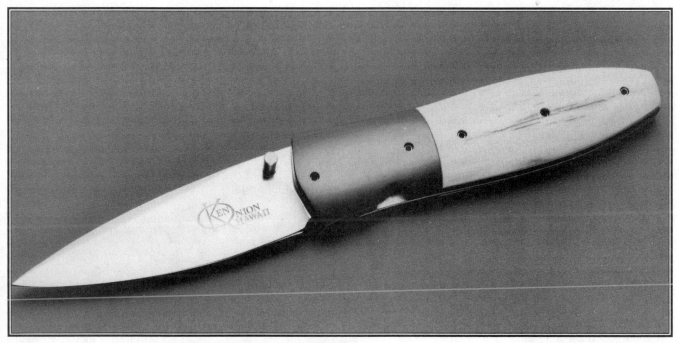

A conventional liner-lock peg opening folder from Ken Onion. *(PHOTO BY WEYER OF TOLEDO)*

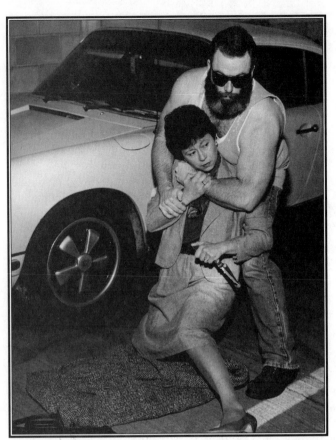

what's available.

Knife training courses come and go, so it is hard to recommend one over another. Northwest Safari's Defensive Clip-It class is probably the best known and one of the most realistic. Eric Remmen teaches his students how to break away from attackers who have taken their victims by surprise.

Gun Site has had an excellent folding knife class in the past but there has been some turnover in instructors. A letter to the training facility requesting current status is worth the effort. Other well-known instructors hold seminars in various parts of the country from time to time. Watch the cutlery publications for announcements of time and place.

One of the best true defensive knife courses available is Eric Remmen's Clip-It class. The main object is always to break free of an attacker and flee to safety.

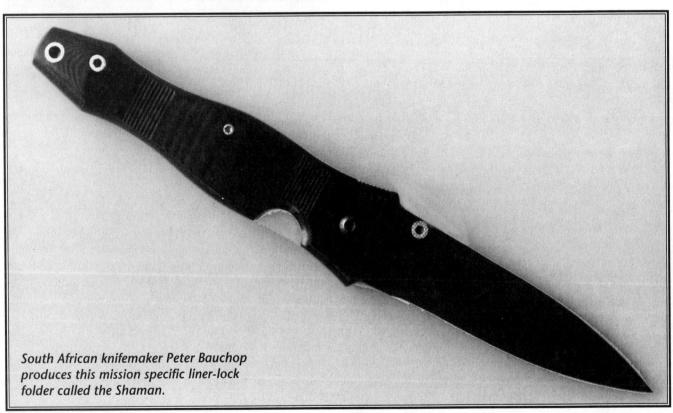

South African knifemaker Peter Bauchop produces this mission specific liner-lock folder called the Shaman.

14

CUSTOM VERSUS FACTORY FOLDING KNIVES

Between the 1890s and the start of World War II, the better brands of folding knives were handcrafted with a fit and finish that only a small number of knifemakers can match today. Given the hundreds of different patterns most companies offered, and their willingness to turn out small runs of each, many of these pocketknives came close to being "custom" items. Those few custom knifemakers that were around put most of their efforts into fixed blade hunters as there was little reason to compete with the excellent factory products.

It took World War II to really bring the custom knife market to life. While a person might be willing to get by with any old sort of knife for field dressing his annual deer, the thought that he might have to depend on a

sharp blade in close combat made a finely crafted custom knife seem like a much more reasonable purchase. Commercial knifemakers of this period were not particularly willing to make weapon pattern knives for anyone outside a government contract. Most commercial combat knives during World War II were simply plain jane versions of pre-war hunting blades. Custom makers such as Randall Knives, that had been turning out a few dozen outdoor blades a year, were now swamped with orders for combat and survival knives.

At the end of the war, the custom knife market dried up overnight. The majority of hand knife crafters turned to other means of making a living, but a few such as Ruana, Randall and John Ek hung on, turning out special blades for

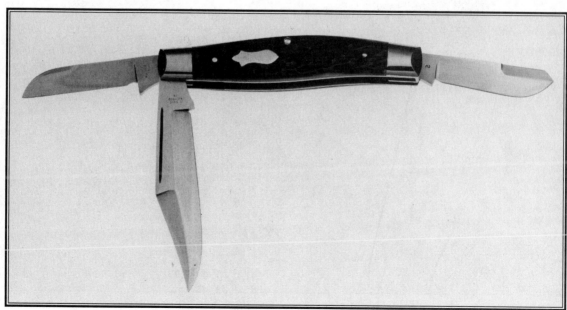

One of the few knifemakers that can equal the cutlery from the "Golden Age" is Tony Bose. This three-blade stockman would be hard to top in any period.

(PHOTO BY WEYER OF TOLEDO)

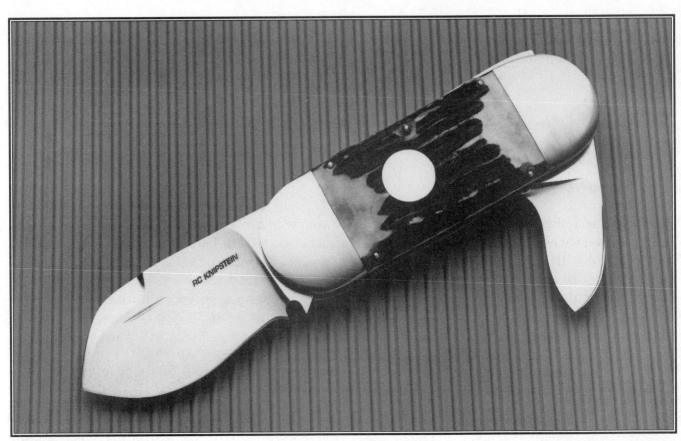

R.C. Knipstein produced this superb Sunfish pattern equal end slip-joint. (PHOTO BY WEYER OF TOLEDO)

A Steve Hill folding Bowie complete with brass backed blade. (PHOTO BY WEYER OF TOLEDO)

those who still wanted something better than what they could buy off the shelf.

The seed had been planted in the American sportsman's mind. If someone such as Randall made knives on which a soldier could stake his life in hand-to-hand combat, his hunting blades must really be something special. Slowly but surely, the market for custom-made outdoor sheath knives grew.

While factory folding knives might not have been made with the same high standards as before the war, they were still excellent tools for the money. Few custom knifemakers were willing to try challenging an old line cutlery company such as W.R. Case, to turn out a basic three-blade stockman.

The Vietnam war also created a greatly expanded demand for custom combat knives.

This time a more affluent economy allowed handmade cutlery to retain much of its forward momentum after the conflict. Custom-made hunting knives were also now perceived as far superior to the average factory fixed blade. At the same time, the Buck 110 style lockback folding hunting knife was rapidly replacing both custom and factory sheath knives on the belts of American sportsman. Not only was the Buck 110 a highly popular outdoor knife, it soon became standard equipment for all manner of tradesmen who worked with their hands. The single blade lockback was now the most common form of everyday working pocketknife.

With only one blade and a much easier mechanism to tune for fit and finish, the basic rocker-bar lockback started showing up

Three Mammoth Ivory-handled folders from Steve Fecas.

(PHOTO BY WEYER OF TOLEDO)

A basic working utility folder from Bob Terzuola. (PHOTO BY WEYER OF TOLEDO)

A 3½-inch closed trapper from Wally Watts.

in custom knife lines. As with custom sheath knives, the handmade lockback could offer the buyer better steels and a wider selection of handle materials than a factory knife. Even then, it was several years before the average custom rocker-bar lockback matched the better factory products in fit and finish.

Combat and survival sheath knives maintained their appeal but makers of both factory and custom fixed blade hunters soon found themselves in the backwater while lockback folders dominated the cutlery market. As custom folders improved, hand makers started taking the lead in developing better locking mechanisms, blade styles and knife materials. Unlike the past, factories were quick to watch and learn from the custom makers. Spyderco started the second wave of the lockback movement by introducing a practical, legal, one-hand opening folding knife. Soon both custom and factory producers were matching each other advance for advance.

The popularity of Spyderco's Clipit spawned a vast array of one-hand opening custom folders. ATS-34 became the accepted standard for a premium blade material with custom makers and soon Al Mar and Benchmade were offering it on their standard factory products. Custom makers accepted the liner-lock system as the strongest way to hold a heavy-duty folder open and many factories quickly followed up with their own spring tang block knives. G-10 appeared on Benchmade's handles and shortly thereafter, most of the custom makers of defensive folders were offering the same material on theirs.

Although it took them a few years to catch up, the workmanship and finish on the better custom single blade folders is now considerably higher than that found on the average

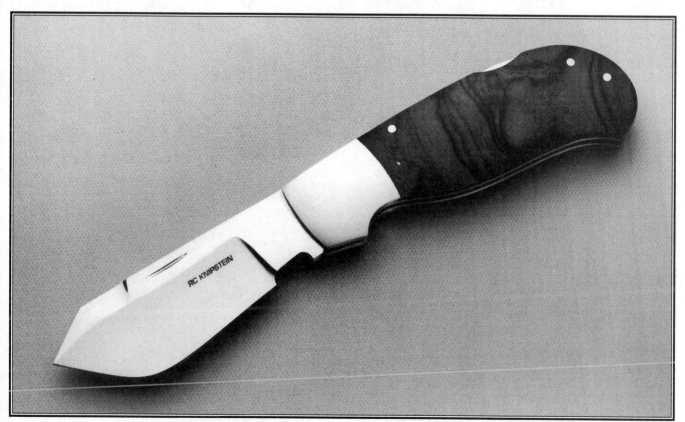

A rocker-bar lock Cotton Sampler from R.C. Knipstein.

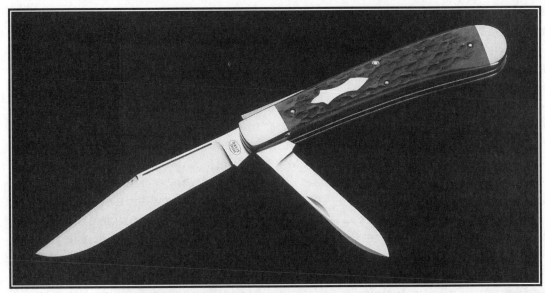

A two-blade English Jack from Terry Davis.

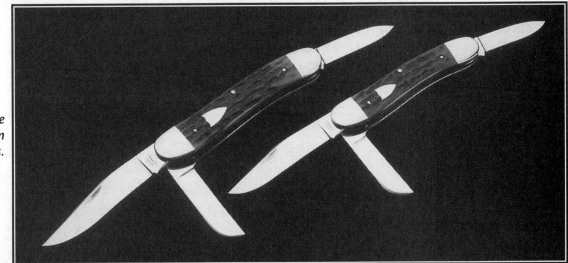

Two three-blade stockmen from Terry Davis.

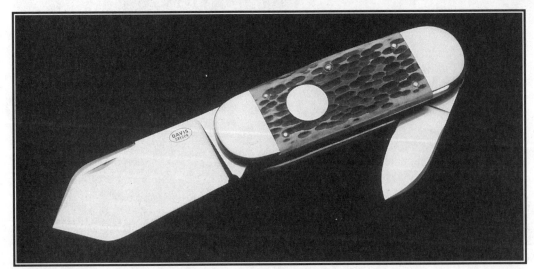

A two-blade Sunfish from Terry Davis.

factory lockback. Frankly, the workmanship on conventional factory multi-blade folders has continued to fall as most operations try to shift as much of the process as possible over to automated machines. This is not to say that the utility of any of these knives has suffered over those produced at the turn of the century. To the purist, however, "They don't make them the way they used to." Multi-blade custom folder makers comprise a small club, but a few such as Tony Bose, Eugene Shadley, Robert Enders, Terry Davis, R.C. Knipstein and Wally Watts are now producing knives that exceed the standards of the Golden Age of knife making.

Handmade cutlery is often preferred to production line products. Usually better steels are used and edge holding is superior. On stock removal blades (those ground or cut from a bar of steel), this really isn't a major concern today as most all of the better factory models use ATS-34 stainless. Of course, if you are one of those who feels stainless can't be sharpened and the only good knife is one of carbon steel, custom makers can provide you with some of the more exotic alloys such as A-2 or D-2. Practically all of the production carbon steel folders still made are produced from plain 1095 carbon or, on rare occasions, O-1 carbon.

If you feel hand forging produces superior blades, you will find yourself limited to custom models. Don't believe the claims some factory knives make; none made in the last 50 years have actually been "hand forged." A few may have been made by the drop forging process, in which the blade is blanked out in one or more dies by a powerful drop hammer, but this doesn't provide the grain structure of a hand-shaped knife.

There are also a number of factory Damascus bladed folders on the market. These are ground from bars of mass-produced pattern welded steel. While this method produces a very attractive knife, it does not necessarily provide the same edge holding

Two Texas Ticklers from R.C. Knipstein.

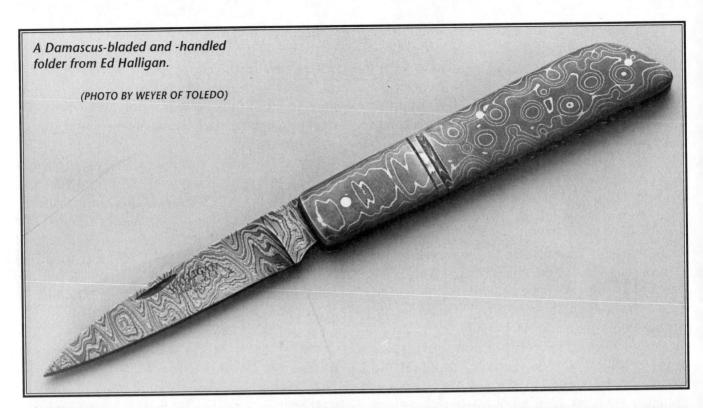

A Damascus-bladed and -handled folder from Ed Halligan.

(PHOTO BY WEYER OF TOLEDO)

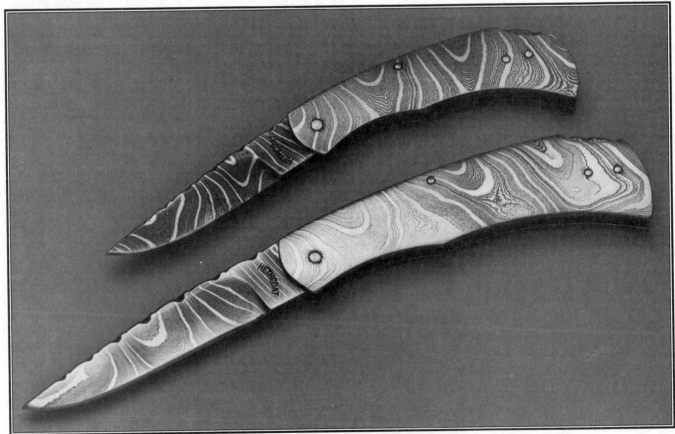

Two more Damascus-bladed and -handled folders, this time from Don Hethcoat. *(PHOTO BY WEYER OF TOLEDO)*

A primitive style friction folder from Daniel Winkler.

(PHOTO BY WEYER OF TOLEDO)

A Damascus steel folder from Jed Darby.

(PHOTO BY WEYER OF TOLEDO)

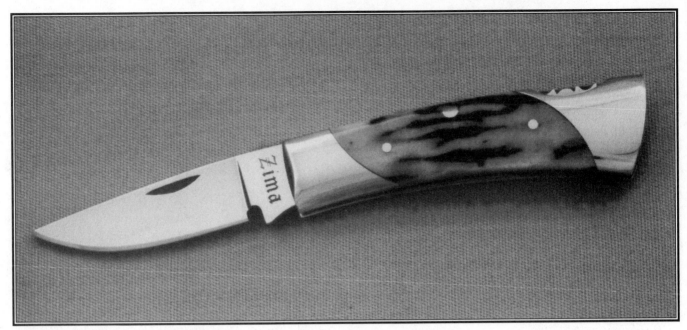

A handy little pocket size lockback from Zima Knives.

and cutting advantages of a true forged-to-shape Damascus blade.

A true custom knife allows the buyer a lot of leeway in having a one-of-a-kind folder designed to meet his specific needs. If you can't find exactly what you want by checking the cutlery catalogs, make a drawing of the knife you desire, contact a maker, and within a few months you might have the knife of your dreams.

Most commercial knife companies have drastically cut back on the number of pocket-knife models they produce. A custom folder is often the only way you can own a previously popular model that is no longer available. Custom makers can also produce the specific blade pattern and size the buyer prefers. This advantage also applies to handle materials. With a factory knife, you have to accept the blade pattern and handle material

A heavy-duty combat/survival folder from Greg Lightfoot.

the company feels is most marketable or do without. For instance, the various synthetic handle materials are cheap and easy to work with when you are making knives by the thousands, but many knife users still prefer the esthetics of natural materials such as stag horn and tropical hardwoods. A custom maker can just as easily make your knife with ironwood handles as he can with stag horn or G-10 fiberglass.

There comes a certain pride of ownership with using a first class tool and or a one-

One advantage of a custom knife is that the maker can provide whatever handle options the user requests. These folders are from Bob Dozier.

(PHOTO BY WEYER OF TOLEDO)

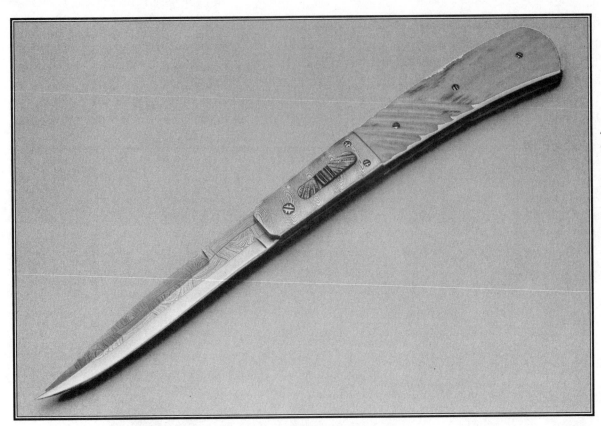

An auto-opener in Damascus and Mammoth Ivory from Ralph Selvidio.

(PHOTO BY WEYER OF TOLEDO)

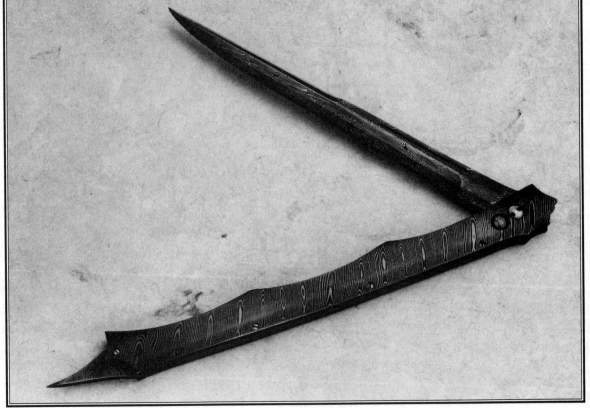

Darrel Ralph turned out this oversized auto-opener.

(PHOTO BY WEYER OF TOLEDO)

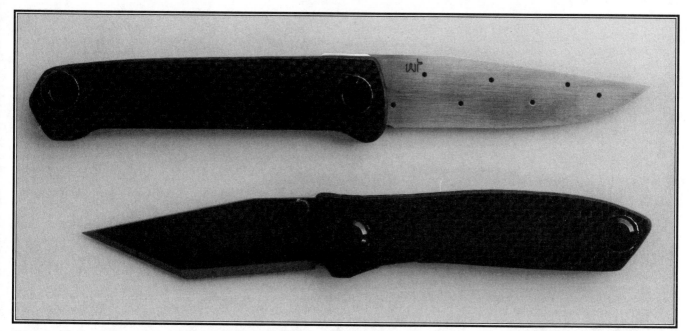

Warren Thomas is experimenting with new techniques such as these two folders with composite steel and carbon fiber blades.

of-a-kind item. Pride of ownership is either important to you or it's not, so it's hard to make a good argument for or against custom knives based on that alone. Still, it is one more reason why some choose custom over factory made folders.

Custom makers are usually the first to take advantage of improved materials and metal working techniques. Titanium frames and liner-locks, ATS-34 blades, Damascus (pattern welded) steel, Micarta handles and double action auto-openers are all examples of cutlery features that were pioneered by custom makers.

There are a number of downsides to custom folders. The first in most knife users' minds (as opposed to collectors) is price. While there are many excellent custom fixed blades available for under $100, the bottom end of custom folder prices stop around $150 (1996 prices). Any folder requires many more individual parts and considerably more time and skill to assemble than a fixed blade. Making each part by hand only complicates the process. Custom knife makers don't like

to admit it, but there are a number of good reasons for mechanizing the production of folding knife parts. More and more of the big names in custom folders are relying on expensive milling machines and contracting their blade cutting out to laser shops. While this is a controversial move with collectors, knife users should only consider whether it produces a superior tool.

Although it is seldom considered, using any knife is a destructive process. Each time it's resharpened, a little more of the blade is removed. On a relatively large fixed blade (compared to most folders) that is only used a few times a year on fishing, camping and hunting trips, this wear will not be noticeable for several decades.

If the knife is a large folder used for similar pursuits, wear will also probably not be noticeable for many years. For many people, though, folders are everyday working tools that they put on with their pants each morning. The more often a knife is resharpened, the quicker it wears out. Use a folder daily for cutting chores and you will probably

Howard Viele's unique style is instantly recognizable in these two custom folders.

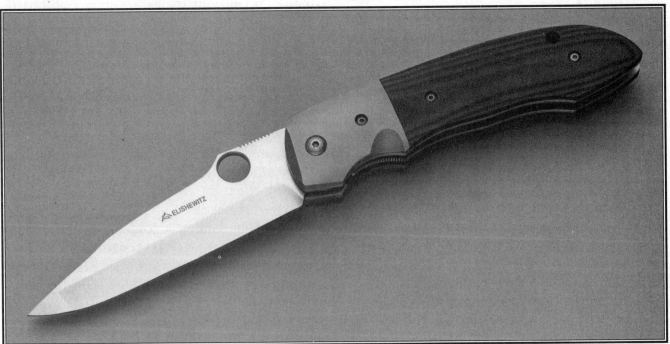

Another custom maker with a style all his own is Allen Elishewitz.

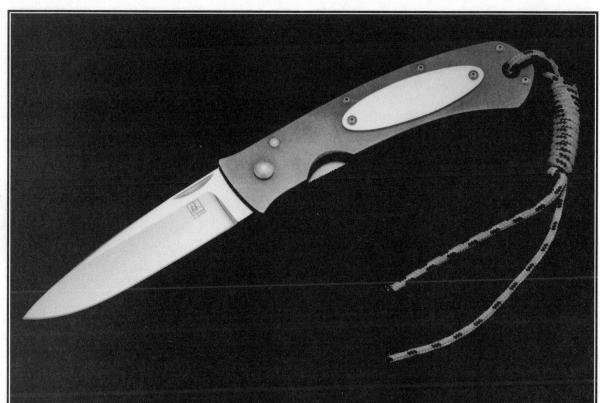

A sleek and functional folder from Bob Lum.

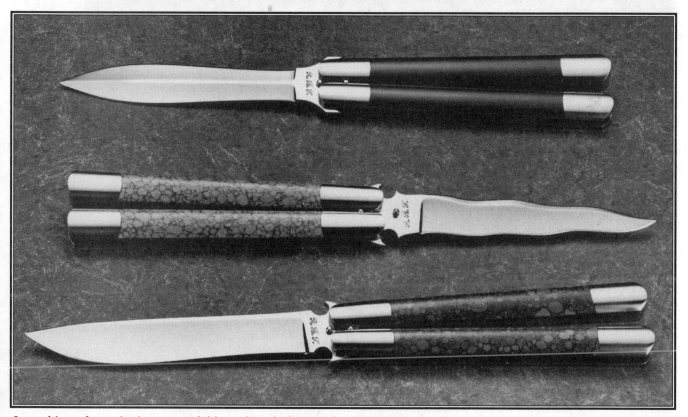

Something of a rarity in custom folders, three balisongs from Ralph Turnbull.

(PHOTO BY GARY LONG)

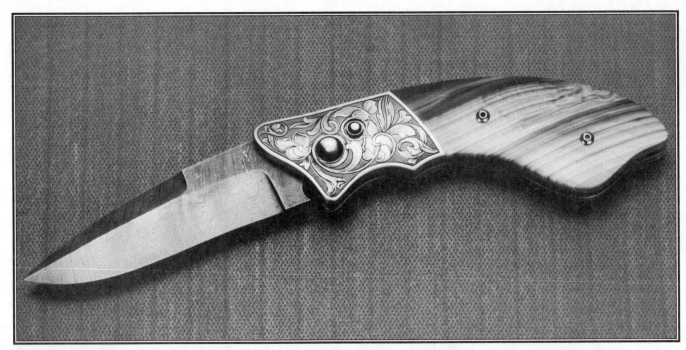

A folder handled in semi-precious stone, such as this Jot Singh Khalsa, would have to be considered strictly a collector's investment. (PHOTO BY WEYER OF TOLEDO)

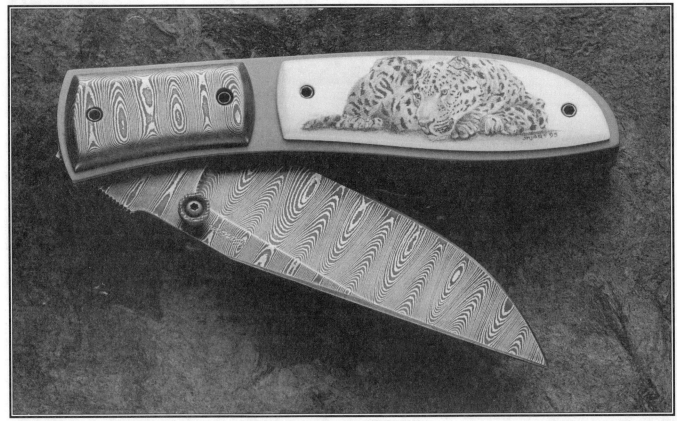

While this Kit Carson Model 4 can be a purely functional working tool, it can also be made into an object of art. (PHOTO BY WEYER OF TOLEDO)

be resharpening the blade at least every week or two. The basic construction of a folding knife gives it more moving parts to wear out and an inherently weaker design than a fixed blade. Pins and springs fatigue and break, handles crack or fall off, locks fail, and joints loosen as a part of normal wear and tear.

Anyone who has spent much time around knife shows has probably seen dozens of old pocketknives with blades sharpened down to toothpicks. A long-propagated myth in cutlery advertising is that a good knife can be handed down for generations, but in reality, using a folding knife will wear it out; hard use will accelerate that wear.

The average custom folder runs between $250 and $450. If it is used only for hunting and other recreational outdoor pursuits, the knife should last the owner many years. While this may not work out to pennies a day, it still amounts to only a few dollars a month. The same heavy-duty knife probably has a decade or so of working life when used as a serious everyday working tool.

Small working knives wear out sooner than large working knives. Most people buying a knife for everyday use will probably not feel they received their money's worth if they spend $400 on a small- to medium-sized pocketknife that only has a five-year working life. On the other hand, the 15-year lifespan of a large single-blade lockback at the same original price might seem much more reasonable, particularly if the knife was especially designed for their personal needs. Pride of ownership is still an important part of this picture. You must be a serious knife buff to even consider investing in a custom folder, so if using a handcrafted piece of pocket jewelry gives you personal satisfaction, there is no reason not to go for it.

Custom knives are often promoted as art objects that will provide their owners a good financial return on their money, but there is one consideration that should be made when comparing commercial against custom: Serious collectors only pay top dollar for knives that are in mint, unused condition. A custom sheath knife that has been cared for may hold its value, although that probably won't rise much beyond the normal inflation rate. Folding knives tend to show wear much quicker and thus lose their value rapidly. The policy for a working folder is to buy it because

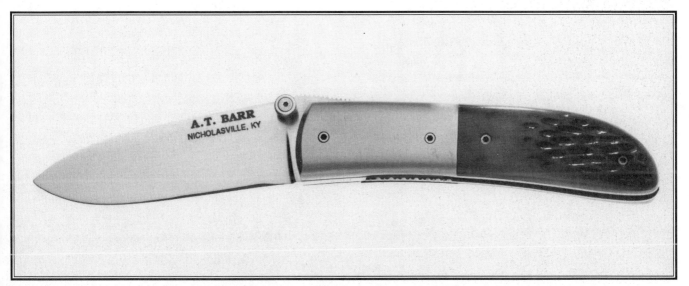

Why not carry a custom folder like this one from A.T. Barr just for the pure pleasure of it?

(PHOTO BY WEYER OF TOLEDO)

you like it as a tool, not because you expect it to dramatically increase in value.

There has been a tremendous increase in the number of custom folder makers over the last few years. This may be because a folder provides a handmade blade that the owner can justify carrying on a daily basis. What fun is the finest fixed blade hunter if you can only use it once a year? On the other hand, when it comes time to clean the mud and vines out of the rototiller or cut roots in a drain pipe ditch, it's hard to beat a good modern factory folder for performance at a reasonable price. Wear it out, lose it or break it — a factory folder may be replaced for an hour or two of the average person's wages.

15

THE COLLECTOR'S WORLD OF FOLDING KNIVES

There have been knife collectors as long as there have been knives. For most of history, it was the fixed-blade combat weapon that received all the attention. Soldiers brought back battlefield souvenirs from their travels and the wealthy decorated their homes with antique daggers and fighting knives. With the exception of those that had belonged to famous people, pocketknives were simply looked on as working tools of no more interest to a collector than hammers and saws.

In the mid-1960s, it occurred to many knife users that the overall workmanship of modern, traditional pattern folders was diminishing. Most of the attractive natural bone, stag and wood handles had already disappeared from the market. With many individuals already collecting Remington and Winchester firearms, it was only natural for some to start seeking out the discontinued pocketknives of these well known companies. The federal gun law of 1968, which made it far more difficult to collect firearms interstate, converted large numbers of gun collectors into knife collectors.

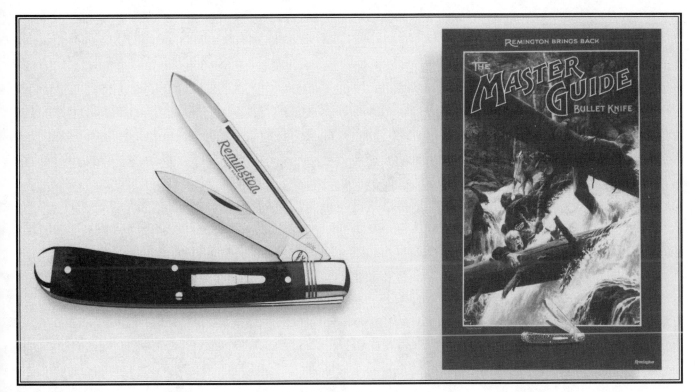

The 1995 Remington® Bullet Knife and Poster "Master Guide" T1273.

Remington's Reproduction Bullets (top, bottom) — knives made by the company during the 1920s and 30s — have been some of the more popular modern collectibles. The originals are still far more valuable.

In 1969, the late Dewey Ferguson started publishing a series of collector handbooks called the "Romance of Knife Collecting" that dealt heavily with Case folders. Not only had Case made a wide variety of extremely high quality cutlery, periodic changes in its blade stamps allowed the knives to be dated within a few years of production. Each change in blade stamping created a sub-group of collectible knives. Those collectors getting in on the ground floor quickly discovered that given that old pocketknives were often not valued any higher than new ones, many out-of-the-way hardware stores contained stocks of long discontinued models and markings. A type of "gold rush" took place during the late 1960s and early '70s to hunt out these forgotten hoards of folding cutlery, which became the core of many fine collections.

While I usually converted my finds into cash as quickly as possible, I fondly remember the thrill of the chase knife collecting provided in that period. Along with a handful of collectible Case and Schrade models, I lucked into a local hardware store that carried Queen Cutlery folders with at least six different discontinued stampings.

The elderly owner refused to sell many of the knives in his case because he didn't want to leave display slots empty. I purchased every knife he was willing to part with. I was soon to regret not persisting in obtaining the remainder as the owner died and the hardware store liquidated its stock without offering me another chance at those old Queens.

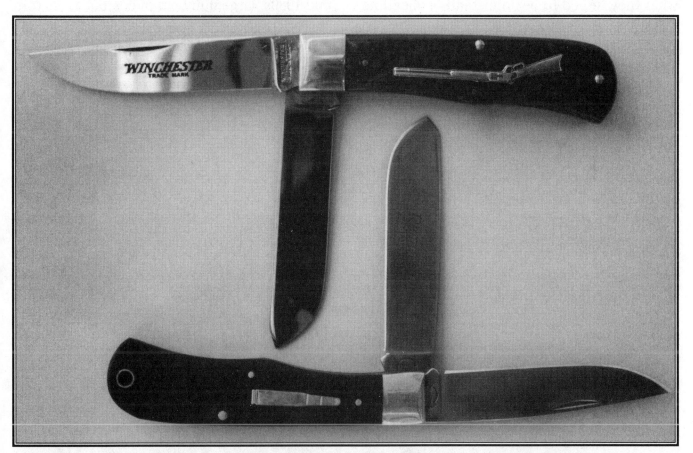

While the top knife from Blue Grass Cutlery is very well made, Winchester never made an original large trapper. The bottom knife is a Remington Bullet replica. Either knife is a good user and fun to collect, but will increase in value very slowly.

When old Case, Remington and Winchester folders started becoming more difficult to find and prices started to rise rapidly, collectors quickly turned their attention to the many other fine brands. Cattaraugus, Diamond Edge, Keen Cutter, Union Cutlery, Miller Brothers, LF&C, New York Knife, Russell, Robeson, Schatt & Moran, Western States, Queen Cutlery, OVB, Napanoch, Holly and a host of others quickly developed avid followers.

To some in the cutlery industry, this presented a problem as money was being spent by customers on knives made by companies no longer in business instead of on new products. In 1973, A.G. Russell contracted with Schrade to produce the first model of what many felt might be the solution to this situation: the commemorative knife. Here was what they hoped to be an instantly collectible knife that could be produced at relatively low cost in quantities to match whatever the market would bear. Not only were these knives easily produced, some companies were not above charging a premium for what was basically a standard model with a change in the blade etching, handle shield or color of the Delrin plastic handle. Since then, we have seen a constant flood of folding knives commemorating every possible event, object or person imaginable. Some of these have proven to be worthwhile investments for the collector and others have been miserable flops.

It took a while for the quality of custom folders to catch up with even the modern factory knives, let alone the products of the Golden Age. Once they did, around the mid-1980s, large numbers of custom collectors

Another Winchester replica from Blue Grass Cutlery, this time of a pattern made by the company during the 1920s and 30s.

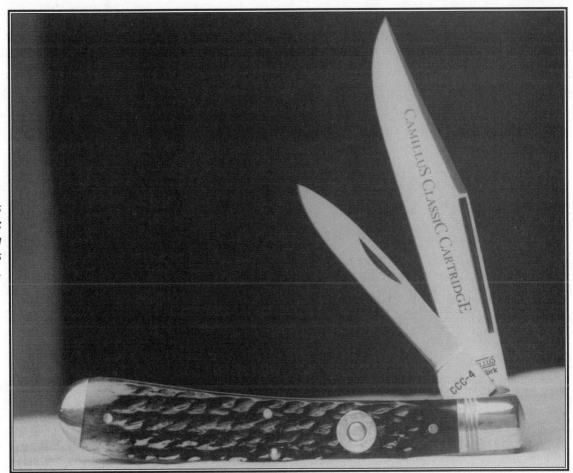

A Camillus English Jack commemorating the .257 Roberts rifle cartridge.

were converted from fixed blade buyers to handmade folder buffs. Today, this is by far the most popular field in custom knife collecting. In addition to taking considerably more skill to produce a high quality folder, many collectors have found that folders take up much less storage and transport space.

There are two extremes in knife collecting: those who collect purely for the love of cutlery; and those who see their collection strictly as an investment. Those who collect knives wholly for pleasure have few problems until they are forced to sell part or all of their prized accumulation. In many cases, they quickly find they cannot even recover their original investment. Those who collect as an investment usually make more money but have less fun than true cutlery lovers. Somewhere in the middle are also large num-

bers of collectors who buy because they love knives, but hope in the end their purchases increase in value. I have nothing against collecting for pleasure or profit, but years of experience has taught me it's much better to follow a few basic rules.

Most beginning collectors, including myself, start out with the desire to buy every knife that appeals to them. They soon accumulate a hoard of odds-and-ends models with no particular direction to their collection. It may take awhile, but they eventually discover they will never own or have room for one of everything. Usually by this point they have found a particular field that interests them, so they start trying to sell off everything that doesn't fit into that collecting specialty. While a few of their original purchases will turn out to have been wise investments, many will turn out to be

Schrade commemorated its 90th anniversary with this Trapper pattern folder.

white elephants of little interest to other collectors.

It is much better to pick one or two collecting specialties from the start, study every reference available on them and make your purchases very carefully. This specialty should be in a type of knife you personally like. Even if your investment doesn't provide the increase in value you first expected, you will still enjoy the collecting.

Collecting specialties may be particular brands (Case, Remington, Queen, etc.), special patterns (barlow, stockman, Boy Scout), handle materials (stag, pearl, yellow Delrin), mechanism (ring pull lock, liner-lock, auto-opener), custom or any other feature an individual can come up with to narrow the field. When it comes to resale potential, large knives are almost always in more demand than

small ones. Folding hunters and fighters are always considered the cream of collectible knives. That doesn't mean that an outstanding and valuable collection can't be built around, say, the standard 3⅜-inch closed barlow. Most collectors tend to have only one real specialty, but two are recommended. Having only one focus will often cause long dry spells in which the collector can't find anything to add to his collection. This, in turn, leads to boredom and some individuals quickly lose all interest in their original goal. Having two specialties will usually allow you to find something to acquire at any large show.

The next rule is to always buy the best condition you can afford. Knives are graded by collectors in a range from pristine mint to very poor. Pristine mint means the knife is in exactly the same condition as when shipped from the factory. No use of any kind, no resharpening and no rust or scratches. Very few knives made more than 50 years ago will be found in this perfect condition, so some collectors use the term "mint" for unused knives with tiny defects. Near mint is a very similar to mint but the knife may have been lightly sharpened once or twice. Excellent condition normally allows up to 10 percent blade wear, but with the springs and handles showing minor pocket wear. Very good is considered up to 25 percent blade wear with minor chips or cracks in the handle. Fair allows for 50 percent blade wear and large chips and cracks in the handle. Poor means a knife is fit only for parts to repair other folders.

Never buy any older knife (more than 30 years) below excellent condition if you consid-er it an investment. On knives less than 30 years old, never buy anything below mint. Condition is everything to collectors. The difference in value between a knife in pristine mint or excellent condition can be as much as 50 to 75 percent. Collector price guides almost always quote a mint value. Any condition below mint tends to become very subjective. You will quickly find that most so-called antique knife dealers pick up a price guide, find the mint price for any given model and then ask that amount for knives that rate no higher than very good.

The Remington model R1123 4½-inch closed two blade Bullet trapper is a good example of the "condition is everything" rule. At one time, this was one of the most popular folding knife patterns among experienced outdoorsman. Remington sold thousands of R1123's during

Buck's David Yellowhorse Trapper probably has more potential in the collector's market than most modern knives.

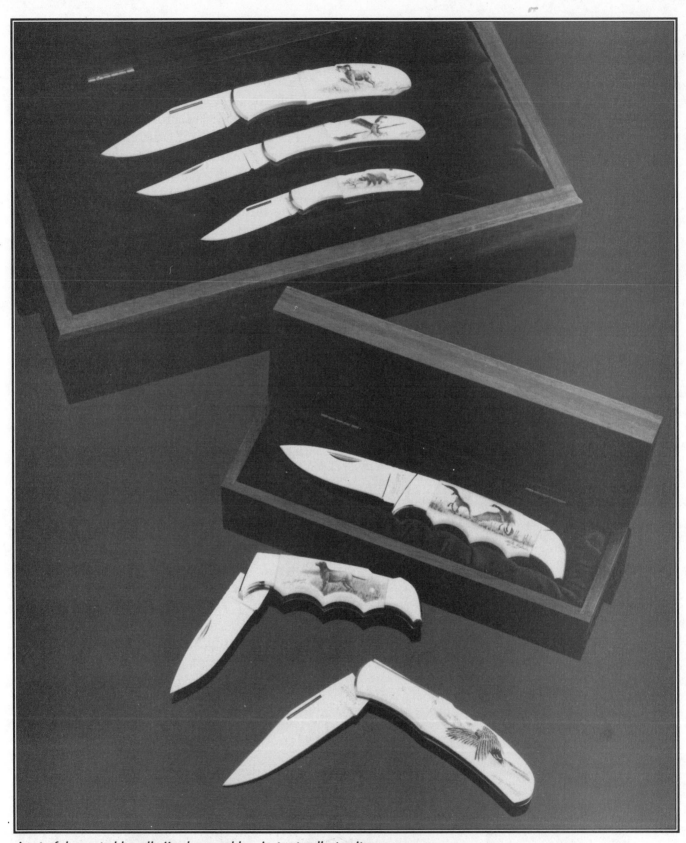

A set of decorated handle Kershaws sold as instant collector items.

its roughly 20-year production run, but the vast majority were put to long, hard use in the field. Today, this knife is one of the most sought-after folders by collectors and a mint condition specimen could be worth well over $1,000.

On the other hand, there are many hundreds of R1123's still in existence that have been used to the point where the blades are worn down to narrow splinters and the handles are cracked and broken. Attend any large show and you will see these scarred old workhorses being offered for sale at several hundred dollars each. At first this may seem like a good bargain, considering what a mint condition R1123 brings. Study this situation for a while and you will discover that many advanced collectors have poor condition Remington trappers for sale, but practically none are willing to buy one for even a fraction of what they are asking for their own. A closer look at their display cases reveals that most of the old knives for sale will rate no higher than very good condition.

Most of these experienced collector/dealers pay premium prices for excellent to mint knives to add to their own collections, and try to buy wholesale and sell retail everything else to the inexperienced. New collectors buy the good to poor condition knife, thinking they will upgrade in the future. When they try, they quickly find there is little market for their old knife at the price they paid, let alone at a profit.

However, old knives in less-than-mint condition can be fun to collect if the knife lover keeps in mind they will have little demand with experienced collectors. Never pay a premium price for a heavily-used knife no matter what the blade stamp or model. Just keep repeating to yourself, "condition is everything."

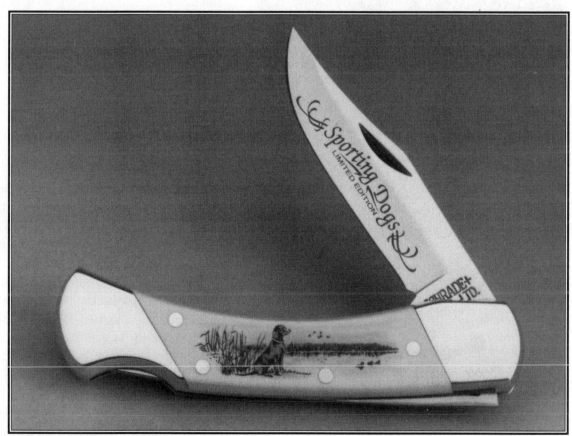

A Schrade lockback commemorating sporting dogs.

Modern commemoratives is a field best approached for fun collecting only since few ever develop much of a resale market. The best are probably replicas of old patterns produced by Blue Grass Cutlery, Parker Brother Knives, the Ka-Bar collector's club and Ontario Cutlery. Look for natural handle materials, traditional patterns, and events and/or persons that seem worthy of commemorating.

Also look for limited runs, preferably under 1,000 knives. Anything more than 5,000 knives is almost certain to never increase in value. Never buy anything but mint, in-the-box, and never pay full retail for a current model. There are too many discount knife dealers insuring commemoratives will not actually be worth "suggested retail" for the first few years after they are issued.

Spyderco brought out this pair of Worker Clip-its as a 10-year commemorative.

The next rule is to study and read any information available on knives, both in and out of your particular specialty. There are a number of price guides available for most of the more famous old brands. It's an unfortunate fact that there are many counterfeit old knives in circulation. The most common means of counterfeiting a folder is to restamp the blades of a less desirable make into something rare. Other times handles of one make are combined with blades from rare but poor condition knives. Some dealers invent non-existent rare models by changing handles and blades. In a few cases, very valuable knife models are turned out as handmade counterfeits.

Studying the old catalog reprints and modern photos of the actual knives used in price guides will help give you an instinctive feel for what a legitimate knife should look like. Also read all of the current knife periodicals. Bernard Levine's "Whut Izzit" column in *Knife World* is particularly useful but *Blade*, *Tactical Knives*, *Knives Illustrated* and the DBI Book *Knives* annuals are all valuable learning resources.

Beginning knife collectors usually have two other problems. First, they simply want everything right now. They read a guide to the field in which they are interested and immediately want every possible variation tomorrow. Old knives must be hunted. For most of us, much of the thrill in knife collecting lies in the never-ending search for that next article. Those who don't learn patience usually burn out on the hobby in short order.

The second problem is not knowing where to acquire old knives. There are a handful of full-time mail order dealers in antique and collectible knives, but expect to pay a premium for their wares as this type of business has a fairly high overhead. Over the last two decades, dozens of cutlery shows have sprung up across the country. Any of the knife publications will give you times and places.

This custom Tony Bose replica of a Remington Hunter-Trader-Trapper folder is a good instant collectible but has a price to match.

While many fine knives are offered for sale at these events, it's best to remember that you are dealing with hard core cutlery buffs behind the tables. Although you may be able to horse trade yourself into a good deal, you will seldom find a real sleeper.

Knife shows have tended to diverge into either general cutlery fairs or strictly custom showings. A few custom shows have gone one step farther and become purely art knife galleries. Along with the knife shows are the hundreds of gun shows spread throughout the country. This is often a good place to hunt old knives as long you are reasonably cautious in your dealings.

Antique shows and shops tend to be hit and miss. As a rule, they will have everything grossly overpriced, but every once in a while they slip up with a piece with which they are not familiar. I check all on a regular basis but only occasionally do I purchase. The less formal flea markets are good places to hunt old knives, although they tend to have the same hit and miss pricing as antique shows. Garage and estate sales can turn up some real gems, especially if the owners are old enough to have had some contact with the Golden Age.

While any knife in less than pristine mint condition will have a few blemishes, most new collectors start thinking about restoring and/or refinishing the knife to a better grade. As a general rule, it is best to do as little as possible to the patina on an old knife. Clean active rust off the blade with oil, but avoid any kind of abrasive coarser than 800 grit. Simichrome polish is good for cleaning light stains and dirt off the surface of blades without doing serious damage.

Handles and blades may be replaced with original parts from junk knives, but don't expect these to be overly desirable to an advanced collector. The same goes for all the buff polished and "restored to mint" knives one finds on antique cutlery lists and at shows. Dealers like to sell these to the new collector, but you won't find many in their own personal displays.

Once cleaned and very lightly oiled, your knives should be stored in a dry, low humidity location. If possible, wrap each in acid-free paper or soft cloth and then check each for signs of rust on a regular basis. Make sure all fingerprints are wiped off after showing the knives to anyone. It isn't always easy to maintain the condition of a fine old knife since rust can be extremely sneaky. Check and recheck.

To summarize:

1. *Learn to specialize.*

2. *Collect what you like.*

3. *Condition is everything.*

4. *Do as little restoring as possible.*

5. *Bigger is almost always better.*

6. *Read everything you can find on the subject.*

7. *Have patience.*

8. *Attend knife, gun, antique, flea and garage sales as often as possible.*

9. *HAVE FUN.*

16

KNIFE SHARPENING AND CARE

For many knife users, edge sharpening is a bewildering science that only a few expert craftsmen ever master. This doesn't need to be true, as once the basic techniques are understood anyone can become proficient with a conventional benchstone. If this fails, there are dozens of tools and gadgets on the market designed to make knife sharpening completely foolproof. While some of these sharpening aids are questionable in effectiveness, many work quite well.

Basically, blades are sharpened by removing small amounts of metal from one or both sides of the edge in a manner that produces a very thin contact point. To accomplish this,

the blade is rubbed against an abrasive material harder than the knife steel. Using the Mohs' scale of mineral hardness, blade steels generally fall between 5.0 and 6.5 (diamond is at the top at 10.0, but this is an arbitrary scale. The difference between 7 and 9 is much less than between 9 and 10).

Practically all abrasives consist of tiny sharp-edged fragments or crystals held together by some type of bonding agent. The Japanese have long preferred a very soft bonding agent on their sharpening stones that constantly exposes new fragment edges. The downside of this is that the stone will quickly become dished and must be lapped

Arkansas stones are a form of quartz found only in — surprise — Arkansas. While they produce a very fine finished edge, they are a little slow for heavy metal removal. This pocket stone is marketed by Remington as part of its cutlery line.

While smaller stones will work, the best sharpening tool on the market is the Norton Tri-Stone Cradle. It's shown here with the Norton Fine India stone up.

flat on a regular basis. Western stones usually comprise a much tougher bonding agent that breaks down much slower under use.

NAVACULITE

The legendary navaculite stones — Washita, Soft Arkansas, Hard Arkansas and Hard Black Arkansas — are all forms of quartz that measure 7.0 on the Mohs' scale. Although there are many other locally popular types of sharpening stones made from quartz-based rocks, the navaculite family is generally considered the finest. Navaculite stones are composed of aggregate, tiny, sharp-edged quartz crystals bonded together by still smaller crystals of the same material. The difference between Washita, Soft and Hard Arkansas is not in hardness, but in the average size of the primary crystals. The smaller the crystals, the finer the stone.

Because a hard steel blade comes very close to equaling the hardness of an Arkansas stone, these natural hones have fallen out of favor in recent years. The better grades of navaculite have mostly been mined out and the general quality of the stones being offered

for sale today is dropping. Arkansas stones still do a good job on the softer alloys as long as the amount of metal to be removed is small. Even the Washita stones are relatively fine gritted when compared to some of the man-made options.

The tiny cementing crystals holding navaculite together are also said to polish an edge as the large ones remove metal. A hard Arkansas makes an excellent finishing stone in situations where a blade needs to be surgically sharp or for fine woodworking tools. There are also man-made stones that use crushed Navaculite bonded together with a synthetic material. These seem to work about as well as the natural stones but are a bit too soft for high Rockwell steels.

ALUMINUM OXIDE

Next up the common abrasive scale is aluminum oxide in its several natural and man-made forms. Corundum was once the most common type of aluminum oxide hone, but synthetic abrasives such as Norton's Fine India and the various Japanese waterstones are far more prevalent today. At a Mohs' hardness of nine, aluminum oxide is harder enough than the hardest steel alloy to usually produce an edge in a relatively short time, assuming the grit size is correct for the job at hand. Most experienced sharpeners consider the Norton Fine India the best all-around benchstone on the market. The problem here is that Norton doesn't market the Fine India widely in the usual hardware store outlets. Try one of the woodworking tool specialty companies such as Woodcraft.

STONE OILS

Both India and Arkansas stones are normally considered oil stones, meaning the surface should be coated with a lubricant when in use to keep the abrasives from glazing over with grit and steel filings. There is a school of thought in knife sharpening that feels stone oils are unnecessary, an idea to which I don't personally subscribe. My first choice in stone oil is WD-40 or a similar light penetrating

While the author prefers WD-40 on his stones, it's not always desirable around food processing cutlery. Norton makes a special mineral oil-based stone lubricant that is safe in contact with food.

lubricant. Norton and other companies offer mineral oils that are safe for use on food processing knives that also do a good job. Kerosene is still another low-cost, lightweight oil preferred by some in the business.

While it isn't really an oil, a trick I picked up a few years ago from an Australian knife expert was to use liquid dishwashing soap as a stone coating. Not only does it do a fairly good job of sharpening a blade, rinsing the stone in water leaves it extremely clean as well.

CERAMIC

The ceramic rods and hones that have become common in the last couple of decades are also forms of aluminum oxide. Most seem to be of considerably finer grit than the Fine India and thus remove metal rather slowly on dull edges. Currently there are two common ceramic grit sizes: gray at around 800, and white at around 1200. Either will do an excellent job of finishing an edge started on an India stone or maintaining an edge that is just starting to loose its keenness.

One of the pluses of ceramic stones is that they do not require surface oil or water to function. Over a period of time, they will glaze over with steel filings so periodic cleanings with scouring powder is a good idea. Most will also go through automatic dishwashers just fine. The Japanese produce ceramic waterstones with a soft bonding agent so that the surfaces wears in a manner similar to their traditional benchstones. These tend to sharpen a bit faster than the dry American models, but do require water on the surface.

SILICON CARBIDE

Silicon carbide is probably the most common material used in inexpensive, man-made sharpening stones. This is also one of the main reasons why many people never seem to

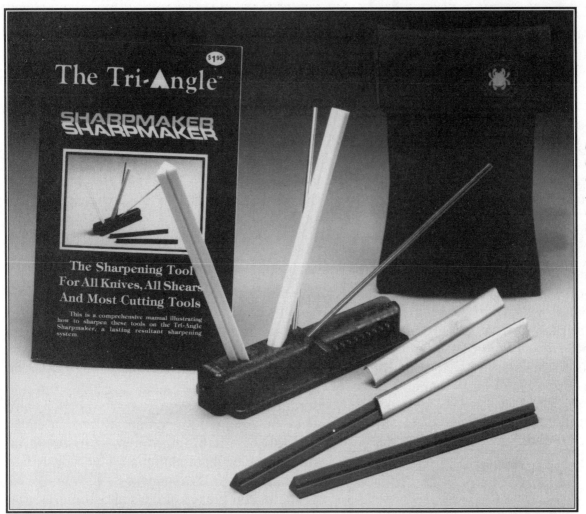

The most common form of modern ceramic sharpeners is the double rod V, such as this Sharpmaker from Spyderco. Spyderco's triangular rods have the distinction of being able to sharpen serrated edges.

Ceramics are also available in conventional benchstones in both medium and fine grits. These are from Spyderco.

The Norton Tri-Stone Cradle is shown here with the coarse grit silicon carbide stone up.

obtain a really sharp edge on their cutting tools. On the Mohs' hardness scale, silicon carbide rates slightly higher than nine.

While it is well-suited to removing large amounts of metal from hard blades, Norton Abrasives recommends it for rough sharpening only. Most silicon carbide stones are of fairly coarse grit, so there may be a manufacturing reason why a fine grit stone is not practical. Many two- and three-sided hones use silicon carbide for the coarse and medium grit stages and then finish on a Fine India, Arkansas, ceramic or diamond surface.

WATERSTONES

Japanese waterstones may be either natural stone or man-made abrasives. High quality natural stones are becoming rare and expensive because these deposits have been mined for hundreds of years. Aluminum oxide grit is the most common man-made abrasive used, but ceramic and silicon carbide are also used on some models.

Those who prefer Japanese stones feel they "cut" faster into metal than Western styles, but I personally have never found the difference

to be very noticeable. Waterstones are primarily created for sharpening wood working tools requiring a smooth polished edge.

Japanese waterstone comes in both natural (center), ceramic (left) and composite aluminum oxide (right) versions. The white stone on the Aoto (Mountain Blue Stone) in the center is called a Nagura. It is rubbed over the surface of the wet hone to create a polishing paste.

As a result, most models use a finer grit size than is common in the United States. The Japanese also use a different grit scale than the West, so don't be confused by what seem like impossibly fine hones. A 6000 grit water stone is roughly the equivalent of a 1200 grit Hard Black Arkansas or white ceramic.

Using liberal amounts of liquid on a waterstone is more important than on the average oil lubricated hone. Water has the advantage of being inexpensive, but it also tends to be more messy than oil, and carbon steel blades require thorough drying to prevent the edge from rusting.

Japanese waterstones tend to be more fragile than Western models and one should never let a saturated stone freeze. If your primary use of a folding knife is carving wood, a set of waterstones may be the best option for you, but for everyday home and field use I would stick with Western abrasives.

Diamond sharpeners from Buck Knives.

DIAMOND

The hardest of the honing surfaces is diamond. Diamond hones have made even the hardest steel alloys easy to resharpen and in the process converted many knife users to a higher grade of cutlery. As with most abrasives, diamonds are offered in a variety of grit sizes depending on the user's needs, but in a pinch applying a little extra pressure to the blade will make even the fine grits cut relatively rapidly.

Diamonds are normally bonded to a thin metal plate, which in turn can be mounted on a variety of handles. Each abrasive company has its own method for bonding diamonds and all claim theirs to be the superior system. Various custom knifemakers say that one diamond hone brand or another will wear out under heavy, use but none seem to agree which is the inferior bonding system. Some surfaces, such as those produced by EZE-LAP, do require a breaking-in period before they are at their most efficient.

A Norton three-way cradle (coarse silicon carbide, medium silicon carbide and Fine India) is a good choice for a shop hone; the diamond hones will do for any field sharpening. Most diamond hones are light to carry, durable, efficient, capable of handling the hardest blade and don't require water or oil to function. The smaller diameter diamond coated rods and butcher's steels may be used to sharpen serrated edges. Diamond rod type sharpeners are also ideal for recurved edges.

BUTCHER'S STEELS

For those wondering about the traditional butcher's steel, it's best to understand this tool normally doesn't remove metal from a blade, it simply polishes and aligns an existing edge. In its most common form, a butcher's steel is simply a rod of very hard metal with parallel groves cut along its length. Many feel

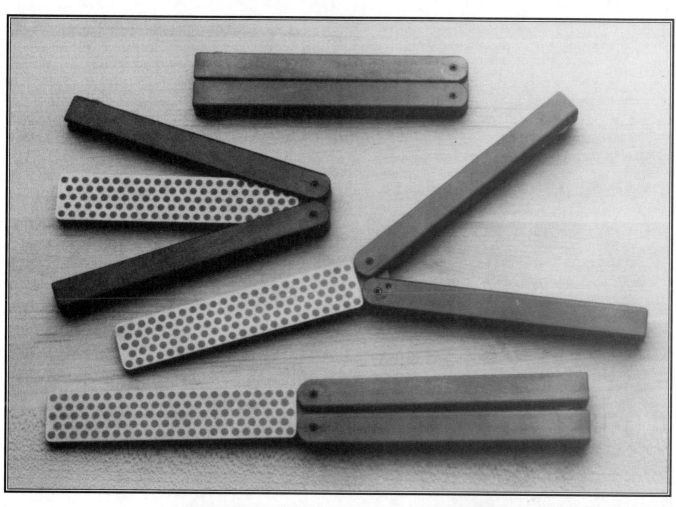

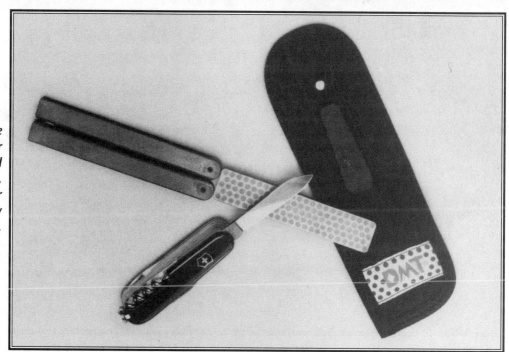

DMT pioneered the folding plastic cover on its diamond field sharpeners (top, bottom), which other companies are now starting to copy.

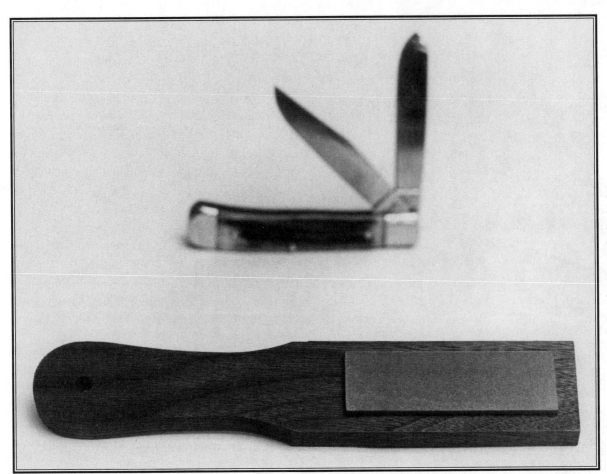

Eze-Lap mounts many of its diamond benchstones on wooden pads.

One of the author's personal favorite sharpening tools is this Eze-Lap diamond butcher's steel.

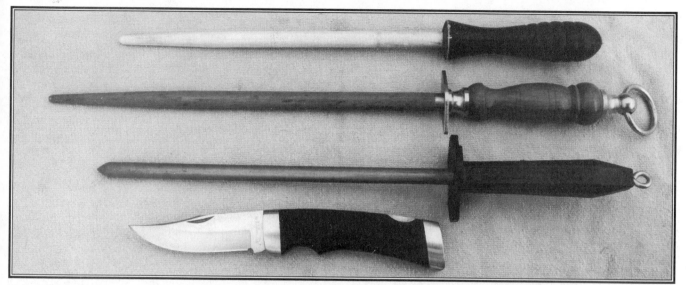

A butcher's steel, such as the F. Dick in the center, does not really remove metal from a blade, so it's not actually a sharpening tool. The ceramic rod (top) and the EZE-LAP diamond rod (bottom) both polish and remove metal from an edge. This makes them a better choice for the average knife sharpener.

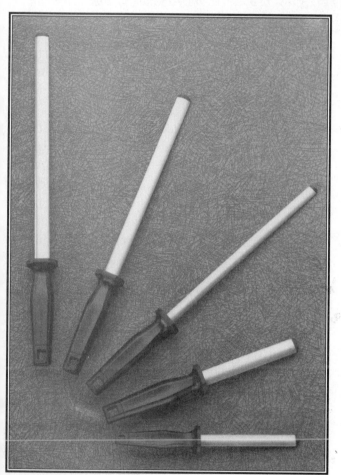

Ultimate Edge is another good source for diamond-coated sharpening rods.

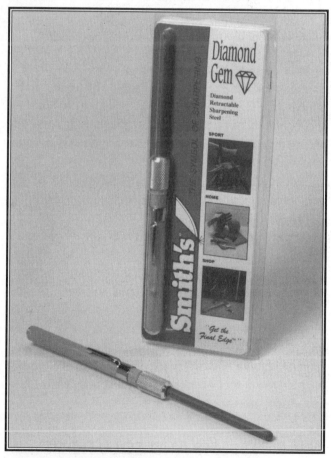

Small diamond sharpeners in their own carry case, such as this model from Smith's, are ideal for touching edges up in the field.

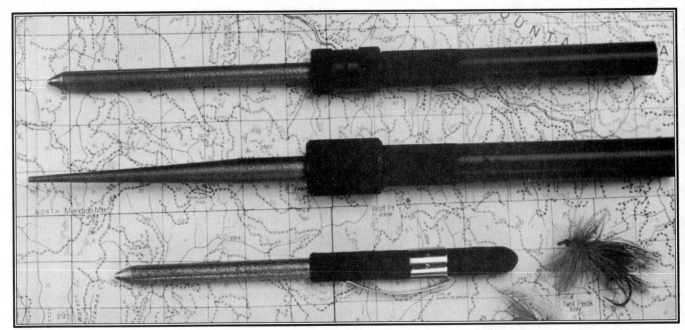

Longlast Sharpeners are tungsten carbide coated and work like a cross between a conventional butcher's steel and a diamond rod.

that a smooth polished surface on the steel works better than parallel groves. Butcher's steels can be a great way to maintain a blade in the field, but they won't help much after it's really dull. There are many butcher's steels on the market that are coated with various abrasives to increase their efficiency. How well these work depends on what abrasives are used.

No matter what type of benchstone or sharpening rod you select for home or base camp use, go for the largest model available. There is a traditional rule in knifesharpening that the hone should be two inches longer than the longest blade to be used on it. While this is a good rule, a 12-inch hone for even the smallest blade is preferable. Large hones are faster, more stable and easier to use. Field hones tend to be smaller since they are rarely used for heavy sharpening.

PROBLEMS AND SOLUTIONS

A badly abused and/or chipped blade might take as much 30 minutes to resharpen, but a knife that has simply lost its edge performing normal cutting chores shouldn't take more than two or three minutes to touch up. Most can do the job in under a minute.

The number one problem for anyone learning to use a benchstone for free-hand blade sharpening is holding the proper edge-to-stone angle. Rocking the blade up and down as the knife blade passes over the stone is probably the most frequently made error. This, in turn, means the sharpener never has the blade in contact with the stone at the same angle on subsequent passes. The blade-to-stone angle must be held constant on each separate pass. Go slowly and watch carefully as the edge sweeps across the stone. Both sides of the blade should be given the same number of strokes. This may be done by alternating sides or by counting sweeps on each side.

The proper edge-to-stone angle is a never-ending subject of discussion. Most references will state that you should hold a precise 20 or 22 degree angle. Rather than worry too much about the exact angle, simply vary the degree until you find what works on that particular blade. Flatter angles, say under 20 degrees, create very sharp but thin edges that are good for fine work and delicate cutting. On the downside, they may not be strong enough for rough work (users will have to define what they consider rough work). Steeper angles, say between 24 and 30, are for heavy cutting and chopping tools. Cutlery makers have settled on the 20 to 22 degree setting as a compromise but they tend to expect the consumer to use their folder a little harder than they really should.

Just because the cutlery maker tells you to resharpen at 20 degrees doesn't always mean his worker did at the factory, which raises the next problem. If you hold the knife at a flatter angle than the factory bevel, you will be sharpening on the shoulder of the bevel rather than the actual edge. Eventually, you will grind the blade down to your own angle, but most sharpeners declare their blade unsharpenable and give up before they reach that point. A close look at the blade should tell you if you are removing metal someplace behind the edge or on it.

Holding a steeper angle than the factory will work fairly well for awhile, but eventually the edge bevels are stubbed off into the shoulder of the blade. At this point, the blade will be both difficult to resharpen to a really keen edge and will not seem to cut very well once honed. A stubbed-off blade may be restored by laying the edge down at a relatively flat angle, say 12 to 15 degrees, and honing the steep shoulder off. Once this shoulder is removed you should go back to sharpening at a more normal angle.

Even custom knifemakers have problems sharpening the two sides of a blade at differ-

One of the first successful sharpening guides on the market was the Razor Edge.

ent angles. While it is not hard to put a good edge on a blade doing this, the knife will not hold that edge as long as a symmetrically honed edge. For me, it is the side of the blade being honed when I pulled the knife to the right across the stone that usually ends up being too steep. I have to intentionally hold the blade a little flatter than seems correct when I make each stroke.

FREE-HAND SHARPENING

To free-hand sharpen a knife, lay the blade on one end of the medium grit stone and slightly raise the edge off the surface to what looks like a 20 degree angle between the two. Now sweep the edge from heel to point across the stone as if you were trying to cut a thin slice off the surface. Running the blade edge first across the stone may not seem right, but working the blade away from the edge simply doesn't work. Turn the knife over and repeat the procedure. Don't be afraid to lean into the knife fairly hard. If the angle is right and you are not rocking the blade, you should see some definite improvement in the edge within a minute or so.

In general, most people are afraid of removing metal from the blade at this point. Thin the shoulders of the edge out and the next step will be much easier. Switch to a fine grit and raise the blade three or four degrees from the initial sharpening. Now sweep the edge across the stone very lightly on both sides a few times. The knife should now be sharp enough for most field uses but, if you truly require a razor edge, this last step may be repeated on a hard Arkansas or fine grit ceramic stone.

Some prefer to go one step farther and strop the edge across a leather belt coated with buffing compound or jeweler's rouge. When stropping a knife, stroke the blade away from the edge rather than into it, as you would on a benchstone. The reason you can now reverse the direction of the stroke is that

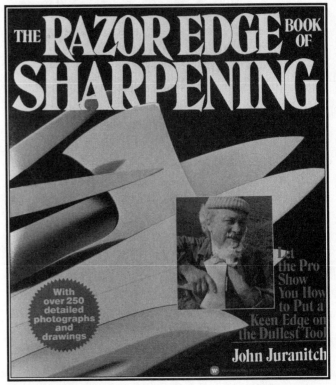

Razor Edge puts out a very educational book on knife sharpening using its system.

you are polishing off rough areas on the edge rather than trying to remove metal from the sides.

An alternative sharpening method preferred by some is to make small circular or figure eight strokes along the entire length of the blade until a burr forms on the reverse side of the edge. The burr occurs when one side of the blade is ground down to meet the bevel on the reverse side. Basically, the edge becomes so thin it bends under hand pressure into a semi-microscopic curl on the opposite side. Drawing the fingers lightly across and away from the edge will allow you to feel it. Remember, the burr should run the entire length of the edge. Once it's established on one side, turn the blade over and repeat the procedure. After this has been accomplished, both sides of the edge may again be either lightly drawn across a fine hone or stropped on leather to remove the burr and finish the edge.

The Japanese have long used this burr system on their one-sided edge bevel knives. In the last few years, similar one-sided grind blades have become popular with both custom and factory folders. Here a burr is ground onto the flat side by working the beveled side either in circles or sweeps across the hone. When the burr can be felt the entire length of the blade, the edge is finished by a few light low angle strokes on a fine hone or strop across the flat side. Many knife sharpeners insist this is far easier than sharpening a Western-style double bevel edge, but I have found it takes just about as much practice to do right.

SHARPENING GUIDES

Because many people do have problems holding the same angle from sweep to sweep across a benchstone or sharpening rod, there have been many tools developed to do the job for them. One of the oldest is probably the Razor Edge Sharpening Guide in which an angle guide is clamped to the back of the blade to hold the edge at a precise position as it is drawn across the hone. This works best when the factory bevel is identical to the pre-set angle on the guide, but if it isn't, the knife will eventually be reshaped to the correct angle. Other companies have used the same principle to create clamp-on angle guides of one type or another and most work fairly well.

More sophisticated versions of the clamp-on angle guide are the various tools put out by Lansky, Gatco, DMT, Frost and a few others. With these tools, the blade is placed in a clamp and the series of hones mounted on steel rods are pushed across the blade. The opposite end of the hone rod is run through a hole on the blade clamp that determines the sharpening angle. As long as the rod stays in the hole, the angle remains fixed on each pass. Most of these systems enable the user to

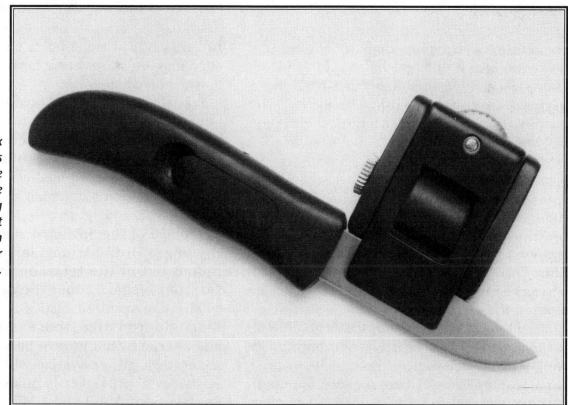

Benchmark Knives offers the Roledge Knife Sharpening Guide that works much like Razor Edge's.

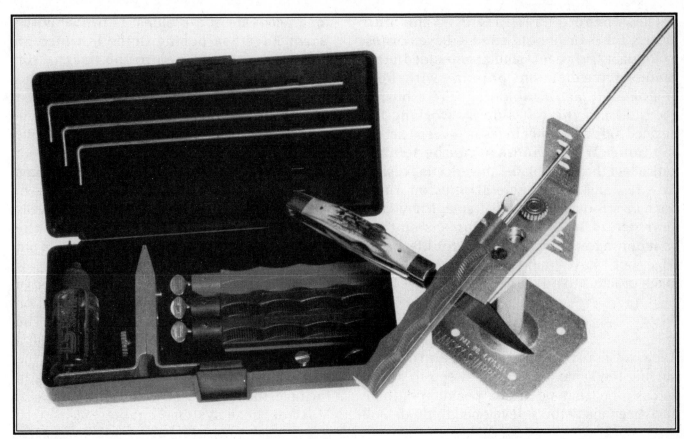

The Lansky Sharpener takes all the guesswork out of holding the proper angle, but at the price of added set-up time.

change the sharpening angle by sliding the hone rod into a different holes on the blade clamp. This type of sharpener works well, as long as you are willing to spend the time setting up and positioning the clamp on your knife.

V RODS

Another common sharpening system is one based on two abrasive rods mounted in a V on a wood or plastic base, in which the blade is simply pushed straight down and pulled across the rods to maintain the proper angle. Most of the early versions of the V sharpener utilized fine grit ceramic rods that worked well for touching up semi-sharp blades, but not so well for really dull edges.

Later, medium grit ceramic and diamond rods were added to some models. A few offer two sets of rod angle holes so that the knife edge may be started at a fairly flat bevel and finished on a higher one.

Probably the most famous and best of the ceramic V sharpeners is the Tri-Angle SharpMaker from Spyderco. Rather than round rods, this system utilizes triangular ceramic rods in both medium and fine grits. Diamond sleeves are also available as an option for really tough jobs. The real advantage of the Spyderco sharpener is that the edges of the triangular rods will ride in and out of the teeth on most common serrated blades. About the only other way to sharpen serrated blades is to find a slim diamond rod like those made by DMT and sharpen each groove between the teeth separately. Either system will work but the Spyderco SharpMaker is quicker and easier. Some people feel the DMT diamond rod leaves the ends of the teeth with sharper points. Spyderco's rods also have a groove for sharpening fish hooks and may be set at a flat angle for scissors.

CHEF'SCHOICE 110

Conventional wisdom has long been not to go anywhere near the shop power grinder with knives. These high-speed silicon carbide wheels will overheat and remove the temper from a blade in seconds. Woodworking tool supply companies often offer slow turning, water-cooled electric grinders that will safely sharpen knives, but these tend to be more expensive than the average folding knife user is willing to invest. The electric sharpeners built into some kitchen can openers are about as bad as the shop bench grinder. There is one reasonably priced electric sharpener that can be recommended, the Chef'sChoice Model 110. This system utilizes three grits of spinning diamond wheels set at different angles. Pre-set magnets hold the blade at the proper angle to the hones so all the user has to do is pull the knife blade through the slots provided.

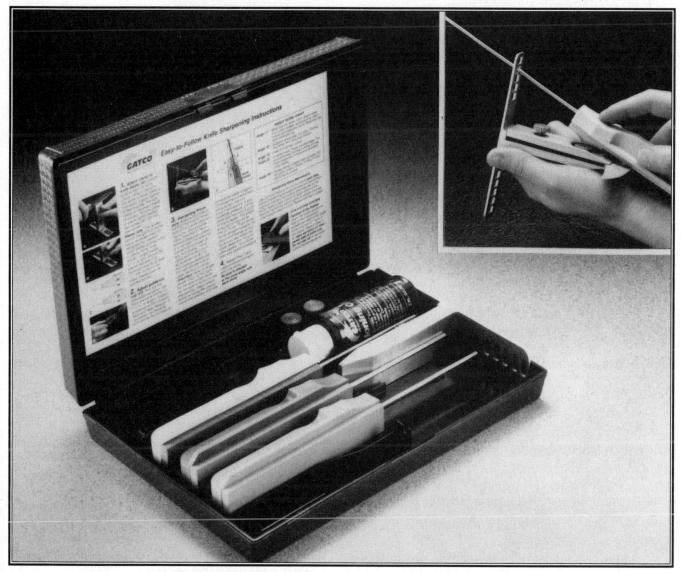

GATCO's sharpener works much the same as Lansky's, but each has its own range of special options.

The Crock Stick was the first of the V rod sharpeners on the market. The inventor didn't patent his invention and soon everyone had a copy.

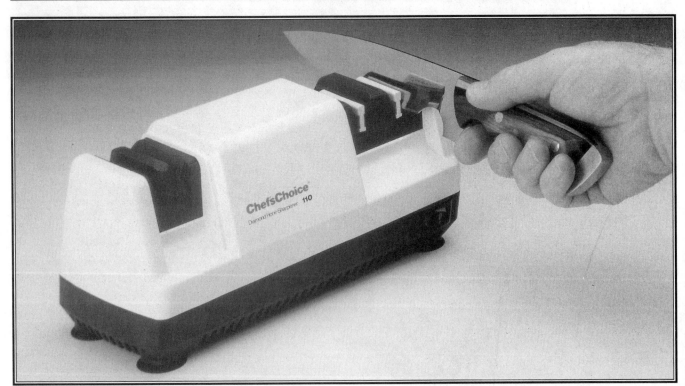

One highly recommended electric sharpener for honing folding knives is the Chef'sChoice 110.

As the name indicates, this sharpener was made primarily for honing kitchen cutlery. While the Model 110 doesn't work all that well with thick blades, such as those found on most sheath knives, folding knives are usually about the same thickness as heavier cooking blades, and the 110 will work well enough for these blades. The diamond wheels make quick work of hard metal and can produce a razor sharp blade.

Anyone can learn to use a benchstone or sharpening rod if they simply take their time and watch what they are doing. Also, sharpening equipment needs to be equal in quality to their knives.

The basic knife sharpening battery should include the following:

IN THE SHOP

- *A 12-inch Norton combination India or three-stone cradle of the same dimensions. A suitable alternative to the Norton is a 12-inch DMT or EZE-LAP diamond benchstone.*

- *WD-40 for lubrication on the Norton stones.*

- *Either a large Hard Arkansas or fine ceramic benchstone for finishing edges.*

- *A Spyderco Tri-Angle Sharpmaker for serrated edges.*

- *A 10-inch diamond coated butcher's steel for quick touch-ups.*

IN THE FIELD

- *One or more of the small diamond hones offered by DMT, EZE-LAP or Ultimate Edge.*

- *If a really fine edge is required, the blade may then be finished on a small ceramic pocket hone such as those offered by Spyderco.*

- *Keep a 10-inch EZE-LAP diamond rod behind for serious sharpening jobs.*

CARE

At one time the primary worry associated with folding knife care was rust. Now that the majority of pocketknives seem to have blades of one type of stainless or another, rust is considerably less of a problem. This is not to say that even stainless won't corrode under the right conditions.

Both carbon and stainless steels may be protected from corrosion by a light coat of oil, but this protection is nullified by almost any type of use. The best policy is to clean and dry your knife after cutting wet, acid (fruit) or salty items. If you use your knife in or around salt water, it is a good idea to give it a thorough rinsing with fresh water at the end of the day.

Carbon steel knives will still stain no matter how much effort you make, but with care this will be a light gray patina rather than a rusty pitting. Sooner or later, both types of steel will pick up a few rust spots and stains you will want to remove. A preferred method is using a Scotch Brite pad and scouring powder. Simichrome polish is also useful for removing light stains and corrosion, and for cleaning and shining bolsters.

The pivot points and locking mechanism on a modern folder are probably more critical than the blade when it comes to care. All it takes is a grain of sand in the lock to prevent a blade from being safely secured in the open position. An un-oiled blade tang rubbing on a dry, gritty bolster will also eventually wear and loosen. The best policy is to flush out all debris and grit around blade tang and lock on a regular basis. A few drops of oil will help keep things working smoothly on any knife where the blade tang pivots against metal liners or bolsters. Small amounts of oil are beneficial to most of the thermoplastic handled folders, but there are a few where this isn't recommended. When in doubt, read the manufacturer's instructions.

Handles are usually even more maintenance-free than blades. About all you can do is avoid using them as pounding tools and don't drop them on hard surfaces. Natural materials such as bone, stag, and wood should not be allowed to soak in water for prolonged periods. Most of the modern plastics will stand up to gasoline and other common solvents, but there are a few that may be damaged by them. As long as a knife is kept clean and sharp, about all that can go wrong is that the owner abuses or loses it.

About the only products needed to maintain a working knife are a Scotch Brite pad and a can of Break Free lubricant. The Scotch Brite pad will clean most light rust and stains from a blade. Break Free oils joints and protects carbon steel blades from rust.

17

FOLDING KNIVES AND SURVIVAL

I don't think I could write a book on cutlery without saying something on the subject of survival knives.

Survival means different things to different people. Some automatically think of military or street situations in which the problem involves close combat with an adversary seeking to take your life. Others consider a general breakdown of society, in which they will be on their own for long periods of time. My personal definition of a survival knife is a knife for solving short-term emergencies, most of which will be environmental or mechanical. In modern society this will seldom be a serious problem close to civilization, so I also assume the situation will take place in the distant backcountry, a Third World country or, possibly, at sea.

While it probably had its beginnings in Vietnam, it was the "Rambo" series of movies that put the phrase "survival knife" into mainstream language. Suddenly, no one could expect to live through the smallest emergency without a huge, indestructible, sawback, hollowhandle wonder knife.

This is about as close to a bear as anyone should want to be with a knife. The knife shown is the now-discontinued Gerber Parabellum; the location Iwas deep in the Canadian wilderness.

The Gerber Parabellum has the unique feature of a sheath that allows the knife to be carried opened or closed. The author is making one of many portages on this particular Canadian canoe trail.

I've always had two questions for those promoting these knives. One: What is it that you do for a living that might suddenly cast you adrift in the wilderness with only a knife to pull you through? Do you really think there is a chance you might have to go hand-to-hand with a hoard of bad guys? (Forget wild animals. Not only are bear and cat attacks extremely rare, you would have next to no chance of surviving the elements for any length of time after a knife fight with big bear.)

True wilderness explorers are few and far between these days. Most of us are hiking, canoeing or driving on established trails, waterways and roads, even in the backcountry. An unexpected forced landing in a

plane might be a realistic scenario, but none of the commercial airlines are going to let you on with that wonder knife strapped to your side. Going back to the Vietnam theory, the military is really the only major group realistically needing the large, special purpose survival knife.

The second question is this: You are a hunter, backpacker, fisherman, canoer or backcountry skier. Would you really want to perform your normal knife chores with one of those 10-inch sawback bowies? If not, are you willing to carry both the special purpose survival knife and your normal outdoor bladewear into the wilds? Realistically, when an emergency situation arises, it will be the knife you have on you that will have to serve as a survival tool. For the vast majority, this is going to be some type of folder — simply because this is what they carry on an everyday basis.

Long before "survival" became a buzzword and much of the country really was wilderness, backcountry travelers carried much simpler cutlery than we do today. The mountain men followed the beaver trade through the Rockies with plain butcher knives on their belts. Once the Indian wars ended, wilderness knives got even smaller. Most of the classic, woodcraft and wilderness hiking writers of the late 19th and early 20th centuries recommended carrying a sheath knife in the four- to five-inch range and a strong folder. A number went as far as to say

they didn't see a need for anything other than the multi-bladed folder. Remember, these were men who could actually hike off into the hills and live off the land for months at a time.

Knife and gun writer Chuck Karwan has stated that he thinks many people feel "survival knife" means a knife that will survive anything rather than a tool that will allow the user to survive. All right, a folding knife is not suitable for military-style hand-to-hand combat, but it also won't substitute for a prybar, machete or an axe. What it can do is be there when you really need it.

During my years working as a forester, it was common for me to head off on a compass line across roadless wilderness, run timber cruising plots, offset my line, reverse the compass bearing, and work back in another

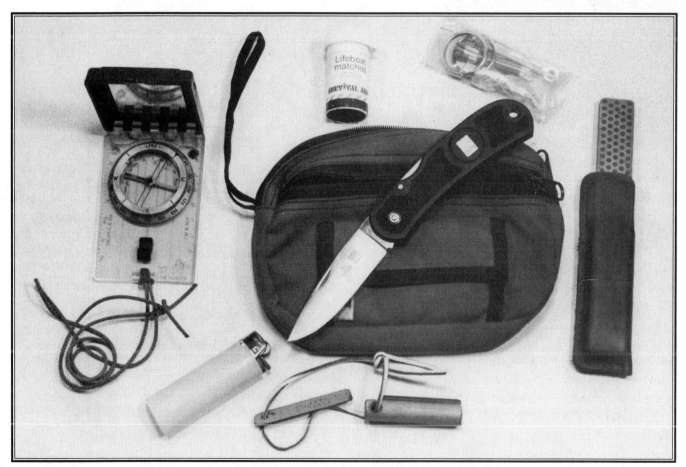

A few years ago, the author built this survival kit around an Al Mar Airweight Sportsman for a wilderness canoe trip. Along with the knife, there are four different ways to start a fire with this kit.

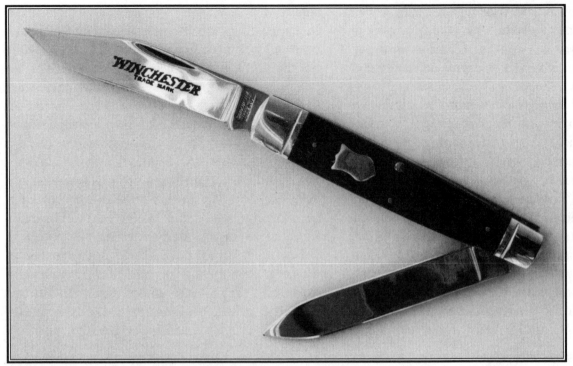

During the Golden Age of Woodcraft writing, between 1890 and 1940, more than one expert recommended a stout two-blade jack such as this Blue Grass reproduction Winchester Texas Jack as the ultimate wilderness survival knife.

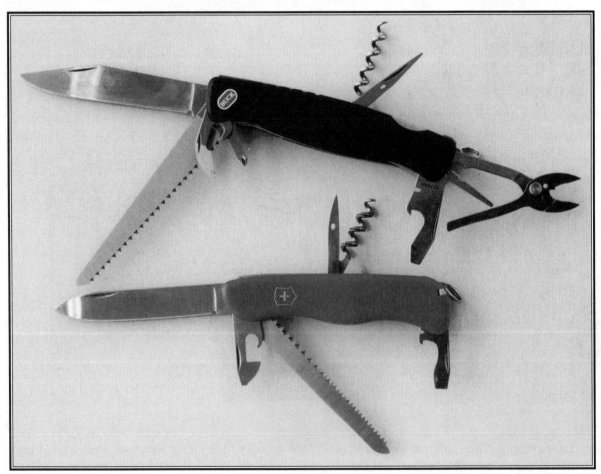

A large Swiss Army such as this Swiss Buck (top) or the Victorinox (bottom) will get you out of just about any scrape with a little ingenuity.

direction until I reached a spot parallel with the company truck. When there was no road close to the area we wanted to cruise, we were often dropped in by helicopter. We could then spend the day following a compass line to a helicopter pick-up point on the next mountain ridge or two over. I seldom carried anything but a strong folding knife, rain gear and a good supply of matches for my wilderness survival equipment. In my experience, this is true of the majority of wilderness pros.

To be completely honest, most of the time I have more than one folding knife on me when I venture into the backcountry. The first is a Swiss Army Spartan or a similar model from Wenger. Probably more people have gotten themselves out of survival problems with a Swiss Army than any other cutting tool. Custom knifemakers cringe when I point it out, but the sawblade on the standard Swiss Army knife will out-cut practically every sawback survival knife I've ever run across.

In situations where fixing something mechanical is the solution to survival, one of the modern generation of pliers/tool/knives might be an even better answer. The Leatherman, Buck, SOC, Gerber, Bear MGC and Utica all have their advantages and disadvantages, so I would advise looking the field over closely for the model that best fits your own special needs. Tool/knives have become extremely popular with outdoor professionals and those in the military. For many, this is their sole cutting tool. Probably the only reason I haven't replaced my own Swiss Army with a tool/knife is that most tend to weigh considerably more than a Swiss Army knife. In any case, I always have one or more of the tool/knives someplace in my vehicle when traveling.

Both the Swiss Army and the various pliers/knives provide a variety of useful survival tools, but for serious cutting I still carry a basic, heavy-duty lockback folder. In my experience, the Buck 110 and its many look-alikes remain the most popular work knife for wilderness professionals. Other good choices in heavy-duty folders include the Gerber Gator-Mate, Al Mar SERE, Spyderco Police and Military models, SOG Tomcat, Benchmade

Kutmaster offers this interesting little camp utility knife with a flint firestarter build into the handle. While I wouldn't carry it as my only cutting tool, it might make a useful back-up.

If any of your survival plans involve fixing something mechanical, it's hard to beat one of the modern pliers/knives. Top left, Gerber Multi-Plier; bottom left, Leatherman Super Tool; top right, SOC Tool; bottom right, Original Leatherman.

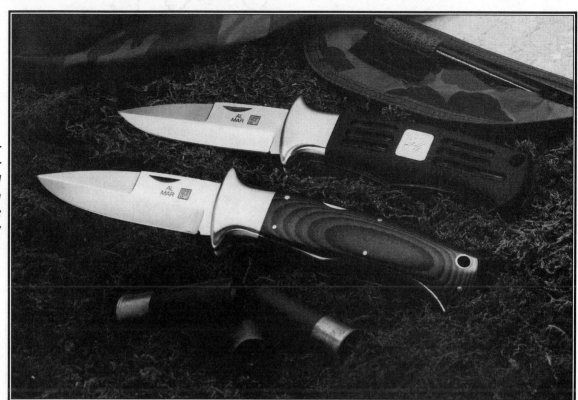

The Al Mar SERE folder was created especially for a survival course taught by Army Special Forces.

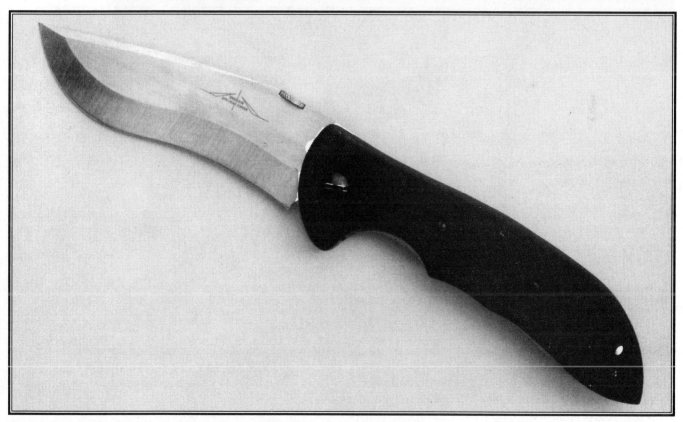

Ernest Emerson's new ES1-C was originally created as a military survival tool.

Any of the modern Zytel-handled lockback folders make excellent survival kit knives. From the top down: Outdoor Edge Field-Lite, Cold Steel Large Voyager, Browning Lockback Hunter.

More Zytel-handled folders suited to survival kit use. From the top down: Al Mar Lightweight, Buck CrossLock, Spyderco Endura.

AFCK, Kershaw Wildcat Ridge and Blackhorse, Lakota Hawk and the Schrade Model 125-OT Mustang.

The proliferation of Zytel-handled folders has added another dimension to the backcountry survival plan. Knives such as Cold Steel's Large and Extra Large Voyagers are for practical purposes, just as strong as the traditional metal bolster models and weigh considerably less. Other good models include the Gerber LST Magnum, SOC Magna-DOT, Spyderco Endura, Buck Goliath, Schrade Outback, Outdoor Edge Field-Lite and Al Mar Airweight Sportsman and Passport.

Among custom knives there are literally hundreds of options, but a few with which I have considerably backcountry experience are the Kit Carson Model 4 and the Chris Reeve Sebenza. Both are capable of performing any task that can reasonably be requested of a folding knife. Other makers I would recommend include Pat Crawford, Greg Lightfoot, Bob Terzuola, Wayne Clark and Dick Atkinson.

I usually don't venture into the backcountry without several knives on me or in my gear somewhere. If you have ever tried to fill one, you know how little space is actually available in the typical hollow handle of a survival sheath knife. Kershaw once offered a nylon belt pouch with a Blackhorse lockback and a variety of survival items as an alternative. Even a relatively small belt pouch offers far more space and options than a hollow knife handle.

The Kershaw kit was fine as far as it went, but it started me thinking. Why not design my own kit specifically equipped for the conditions and area in which I would be traveling? I put together a pouch that included an ultra-flat Al Mar Airweight Sportsman, diamond sharpener, lifeboat matches and magnesium firestarter, compass, spare boot laces, wire, fishhooks and line. The kit was

Custom knives offer a more expensive but high quality alternative to the factory folder for the survival kit. From the top down: Kit Carson Model 4, Phil Boguszewski, Greg Lightfoot and Blade Tech/ Boguszewski.

hardly noticeable on my belt, but gave me the assurance that no matter what other gear I lost, I would still have these basics with me. One of my criteria was to not use any of the items in the kit for my daily needs, so I also carried a Gerber Parabellum on my belt and a Swiss Army in my pocket.

While it probably seems that I have been critical of the hollow handle survival sheath knives, I actually think many would be quite useful in an emergency if there was a guarantee they would be there when needed.

Unfortunately, I also think it's safe to assume they won't. For me, the most practical alternative is either a Swiss Army in my pocket or a tool/knife in my pack, a large, heavy-duty lockback on my belt or clipped to a pocket top, and a realistic survival kit with a second light-weight lockback close to hand.

Add matches, magnesium, compass, spare boot laces, fishhooks and line, and the proper clothing for the area into which you will be going, and you should be ready for short-term survival under any conditions.

For traveling in more urban areas, a knife such as the Al Mar Eagle is a handy tool to have along. Not only will it slice a sausage and cheese lunch and peel fruit, it can serve equally well as an emergency tool and weapon.

SOURCE DIRECTORY

– FACTORY KNIVES –

AITOR
P.O. Box 1
48260 Emua
Spain; 34-43-17-00-01

**B&D TRADING CO.
(EXECUTIVE EDGE)**
3935 Fair Hill Rd.
Fair Oaks, CA 95628; 916-967-9366

BEAR MGC CUTLERY
1111 Bear Blvd. SW
Jacksonville, AL 36265; 205-435-2227

BENCHMADE KNIVES
300 Beaver Creek Rd.
Oregon City, OR 97045; 503-655-6004

BENCHMARK KNIVES
936 North Marietta St
Gastonia, NC 28054; 704-867-1307

BERETTA KNIVES
17601 Beretta Dr.
Accokeek, MD 20607; 301-283-2191

**BLUE GRASS CUTLERY
(WINCHESTER)**
P.O. Box 156
Manchester, Ohio 45144; 937-549-2602

BOKER USA (OPINEL)
1550 Balsam St.
Lakewood, CO 80215; 303-462-0668

BOYE KNIVES
P.O. Box 1238
Dolan Springs, AZ 86441; 520-767-4273

BROWINNG KNIVES
Rt.1
Morgan, UT 84050; 800-333-3288

BRUNTON (LAKOTA)
620 E. Monroe Ave.
Riverton, WY 82501; 307-856-6559

BUCK KNIVES
1900 Weld Blvd.
El Cajon, CA 92020; 619-449-1100

CAMILLUS CUTLERY CO.
54 Main St.
Camillus, NY 13031; 315-672-8832

CASE CUTLERY
Owens Way
Bradford, PA 16701; 800-535-6350

COAST CUTLERY (PUMA)
P.O. Box 5821
Portland, OR 97228; 503-234-4545

COLD STEEL
2128-D Knoll Dr.
Ventura, CA 93003; 800-255-4716

COLONIAL CUTLERY
Agnes at Magnolia St.
Providence, RI 02909; 800-556-7824

COLUMBIA RIVER KNIFE AND TOOL
9720 S.W. Hillman Crt. Suite 805
Wilsonville, OR 97070; 800-891-3100

DMT
   (SHARPENING PRODUCTS)
85 Hayes Memorial Dr.
Marlborogh, MA 01752; 508-481-5944

EDGECRAFT CORP.
   (CHEF'SCHOICE)
825 Southwood Rd.
Avondale, PA 19311; 800-342-3255

EZE-LAP
   (SHARPENING PRODUCTS)
3572 Arrowhead Dr.
Carson City, NV 89706; 702-888-9500

FROST CUTLERY
   (HEN AND ROOSTER)
P.O. Box 22636
Chattanooga, TN 37422; 423-894-6079

GATCO
   **(SHARPENING PRODUCTS
   AND TIMBERLITE KNIVES)**
P.O. Box 600
Getzville, NY 14068; 716-877-2200

GERBER LEGENDARY BLADES
14200 SW 72nd Ave.
Portland, OR 97223; 503-639-6161

GT KNIVES
7716 Arsons Dr.
San Diego, CA 92126; 619-566-1511

HENCKELS ZWILLINGSWORK INC.
171 Saw Mill River Rd.
Hawthome, NY 10532; 914-592-7370

IMPERIAL SCHRADE
7 Schrade Ct.
Ellenville, NY 12428; 914-647-7600

KA-BAR KNIVES
1116 East State Street
Olean, NY, 14760; 800-282-0130

KATZ KNIVES
P.O. Box 730
Chandler, AZ 85224; 602-786-9334

KELLAM KNIVES
3422 Old Capitol Trail Suite 831
Wilmington, DE 19808; 302-996-3386

KERSHAW KNIVES
25300 SW Parkway
Wilsonville, OR 97070; 503-682-1966

LANSKY SHARPENERS
P.O. Box 800
Buffalo, NY 14231; 716-877-7511

LEATHERMAN TOOL
P.O. Box 2095
Portland, OR 97294; 503-253-7826

LITTLE RIVER CUTLERY
   (BUCKCREEK)
2015 Asheville Highway
Hendersonville, NC 28793; 704-697-8833

AL MAR KNIVES
5755 SW Jean Rd. Suite 101
Lake Oswego, OR 97035; 503-635-9229

MICRO-TECH
932 36th Court S.W.
Vero Beach, FL 32968; 561-569-3058

MYERCHIN MARINE CLASSICS
850 W. Randall Ave.
Rialto, CA 92377; 909-874-6058

NICKOLS CO.
  (EKA, SWEDEN)
P.O. Box 473
Woodstock, VT 05091; 802-457-3970

NORMARK
10395 Yellow Circle Dr.
Minnetonka, MN 55343; 612-933-7060

OUTDOOR EDGE
2888 Bluff St. Suite 130
Boulder, CO 80301; 303-652-8212

PARKER KNIFE COLLECTOR SERVICE
6715 Heritage Business Court
Chattanooga, TN 37422; 800-247-0599

PRECISE INTERNATIONAL
  (WENGER SWISS ARMIES)
15 Corporate Dr.
Orangeburg, NY 10962; 800-431-2996

QUEEN CUTLERY
  (ONTARIO KNIVES)
P.O. 145
Frankinville, NY 14737; 716-676-5527

RAZOR EDGE SYSTEMS
  (SHARPENING PRODUCTS)
303 North 17th Ave. E.
Ely, MN 55731; 800-541-1458

REMINGTON ARMS CO
1011 Centre Rd.
Delle Donne Corp Ctr
Wilimington, DE 19805; 800-243-9700

A.G. RUSSELL
1705 Highway 71 N.
Springdale, AR 72764; 501-751-7341

SOG SPECIALTY
P.O. Box 1024
Edmonds, WA 98020; 206-771-6230

SPYDERCO
P.O. Box 800
Golden, CO 80402; 303-279-8383

SWISS ARMY BRANDS
  (VICTORINOX)
One Research Dr.
Shelton, CT. 06484; 800-243-4032

TAYLOR CUTLERY
  (SMITH AND WESSON)
P.O. Box 1638
Kingsport, TN 37662; 615-247-2406

UTICA (KUTMASTER)
820 Noyes St.
Utica, NY 13503; 315-733-4663

UNITED CUTLERY
1425 United Blvd.
Sevierville, TN 37876; 423-428-2532

– CUSTOM KNIFEMAKERS –

DICK ATKINSON
General Delivery
Wausai, FL 32463; 904-638-8524

A.T. BARR
P.O. Box 828
Nicholasville, KY 40340; 606-885-1042

PHIL BOGUSZEWSKI
P.O. Box 99329
Tacoma, WA 98499; 206-581-7096

TONY BOSE
7252 N. County Rd. 300 E.
Shelbum, IN 47879; 812-397-5114

WALTER BREND
Rt.7 Box 224
Walterboro, SC 29488; 803-538-8256

BOB BROTHERS
989 Philpott Rd.
Colville, WA 99114; 509-684-8922

KIT CARSON
1076 Brizendine Lane
Vine Grove, KY 40175; 502-877-6300

FRANK CENTOFANTE
P.O. Box 928
Madisonville, TN 37354; 423-442-5767

WAYNE CLARK
1441 Paso Real Av., Space 273
Rowland Heights, CA 91748

WAYNE CLAY
P.O. Box 474B
Pelham, TN 37366; 615-467-3472

PAT CRAWFORD
205 N. Center
West Memphis, AR 72301; 501-735-4632

C.M. DAKE
19759 Chef Menteur Hwy.
New Orleans, LA 70129; 504-254-0357

TERRY DAVIS
P.O. Box 111
Sumpter, OR 97877; 541-894-2307

JED DARBY
7878 E. Co. Rd. 50 N.
Greensburg, IN 47240; 812-663-2696

BOB DOZIER
P.O. Box 1941
Springdale, AR 72765; 501-756-0023

ALLEN ELISHEWITZ
17194 Preston Rd. Suite 123 #227
Dallas, TX 75248; 214-380-4304

ERNEST EMERSON
4142 W. 173nd St.
Torrance, CA 90504; 310-542-3050

ROBERT ENDERS
3028 White Rd.
Cement City, MI 49233; 517-529-9667

WALTER ERICKSON
23883 Ada St.
Warren, MI 48091; 313-759-1105

MEL FASSIO
4585 Twin Cr. Rd.
Bonner, MT 59823; 406-244-5208

STEVE FECAS
1312 Shadow Lane
Anderson, SC 29625; 803-287-4834

WAYNE GODDARD
473 Durham Ave.
Eugene, OR 97404; 541-689-8098

ED HALLIGAN
14 Meadow Way
Sharpsburg, GA 30277; 770-251-7720

RALPH DEWEY HARRIS
2607 Bell Shoals Rd.
Brandon, FL 33511; 813-6815293

BILL HARSEY
82710 N. Howe Ln.
Creswell, OR 97426; 541-895-4941

ROY HELTON
11535 Phantom Ln.
San Diego, CA 92126; 619-541-2770

STEVE HILL
7814 Toucan Dr.
Orlando, FL 32822; 407-277-3549

JESS HORN
87481 Rhodowood Dr.
Florence, OR 97439; 541-997-2593

R.C. KNIPSTEIN
731 N. Fielder
Arlington, TX 76012; 817-265-2021

KEN LARGIN
67 Arlington Dr.
Batesville, IN 47006; 812-934-5938

TOMMY LEE
1011 Grassy Pond Rd.
Gaffney, SC 29340; 803-489-6699

BILL LEVENGOOD
15011 Otto Rd.
Tampa, FL 33624; 813-961-5688

GREG LIGHTFOOT
5502-45 Street
Lloydminster, AB T9V OC2

BOB LUM
901 Travis Ave.
Eugene, OR 97404; 541-688-2737

BILL MCHENRY
P.O. Box 67
Wyoming, RI 02898; 401-539-8353

CHARLES OCHS
124 Emerald Lane
Largo, FL 33771; 813-536-3827

DARREL RALPH
7032 E. Livington Ave.
Reynoldsburg, OH 43068; 614-577-1040

A.D. RARDON
1589 S.E. Price Dr.
Polo, MO 64671; 816-354-2330

CHRIS REEVE
6147 Corporal Lane
Boise, ID 83704; 208-375-0367

RALPH SELVIDIO
15 Budlong Ave.
Warrick, RI 02888; 401-941-9341

EUGENE SHADLEY
645 Norway Dr.
Bovey, MN 55709; 218-245-3820

KEN STEIGERWALT
P.O. Box 172
Orangeville, PA 17859; 717-683-5156

CHUCK STEWART
2128 Garrick Ave.
Warren, MI 48091; 810-757-4418

WARREN THOMAS
1705 S. Richey,
Pasadena, TX 77502; 713-946-3964

BOB TERZUOLA
Rt.6 Box 83A
Santa Fe, NM 87501; 505-473-1002

BRIAN TIGHE
RR1 Ridgeville
LOS 1MO Ontario Canada; 905-892-2734

RALPH TURNBULL
5722 Newburg Rd.
Rockford, IL 61108; 815-398-3799

BUTCH VALLOTTON
621 Fawn Ridge Dr.
Oakland, OR 97462; 541-459-2216

WALLY WATTS
Rt.1 Box 81
Gatesville, TX 76528; 817-487-2886

TIM WEGNER
8612 S. 222nd Street
Kent, WA 98031; 206-872-4883

JASON WILLIAMS
P.O. Box 67
Wyoming, RI 02898; 401-539-8353

BILL WOLF
4618 N. 79th Ave.
Phoenix, AZ 85033; 602-846-3585

BARRY WOOD
3002 E. Gunnison St.
Colorado Springs, CO 80909; 719-578-9226

MICHAEL ZIMA
732 State St.
Ft. Morgan, CO 80701; 970-867-6078

– CUTLERY PERIODICALS –

BLADE MAGAZINE
700 E. State St.
Iola WI 54945; 800-272-5233

DBI KNIVES ANNUAL
4092 Commercial Ave.
Northbrook, IL 60062; 847-272-6310

KNIFE WORLD
P.O. Box 3395
Knoxville, TN 37927; 800-828-7751

KNIVES ILLUSTRATED
774 S. Placentia Ave,
Placentia, CA 92670; 714-572-2255

TACTICAL KNIVES
1115 Broadway
New York, New York, 10010; 888-456-6247

INDEX